A Time to Grieve

Loss as a Universal Human Experience

Bertha G. Simos

Family Service Association
of America
New York

The excerpt from "Renascence ii" appearing on page 92 is from
Collected Poems, Harper and Row. Copyright © 1917, 1946 by Edna
St. Vincent Millay. Reprinted by permission.

Library of Congress Cataloging in Publication Data

Simos, Bertha G.,
   A time to grieve.

   Includes index.
   1. Grief.   I. Title.
BJ1487.S57   155.9'3   75-27964
ISBN 0-87304-141-0
ISBN 0-87304-153-4 pbk.

Printed in the United States of America

Designed by Grace Markman

To Miriam and Mark

To every thing there is a season, and a
  time to every purpose under the heaven:
A time to be born, and a time to die;
A time to plant, and a time to pluck up
  that which is planted;
A time to kill, and a time to heal;
A time to break down, and a time to build up;
A time to weep, and a time to laugh;
A time to mourn, and a time to dance.

(Eccles. 3:1-4)

Contents

Acknowledgments

This book has been years in the writing and draws from many facets of my life. It would be impossible to thank individually all of the people who have been helpful to me in this work. But thanks are in order. One way of saying thanks without omitting any single individual is through categories.

It is an old saying in psychotherapeutic circles that the therapist learns from his patients. I am deeply grateful to all of the people who have allowed me into their lives during the past three decades of my clinical work. I want particularly to thank those who have given me permission and urged me to cite their experiences with loss and grief in the hope of helping others who are bereaved. Their eagerness to participate is shown in their objections, when I let them read what had been written about them, to changes made in the details of their situation in order to protect their privacy. The names of all persons used in the case illustrations are, of course, invented.

Teachers also learn from their students. The need of social work and gerontology students for reading material on loss and grief and the dearth of material combining both theory and practice led to lecture material, seminars, courses, articles, and finally to this book. Students also include supervisees and social workers who come for consultation on their work. Their gratitude, challenge, and most of all pleasure in using this material to their own greater effectiveness in practice have been most encouraging and rewarding to me.

Colleagues, teachers, and friends have also offered encouragement, help, and challenge that have kept me at the task of research and writing with a sense of enthusiasm and fresh discovery. I want to particularly thank Margot Kohls, a fellow clinical social worker and friend, for her insightful criticisms that have never failed to enrich my own thinking.

My family, particularly my two children, deserve a special thanks. My children's ability to be open and articulate about feelings and thinking has often made me wonder if I haven't learned as much from rearing them as from all the books I have studied.

And finally, I wish to express my thanks to the editorial staff at

Family Service Association of America, particularly to Eileen Graham, who edited the book. Margaret M. Mangold, now retired as Director of Publications, accepted, guided, and encouraged me from the beginning of this project. During this past year Jacqueline M. Atkins took over the task with an equally sensitive touch and hardly a break in continuity. Knowing that one's work is in the hands of careful and competent critics makes for a feeling of safety that allows freedom of expression and spontaneity.

Give sorrow words; the grief that does not speak
Whispers the o'erfraught heart and bids it
break.

Shakespeare, *Macbeth,*
Act 4, Scene 3, line 209

1/
Introduction

The Theme of Loss

Mental health is usually presented in terms of a positive approach to life. We are told to minimize the negative, to set aside gloom, to concentrate on the opportunities open to us, to seek fulfillment within ourselves, and to seek closeness and intimacy with others despite limiting external realities and the residue of past traumas.

This book deals with one particular aspect of mental health, the theme of loss. Loss is defined as being deprived of or being without something one has had and valued and includes the experiences of separation. The term is applied both to the act of severance leading to the loss, as well as to a temporary loss, and to the fear of loss. These experiences, loss, separation, and fear of loss, are universal to all people at every stage of the life cycle. Some losses, such as death, are obvious. Others, such as a disappointed expectation, are so subtle they may go unrecognized as losses, but they leave their mark just the same. Separations can also range from the obvious, such as a child entering kindergarten for the first time, to the subtle, such as the daily departure from home to work in the morning, and work to home in the evening. In the unconscious, all these experiences are dynamically related.

Loss sets in motion a train of feelings called *grief*. In grief, normal means feeling *not happy* rather than *happy*. In grief what is normal goes contrary to what we usually think of as good adjustment, namely, a rational approach to problem solving, the ability to cope with one's problem, a sense of organization and orderliness, an optimistic outlook, and the capacity to relate in a constructive way to other people. Because of cultural and personal reasons that preclude grieving, however, many bereaved people are prevented from experiencing the feelings that should necessarily follow loss in order to ensure a healthy resolution of the trauma. Increasingly, unresolved grief is being recognized as the forerunner for a wide range of physical, mental, and emotional disorders.

The problem: gaps in scientific and professional knowledge

Loss and its sequelae of grief, mourning, restitution, or depletion are an integral part of the human condition. This has long been recognized by religion, folklore, and the arts. All great literature deals with the themes of death, separation, love, betrayal, and other forms of loss. The Book of Job in the Bible provides a classic description of multiple losses. Poetry has traditionally been the repository for expressions of pain and yearning in grief. Great novelists have understood these themes well. These themes have, however, been long overdue in gaining proper recognition from the social sciences and the helping professions. Following some attention to these topics by Darwin and Freud, scientific interest has been erratic and piecemeal. Thus far there is no comprehensive psychology of loss and grief. The most consistent effort to develop such a psychology has been within psychoanalysis itself. Even here, Freud dealt with mourning tangentially in the context of his major focus on other interests, such as melancholia and anxiety. His views did not, however, account for all of the phenomena found in grief, and although later Freudians explored various aspects of grief in depth, they did not round out Freud's views to a comprehensive theory.[1]

Significant contributions to theory have been made by non-Freudian psychoanalytic schools as well. These will be discussed later under various themes. Knowledge has also come from the observation of children separated from parents because of war, hospitalization, day care, and other reasons.[2] A comprehensive theoretical development is presented by John Bowlby in his study of attachment and loss.[3]

Loss, separation, and the fear of loss have also been recognized as underlying dynamics in a variety of physical disorders, such as asthma, ulcerative colitis, heart attack, cancer, rheumatoid arthritis, and emotional and mental disorders ranging from phobias to the depressions, to schizophrenia, and to the senile psychoses. The loss component has also been noted in other situations of stress, such as divorce, death of a family member, adoption, foster home placement, amputations, burns, rape, child and wife abuse, and other types of victimization, whether due to personal pathology or political ideologies. The Holocaust, World War II, the atomic bomb tragedies, terrorism, mass murders, and mass suicides, and other disasters, such as fires, floods, and earthquakes, are the sources for further study.

Loss was the focus of a major scientific study by Erich Lindemann of the survivors and relatives of victims of the Cocoanut Grove nightclub fire, which occurred in Boston in the early 1940s.[4] One conclusion from that study was that grief is not only a natural but also a necessary reaction after loss. Following that research there was an outpouring of professional writing under the label of "crisis theory." Although loss was recognized as a necessary component of every crisis, an examination of this literature shows that the emphasis was placed on coping, not grieving, the goal being to help the bereaved resume his pre-loss level of task-oriented behavior as speedily as possible. The grief process itself is omitted in much of crisis literature, and some of the feelings and behaviors necessary in grief are judged dysfunctional in the crisis model.

In this focus on coping, crisis theory reflected the bias of the culture in which it developed. Until recent years Western society has been known as a death-denying culture, in contrast to societies in other parts of the world where death is regarded as an accepted part of the recurring life cycle of one generation after another. Thanks to the persistence of pioneers such as Elisabeth Kübler-Ross, who dared to talk directly with dying patients about their experiences of dying,[5] the taboo in this area is slowly beginning to be lifted. We are still far from feeling comfortable, however, with the dying patient and his family.

Despite increasing attention to death and dying, we have only recently becoming aware that there are losses short of death with which people need help. Groups for the widowed, the divorced, the children of divorced parents, rape victims, stroke victims and their families, mastectomy and colostomy patients, and other bereaved groups are beginning to mushroom. But these are only a few of the myriad losses we encounter in our lives. There are still large gaps in our knowledge of loss and grief.

The significance of the problem: dangers of unresolved grief

Not only have the concepts of loss, grief, and mourning been slow to gain proper professional attention, recognition of the impact unresolved grief reactions have on health and personality has been even slower. Unresolved grief festers like a deep wound covered by scar tissue, a pocket of vulnerability ever ready to break out anew. Incomplete or partial grieving leaves residue for future difficulties and becomes the forerunner for a wide range of physical, emotional, and mental disorders. Many people with such problems are seen by a variety of mental health professionals—psychoanalysts, psychiatrists, psychologists, clinical social workers, marriage counselors, the clergy, school counselors, and others. Some people find their way instead to the physician, the courts, or become part of the statistics of crime, accidents, and finally items for the obituary column. Although we no longer find grief listed as the cause of death on death certificates, recent research points to a direct connection between the sudden loss of a loved one and chronic loneliness as a factor in premature death.[6]

On a broader social scale, suicide prevention centers find an increase in both suicides and suicide attempts coinciding with the state of the economy. When unemployment increases, or when there are massive job layoffs in a particular industry (automobiles, aircraft, engineering, the space program, teaching), people whose financial security and sense of self-esteem have been tied to one kind of work are caught in a downward spiral. Despite all rational awareness that the problem is a result of outside forces, each person feels a personal sense of failure. As stress mounts, savings are depleted, expenses go on, and no job is available, any additional stress can be the straw that breaks the camel's back and triggers a suicide attempt.

Suicide is the reverse side of homicide, and daily we see news items about family quarrels ending in murder and suicide, or of crime sprees of compulsive, repetitive, and even mass killings. A close examination of the lives of these killers shows clearly the invariable theme of loss, often of early childhood losses. As will be discussed later, children who suffer catastrophic losses, particularly of a parent, are a group at risk. As Gregory Rochlin points out in his book *Griefs and Discontents: The Forces of Change,* those more fortunate can become not only productive but often creative members of society.[7] Others less fortunate, however, go on to adulthood with an inability to form lasting ties of intimacy, with problems regarding task completion, phobias about success, difficulties with normal separations, lives of achievement below one's full potential, psychiatric disorders, and, most serious of all, the propensity for self- or other-destructive behaviors. In *The Anatomy of Human Destructiveness,* Erich Fromm goes so far as to suggest that the increase in violence in society today is directly related to our inability to grieve.[8]

It is not only loss and grief unresolved that can create difficulties. As human beings with the mental capacity to remember, that same memory projected into the future can result in the fear of future losses and separations. The fear of loss can pervade one's mind and interfere with enjoyment of even the most precious moments of existence. "Once burned, twice shy" applies to loss directly. Having known loss, we expect future loss. Some widowed and divorced people fear remarriage. The rape victim is terrified of another attack. The woman who has had a mastectomy fears the recurrence of cancer. Parents who have lost a child fear for their other children. Below are two examples seen in clinical work.

Johnny, age ten, was referred for psychotherapy because of a long history of academic underachievement, rebellion against teachers, and fighting with peers. Johnny was conceived after his parents lost their firstborn child, David, who drowned at age three. The doctor thought another baby might take the mother's mind off her loss. Johnny was a "replacement child." Nothing he did could measure up to the perfection of the idealized dead brother. Johnny's misbehavior was his form of protest at the impossible demands made on him; he could not be David. Johnny's mother suffered a severe depression every July, the anniversary of David's death. Before Johnny's therapy and the mother's concomitant work with a social worker regarding his problems, she had been hospitalized every year, treated with antidepressant medications, and told her condition was physical and that she could expect such cyclical depressions for the rest of her life. When, in treatment, her unresolved grief about David's death was allowed expression through crying and talking of her loss, her depressions disappeared and did not recur. As Johnny was allowed to find his own autonomy, instead of needing to fight against being a replacement for the dead brother, his problems too subsided.

A woman sits in a therapist's office, referred by her physician because of colitis. He had connected her symptoms to menopause and the impending realization that childlessness was now a reality. The patient talked without emotion, as if reporting events happening to another, not herself. Nothing was particularly wrong in her life. She had a husband who loved her. Both had professions which provided them with adequate incomes as well as with satisfaction in the work itself. She had for some time now accepted the fact that there would probably be no children in the marriage, and lately she was not even sure that she had wanted to bother with the demands of parenthood.

The colitis had begun during a summer visit to the town where she had been born. To her great distress, she found that her childhood neighborhood had been torn down for urban renewal. Gone was the house in which she had lived before the death of her father, when she was four. Gone were the homes of aunts and uncles who had given love and support to the fatherless family. Gone was the home of the grandparents who had been the center of family life and strength. "They tore down my childhood," she mourned. "There is nothing left there. Everything is gone." As the tears flowed she said, "This is the first time I have cried over my father's death, and it happened more than thirty-five years ago." Her delayed grief reaction is not uncommon in people who have suffered parent loss in childhood. She has much more grieving to do.

Responsibility of the Helper

This book is the result of a number of forces that have highlighted the need for an easily understood, nontechnical book for practitioners in the helping professions, as well as for the general public. One impelling force has been the slowly growing realization that often people in the helping professions are inadequately prepared to deal with loss and grief.

Grief must be shared with another person. Thus, we cannot speak of the bereaved without at the same time taking into account the comforter, whose reactions will influence the ability of the bereaved to deal with his pain. Because our society emphasizes competence, adequacy, strength, and accomplishment, the bereaved are often prevented by family and friends from expressing their true feelings.

Therapists, socialized into the same society as the patient, family, and friends, are just as likely as they to overlook the loss and grief in the situation and to compound the problem by slapping a psychiatric diagnosis on the patient. Contrary to what one might expect, the education and training of mental health professionals to date has not routinely included courses on how to deal appropriately with people who have suffered loss. The bereaved need to know this in seeking help rather than to trust blindly that the helper is qualified. It is a serious matter to label an individual pathological when he is undergoing a normal life process such as grief. Normal acute grief provides a moratorium from routine living and the person experiencing it is often erroneously assumed to be sick and nonproductive.

We have no experts in grief counseling per se. We are beginning to have grief counseling centered on specific losses, such as divorce, widowhood, certain illnesses, rape, and so on, but loss and grief cannot be relegated to separate categories. In the unconscious all losses, separations, and reactions to loss and to the fear of loss and separation merge into a total complicated entity.

The bereaved are keenly sensitive to feelings aroused and impressions created on others. Grief also makes people highly suggestible. To bare one's soul, expose one's innermost fears, doubts, and tumultuous feelings as is necessary in overcoming grief, only to find that one has been brushed aside, offered platitudes, been misunderstood, judged harshly, or considered critically by someone professing to understand, can be a devastating experience. This happens under the guise of professional help more often than is generally recognized, regardless of the title, prestige, or discipline of the helper. Such an experience, when least damaging, may simply fail to be helpful, cut off the grief work, and delay the reparative process. More seriously, it can create in the bereaved self-doubt about his perceptions and feelings and can foster fears of mental illness, loss of a sense of self, and feelings of hopelessness.

As a rule, many people hesitate to intrude in areas where they lack knowledge or skill; however, in personal relationships and emotional problems everyone believes himself to be an expert. Without invitation we get advice on how to deal with a spouse, how to discipline children, and how to deal with loss and grief. Because of these well-meaning friends and even professionals, the bereaved are subject to additional stress at a time of great vulnerability in their lives.

Observation of the plight of professionals and of one's acquaintances in dealing with loss and grief is merely one impetus for the writing of this book. Further conviction of the need for such a book comes from the pleas of students in social work, occupational therapy, and nursing, school counselors, and others, for guidance in dealing with people confronted by loss. These students have expressed guilt and anguish over their past helplessness in failing to offer comfort to those who turn to them in grief, and resentment that their earlier training had failed to prepare them to be helpful in such situations.

The physically disabled leave the student particularly confused and helpless, especially when the patient seems to be dealing so heroically and stoically with his losses. Students struggle with the question of when help is really necessary, and when the offer of help becomes an intrusion out of the student's need for "a case." Do all people faced with catastrophic bodily assault, such as amputation or surgery, face loss, they wonder. Or are there perhaps some strong-minded enough who do not need to grieve? If a person claims he has no problem and seems to be coping adequately, what do you do then? Isn't the ability to cope with life's problems the measure of one's mental health and ego strength? Is it possible that we can create problems where none exist?

Detractors of those in the mental health professions enjoy the belief that people who choose such work do so in the search for answers to their own problems; to a large extent this may be true. There are undoubtedly unconscious components in any vocational choice. No one, however, is without problems. Out of our own pain can come empathy and compassion, necessary attributes in dealing with people.

In the course of socialization into the helping professions, we learn that in areas where we are blind to our own problems, we cannot see clearly into those of our patients. Where we hurt, we cannot listen to the hurt of another. Only by having problems and overcoming them, suffering and finding healthy relief from suffering, struggling and finding socially and personally acceptable solutions to our dilemmas, can we hope to help others find healthy solutions to their problems in living.

Thus, the helper must have both knowledge and personal experience in having lived through the cycles from loss to restitution in his own life. This means recognition of the loss, appropriate grieving, and healthy restitution completing the cycle from loss to restorative living. There is a further demand on psychotherapists to recognize and help the patient become aware of loss and grief or the absence of grief as underlying dynamics in some of the problems that come to their attention. Loss cannot be escaped. It is an ongoing and essential part of the human condition. By helping people deal more effectively with loss and grief we can be instrumental in enabling them to move on to more creative living.

The Plan of the Book

The therapeutic task in regard to loss is threefold: to help the bereaved know that they have experienced a loss, to facilitate the expression of normal and appropriate grief, and to find healthy restitution for that which has been lost. How to approach this task is one of the themes of this book.

There are stumbling blocks. One has to do with resistance to looking at such a painful topic as loss and grief, leading to a lack of interest on the part of researchers. Another concerns conflicting theories about the components of normal grief. If the experts disagree, how can practitioners and laymen have guidelines for action? Yet the practitioner has always been confronted with the need to act with incomplete data. Human suffering demands attention, and the truths of today are the doubts of tomorrow. Thus does knowledge grow while we do the best we can with the tools at hand.

The plan of the book, then, is to begin in chapter two with a description of the wide range of life experiences that can be classified as losses. Chapter three gives an overview of normal grief and deals with some of the complexities surrounding the duration of grief. Chapters four through thirteen take each of the major components of the grief process through an in-depth study of the phenomenon from a standpoint of theory, practical manifestations in case situations, and guidelines for the practitioner in dealing with this aspect with the bereaved. Chapter fourteen offers some help in recognizing the various avenues to restitution, and in understanding substitution and depletion. Finally, chapter fifteen discusses loss as being an agent for change. The book is arranged within each chapter so that the more theoretical material is separated from the practical discussion for the practitioner who is seeking an immediate answer to a problem. The goal throughout is to help identify healthy ways to cope with loss and grief so as to make it possible for these life experiences to be used as an impetus toward growth and creativity.

Notes

1. Sigmund Freud, "Mourning and Melancholia," and "Inhibitions, Symptoms, and Anxiety," in *The Complete Psychological Works of Sigmund Freud, Standard Edition,* ed. James Strachey (New York: Macmillan Co., 1964).

2. See Anna Freud and Dorothy Burlingham, *War and Children* (New York: International Universities Press, 1942); James Robertson, *Hospitals and Children—A Parent's-eye View: A Review of Letters from Parents to the Observer and the BBC* (New York: International Universities Press, 1963); and Christoph M. Heinicke and Ilse J. Westheimer, *Brief Separations* (New York: International Universities Press, 1965).

3. John Bowlby, *Attachment and Loss,* vols. 1 and 2 (New York: Basic Books, 1969, 1973).

4. Erich Lindemann, "The Symptomatology and Management of Acute Grief," *American Journal of Psychiatry* 101 (1944): 141–48.

5. Elisabeth Kübler-Ross, *On Death and Dying* (New York: Macmillan Co., 1969).

6. James J. Lynch, *The Broken Heart: The Medical Consequences of Loneliness* (New York: Basic Books, 1977).

7. Gregory Rochlin, *Griefs and Discontents: The Forces of Change* (Boston: Little, Brown and Co., 1965).

8. Erich Fromm, *The Anatomy of Human Destructiveness* (Greenwich, Conn.: Fawcett Publications, 1973).

2/
Recognition of Loss and Fear of Loss

Categories of Loss

The first task in understanding loss and grief is to know what constitutes a loss. One needs to know what to look for; how to recognize a loss when it has occurred, is about to occur, or is feared; and to be on the alert for casual, symbolic, and oblique references to loss of which even the bereaved themselves are not aware. If one overlooks the loss itself, the reactions thereto, whether normal or dysfunctional, will, in all likelihood, also be overlooked or at best misunderstood. Loss has been grouped into four major categories: the loss of a significant loved or valued person, the loss of a part of the self, the loss of external objects, and developmental loss.[1]

We will begin by discussing loss on the basis of this differentiation.

The loss of a significant person

The loss of a significant person can be one of life's most devastating experiences. Yet, every human relationship is destined to end in loss. Loss is the price paid for relationships that insure survival and participation in the human experience.

The death of a loved one is, of course, the ultimate loss. Death is final and complete. But many little deaths are suffered by all of us along the way. Divorce, desertion, separation, abortion, stillbirth, and rejection mean losses of significant people. Jobs, military service, travel, and geographic moves also take us away from important others. So does placing the aged, mentally retarded, emotionally ill, criminal and delinquent, and putting dependent and neglected children up for adoption or foster care. Further, illness, accidents, and aging can change a loved one so drastically that the person we once knew is gone.

From infancy on our lives are bound up with those of others. We are social beings whose very existence depends on attachment to others. The loss of such an attachment can feel like a threat to life itself.

That is not to say that all close ties are ties of love. Love and hate are closely interwoven, and every relationship has some of both. Ambivalence is the essence of every relationship. Whether the relationship is weighted toward positive or negative feelings, however, it has to end. No matter how much we love someone we cannot keep that person alive forever or at our side forever. So loved ones die or go away, and those who are more hated than loved do also, and sometimes we get rid of those whom we do not love in other ways. Such losses bring their own kind of pain because we have had a say in them.

Death can be a welcome way out of hateful relationships. Men or women sometimes say "I wish my partner would die and then I wouldn't have to go through the trouble of divorce." Such remarks reveal how little is known of grief. The death of a person toward whom we have a high ratio of hate to love can set off the most complicated grief reactions.

The loss of a part of the self

Body image is one of the earliest aspects of self; it develops from the infant's beginning awareness of the distinction between the self and nonself. Body image develops from an accumulation of sensorimotor experiences. Parental attitudes add a further component to body image and to bodily functioning. One may conceive of one's body as good or bad, beautiful or ugly.

Equally as devastating as the loss of a significant person can be the loss of a part of the self. This kind of loss can be physical, psychological, social, or cultural. Physical losses can be structural, the actual loss of a part of the body, or the loss of function, with the body part remaining intact.

Structural losses are found in limb amputation, mastectomy, colostomy, disfigurement through burns, accidents, and surgery, hysterectomy, loss of kidneys, loss of hair or teeth, or any outward change that disrupts body image. Loss of body function can be as a result of such physical manifestations as stroke, paralysis, impotence, frigidity, emphysema, blindness, deafness, arthritis, and so on.

Loss can also be psychological. Examples are loss of memory, judgment, pride, or a feeling of control, of effectiveness and usefulness, of independence and autonomy, and of self-esteem and status. There can be loss of the self in coitus and love, loss of values through war, immigration, rioting, and brainwashing. Loss can be related to fantasies and expectations (of romance, of having ideal parents, of a promotion, pregnancy, and so on).

Peter Marris, a social scientist, makes the point that any event that destroys a person's understanding of the meaning of life can be experienced as a loss.[2] Death, murder, destruction, evil, and natural disasters are examples of such events. "How can there be a God if such things can happen?" expresses this loss of meaning. Other situations where meaning is lost happen when people act in unpredictable ways. "How could they do such a thing?" expresses this confusion.

Another kind of loss to the self is found in social losses. Role loss is one important form. Some common role losses are the role of spouse following death or divorce, the role of employee with unemployment or retirement, and the role of active parent after the children have left home.

Social losses merge into community and cultural losses. Immigration is a severe cultural loss, of continuity of lifestyle, of environmental cues lending meaning to experience (such as road signs and money), of language, familiar faces, places, and relationships, and of values and role patterns. The expectations we have of each other as husband, wife, lover, child, employee, grandparent, and so on, vary from one society to another.

Loss attends urban renewal and the moving of people from a familiar to a new neighborhood. Executives who are assigned to overseas positions experience culture shock, not only with the move to foreign service, but also on returning home—with the loss of extra financial benefits and the status enjoyed in the foreign country. Upward mobility through education, job or career advancement, or downward mobility through demotion, a pay cut, political scandal, and imprisonment are also social losses. Intermarriage, whether racial, ethnic, or religious, can also embody social and cultural losses in the discontinuity of values, role expectations, foods, customs, and rituals. The minority child, protected and beloved at home, can experience a loss when he goes outside the home and encounters prejudice and racism. The mounting problem of teenage pregnancy, whether the girl elects to abort, relinquish the child for adoption, or keep the child as an unmarried parent, means loss to all the principals involved—parents, grandparents, and child, if there is one.

The loss of external objects

The loss of external objects can be of a wide range of possessions, such as money, jewels, or property. Inflation is an indirect but nevertheless significant form of economic loss. The death or disappearance of a family pet is a frequently experienced loss. Purse-snatching is becoming a daily occurrence in larger urban communities. Apart from the shock of the experience itself, loss of the contents—credit cards, money, driver's license, keys, billfold, cosmetics, appointment book, a favorite pen—in sum, symbols of one's very identity—can be quite disturbing.

An automobile stolen or "totaled" in an accident is often not covered to the full amount by insurance. How can one measure the value of material objects lost when a home is destroyed by fire, flood, or earthquake? Even when there is insurance, money cannot replace family treasures, photographs are one example. Often insurance does not cover flood damage, and instances are known where even the hillside land itself was washed away.

Developmental loss

Finally, loss is part of development itself. Some experts go so far as to say there can be no change or growth without loss, that loss is necessary for ego development, and that loss is a complex, lifelong process, extending from conception to death—birth itself being the original separation trauma.[3] The infant loses the breast or bottle in the process of moving to solid foods and drinking from a cup. Toilet training, if attempted too early or too strictly, can be experienced as an intrusion and loss by the child. If the child does as mother says in order to get her approval at a stage when every impulse clamors to say "no" to everything, the child relinquishes his budding sense of autonomy. If, however, autonomy wins out, the child runs the risk of antagonizing the person on whom he is most dependent. In either case there is the risk of loss.

The most serious threat to the young child up to at least age three is the loss of the mother. Because the child's need for the mother is so basic and so immediate, the loss need not be permanent or dramatic to be experienced as traumatic. Every separation has the potential for loss if it continues beyond the infant's capacity to tolerate frustration at that particular stage of development. The loss can be of the mother's physical presence by some event that removes her from her child, such as death, illness, confinement with another child, travel, work, or overwhelming demands of other people or household chores. Or the loss of mother can be emotional through her total or intermittent withdrawal from the child because of her own ambivalence, depression, other mental illness, grief over a loss, or any other psychological problems.

Although the mother remains the center of the infant's well-being in early infancy, the loss of the father can also have significant consequences for the child not only directly, as a figure around whom the child's personality is structured, but also indirectly, through the impact of loss on the mother. The mother who loses her husband, for whatever reason, has emotional and realistic preoccupations which make her emotionally and often practically unavailable to her infant in the optimal manner needed for his early development.

As the child develops, other losses await him. It is a well-known concept in child development that a soft toy, torn blanket, or piece of sweater are transitional objects which symbolize a substitute for the mother as the child moves from infancy to toddlerhood, and from needing mother as the center of his life to being able to tolerate periods of separation from her. Such transitional objects are an important part of healthy development and lead to trauma when removed or lost. Children who show no interest in a transitional object are apt to have serious problems in regard to attachment to people.

Another developmental loss is the loss of baby teeth. The custom of having the "tooth fairy" leave money under the child's pillow attests to the unconscious recognition of the loss and restitution components in this experience.

The fantasied loss of the penis, a concept important in psychoanalytic theory, may be classified also under developmental loss. It is only with age and experience that we learn to comprehend fully differences among people. Even as adults many of us still believe that everyone else is like ourselves. Thus, if we are honest, we assume others to be so, until sad experience teaches us otherwise. The young child becomes aware of sexual differences at an age when he is not yet ready mentally to comprehend the fact of difference. For the young child the sameness among people extends to the physical as well. The child thus concludes that anatomically we all start out alike, and that some people (girls) suffered the loss of an important body part, the penis. The little girl sees herself as the victim of a loss which has already occurred. The little boy, on the other hand, fears that a similar disaster might befall him. Parental insensitivity to this fear or, worse yet, playing on this fear can create serious problems for a child. "Stop playing with yourself or that thing will fall off" and other similar threats to the integrity of the male organ are examples of child-rearing practices that make the child fearful about bodily integrity. Because in the unconscious one bodily protrusion can substitute for another, children may develop fears of losing their noses, fingers, toes, hair, or any other body part. The resistance of some little boys to getting their hair cut or their nails clipped may stem from such unconscious fears. Although a number of people have taken issue with this point of view, it has been an important theme in Western society and thus merits attention.

For children, growing up demands the relinquishment of immediate gratifications in exchange for future gains they often cannot understand and which, at the moment, can little appreciate. Children do not thank their parents for the limits and discipline necessary for their maturing into adulthood. This process is accompanied by pain and protest, as any parent can testify. One eleven-year-old girl, contemplating the loss of childhood with approaching puberty, remarked ruefully, "Isn't it sad that the only direction you can go is forward?"

Loss can be experienced in the birth of a younger sister or brother. There is some thinking that the firstborn, accustomed to exclusive attention from parents, may feel this loss more keenly than do later-born children, and the impending arrival of a competitor in the family may set off a high degree of anxiety.

The school years are replete with loss experiences. There are separations from familiar teachers and schoolmates through the change of classroom assignments and the normal progression from one grade to the next. There is the constant threat of loss of self-esteem in the competitive grading system. Any failure, whether actual or relative, is felt as a loss of self-esteem. Similarly, a promotion that is not earned is also felt as a loss of self-esteem because of the shame set off by the dishonesty.

As the growing child moves from home to peer relationships, from same-sex to opposite-sex friendships, from experimenting with relationships, there is constant danger to self-esteem. First, the parents may unconsciously resent the child forming emotional ties outside the family and verbally throw barbs at the child whenever he does so. These attacks are experienced as losses (of love) even though the child may not even be aware of them at the time they occur, or not know why the parent suddenly became critical. Experimentation with friendships, union and separation, selecting and being selected, or, even worse, watching while others are selected while waiting anxiously on the sidelines (at school dances or even when gym teams are being formed) occurs daily. Each of these normal experiences has in it the potential for, and the fear of, loss.

The ending of a school year brings the loss of familiar structure to the day, of people and activities. Graduation from high school, or the dropping out of school at an earlier grade, is a significant separation, if not loss, experience. Rejection by the college of one's choice or nonacceptance into a college major of one's preference is also a loss. The failure of society to provide young people with an entrance into the working world through employment opportunities is also a severe threat to self-esteem.

The chaos that characterizes family life in many households at the point where young people are trying to emancipate themselves from home is indicative of the struggles of both parents and children in this significant separation experience. It is the fear of loss that makes this period so tumultuous. For some youngsters, particularly in past years, the conflict between the urge to leave the structured home situation offering safety and the panic of facing the larger world could be resolved by flight into the military, dormitory or sorority or fraternity group living, or marriage. Today, peer group cultures provide a quasi-family substitute, as do group living arrangements without marriage.

The adolescent on the way to maturity faces a number of losses. He must relinquish (lose) and mourn the infantile body, the infantile identity and role, and the childhood image of his parents. The failure to work through these losses results in a person who has achieved chronological but not emotional maturity.

As we go through life, each developmental step brings the loss of the gratifications of the previous stage, while new challenges have in them always the potential of failure with accompanying loss of self-esteem. The pleasure inherent in an occasion marking the passage from one life stage to another—confirmation, graduation, engagement, marriage, parenthood—is no guarantee against a feeling of loss.

Marris concludes that:

> The self-confidence of maturity is not a rejection of support but an ability to turn for assurance when need arises, trusting that it will be met. The confirmation that more primitive wants are securely satisfied renews confidence to confront the uncertainties of growth. Conversely, if these wants have never been fully met, growing up does indeed become a succession of bereavements; the grown person is a banished child with forged papers of maturity.[4]

Loss as part of development is also inherent in the stress of moving. The homemaker wife of a middle-class professional man often pays a price for the geographical moves required by her husband's move up the corporation ladder or the ranks of academic life. It is she who frequently suffers from depression with each move as she leaves behind old neighborhoods, friendships, activities, lifestyle, and familiar shopping areas, and struggles to sink roots into a new community, only to be confronted by another move in a few years. Rarely does she connect her depression with the move itself. She is more likely to relate it to financial problems, marital problems, loneliness, or career frustrations.[5] (Obviously, frequent moving is disruptive to a child as well.) Even when economic and career success are achieved at the price of repeated moves, the daily economic struggle of the working man or woman also contains other elements of potential loss. The person who is fortunate enough to attain the pinnacle of success still cannot escape the fear of loss. The top position cannot be maintained forever. There is not only the danger of being succeeded by another; there is also loss in the envy of others' successes.

Losses occasioned by divorce are not uncommon among the middle-aged and elderly, as the post-parental couple finds itself without the distraction of growing children. The mate who was chosen in youth may not meet the needs of the later years. Children often provide a buffer against the full recognition of an outworn relationship, as well as a reason to stay together until child-rearing responsibilities are over. A break occurs and, despite protests to the contrary, there is a definite social gulf between the married and the no-longer married. Our social institutions such as churches, synagogues, clubs, and other groups are largely designed for the married couple or nuclear family. The leftover mate from a broken marriage constitutes a threat to the married, for no marriage is safe from the same fate. In addition, a broken marriage frequently has economic repercussions, particularly if the woman spent her married years in homemaking and has limited economic skills. Lack of money may mean the loss of the homestead, an important anchorage point.

If death, the overwhelming fear of the middle-aged man and his wife, does not intervene, both face the decline of the later years. Losses associated with aging are multiple and cumulative and encompass all realms of life—physical, psychological, social, economic, and a combination of these and others. The elderly are confronted by loss in the decline in physical stamina, in the reduction of sensory acuity of sight, hearing, and taste, in the loss of ease of motion, and in the loss of health from one of the chronic diseases that characterize the later decades of life.

Psychological losses of aging include loss of memory (names, dates, even exact words), of judgment and decision-making ease, of the ability to learn new material readily, to control one's impulses, or to control one's environment. The biggest blow is the realization that we cannot stop the aging process. It is at this time that social losses compound other losses by going hand in hand with role changes: children move away, contact with work colleagues becomes less and less following retirement, and lessened income as a result of loss of partner, or retirement, or both, places a further restriction on a previously strong social position.

Aging of a family member triggers crises for every family, and institutionalization of those elderly who can no longer live independently constitutes a serious loss for them as well as for other family members. All too often such a move heralds psychological and social death well in advance of physical death.

On a more hopeful note, one more developmental loss may be mentioned, one that does not follow the life cycle. This is the loss that occurs in the process of psychotherapy when a neurotic problem is resolved. It is often said in the helping professions that people do not really want to change; they merely want to feel better, to stop hurting, but to retain their old neuroses and habits. When they find that the former is impossible without the latter, a crisis occurs, and they must choose between health and their old dysfunctional ways. Should they select health, a loss occurs, and this loss of the old dysfunctional behavior patterns is accompanied by a grief reaction. There is the joke about the woman who stormed into the office of her therapist with the demand: "I want you to give me back my headaches!" It may appear strange, but the loss of an old pattern, even though it may have been dysfunctional, can also be keenly mourned.

As we go through life we need to relinquish and mourn those wishes, hopes, and fantasies that can never be fulfilled: to be very different in physical appearance or personality, to have been born of different parents, or of a different race, nationality, or religion. We all need to relinquish the wish to remain the center of our own universe as we take our place as one among many.

There are a number of unfulfilled wishes that need to be mourned in psychotherapy. Among these are the sexual and loving experiences that one allowed to go by and which will never come again, the wish for the good mother (the perfect mother who does not exist), the wish that others might now supply that which mother lacked, the loss of youth, the dream of a happy marriage, the wish for a child, for a career, for wealth, and for fame. The loss of intangible wishes can be felt as keenly as the loss of people or things. Each loss must be recognized, mourned, and then relinquished before the person can move on to new hopes.[6]

Varied Characteristics of Loss

As can be seen from the above examples, which are not meant to be all-inclusive, loss can take many forms. It is most profound and most easily recognized when it involves the loss of life—our own or that of a significant other person. (Significant does not mean loved; it means, rather, important in some way.) Loss is also recognized without difficulty when it involves valuable material objects, such as the loss of a home or business, of valuable possessions having monetary or sentimental value.

There are other losses, however, that are much more subtle. When they occur we may be aware of having gone through a painful experience, but we do not always recognize that experience as a loss. Friends and professional helpers may miss the loss aspect as well. Examples of such experiences are minor failures, events causing shame or embarrassment or disappointments. The Oriental value of "loss of face" gives recognition to the loss aspect of these experiences. Such losses may go unnoticed but leave their impact anyway. If the loss itself is unnoticed, in all likelihood the reaction to the loss will also be misunderstood because it is cut off in our thinking from the precipitating event. The ensuing result may be that we see someone in a full-blown normal grief reaction, but inasmuch as no one has recognized that a loss has occurred, the behavior may be seen as disturbed or pathological rather than as normal. (As will be discussed in chapter three, even normal grief is all too often judged as pathology.)

Children and adolescents particularly may be misjudged because their behavior in grief differs from that of adults and may appear as misbehavior requiring discipline. Insensitivity to the emotional and mental lives of young children, particularly the child too young for speech, can make people overlook traumatic losses in their lives out of the conviction that they are too young to know the difference. Yet, infancy and early childhood are periods when children are particularly vulnerable to loss because they have not yet developed the strength to cope with major stress.

Loss can be sudden, as in an accident; gradual, as in a chronic debilitating illness; or prolonged, as when a person is kept alive by sophisticated medical techniques. Loss can be predictable, as with the elderly, or unexpected, as when catastrophic illness befalls a child, upsetting our sense of the order of life, that is, children should grow, and the aged die. Thus, it follows that loss can be tragic but also benign. For the old person fortunate enough to experience what is beginning to be termed an *appropriate death,* the loss of life itself can be benign.

Loss can be complete, partial, or even uncertain and unending. Loved ones missing in war, children disappearing from the streets, young people leaving home for unknown lifestyles are examples of loss without definite endings. So is kidnapping when the victim is never found.

Loss can be brought about by the ravages of nature in floods, tornados, earthquakes, and fires, or by man himself in war, murder, rape, and burglary. Loss can occur singly or be multiple and cumulative. It can be tangible as well as intangible, as in a plan gone astray, a romance turned to disappointment, the envy of another's good fortune, trust betrayed.

Loss can be symbolic, and loss is always personal. No one can decide what constitutes a loss to another person. To one woman the inability to bear a child might be felt as a catastrophic loss; to another motherhood itself would be.

Because loss is part of the human condition, we encounter it daily. For some people, traumatic loss may occur early in life, leaving permanent scars on the developing personality. For others, serious loss may occur later in life when the personality, already having attained some degree of integration, is more prepared to deal with the stress. This delay by no means guarantees that the effects of the loss will not be traumatic. Each loss experience is unique in its impact and meaning. The same type of loss can be experienced as benign one moment and as traumatic another, depending on a variety of factors such as health, energy level, surrounding supports, and others.

Because loss is a universal experience, it is easily overlooked. Yet, loss can disrupt our living arrangements, social environment, or key relationships, and upset the basis for security and interdependency. Loss can be an underlying factor in disease, in pathological emotions and behavior, and even in death itself.

Loss always carries with it a threat to self-esteem. Self-esteem is not an attribute we acquire permanently as part of an ideal childhood. It remains forever fragile, is easily damaged, and demands constant safeguarding. In its broadest sense, loss can be said to occur any time we suffer a blow to self-esteem.[7]

As has been stated earlier, in normal grief, feelings and behavior go contrary to what we usually think of as good adjustment. Grief is such an overwhelming experience that it has been likened to an illness, and, as with any illness, the outcome can range from total to partial recovery, with or without serious residue on later adjustment.

Although grief has been compared to illness, because illness is something with which we are familiar, in reality illness in itself may be considered one form of loss, that of the state of health. We need to look beyond the grief set off by the loss to understand fully the hidden values in loss. These are to be found in the creative forces unleashed by the grief process, which find culmination in eventual restitution. Creative restitution through appropriate mourning and resolution is not an inevitable consequence of loss and grief, for loss can just as well lead to the opposite outcome, that of despair. Both of these eventualities will be dealt with in this book.

Loss and Deprivation

The dictionary makes no distinction between words describing the condition of *having had and then not having* and the other condition of *never having had at all,* using *loss* and *deprivation* for both. Yet, the inner experience of those who have had and lost and those who have missed out on an experience from the outset are markedly different.

Clinical studies, from experiments with animals and from observation of infants, show that the lack of proper and necessary supplies from the outset leads to developmental retardation which, if lasting and severe enough, can never be corrected.[8] These lacks can be in material necessities, such as food, water, warmth; in sensory stimulation, such as light, sound, movement; or in emotional stimulation, such as loving care. The lack of protein during prenatal development, for example, leaves a stunted individual who can never be brought up to normal despite later protein supplementation. What is lacking at a point of phase-appropriateness cannot be supplied later with the same outcome.

Although loss is not the same as basic deprivation, loss can, nevertheless, result in later deprivations as well as in further losses. An example of basic deprivation are children born with a physical or mental deficiency. From the beginning they are set apart from other children by their deficiency, and they must learn to cope, if possible, without that which they lack—which others have and take for granted. By contrast, persons born normal who later meet with a catastrophe that causes physical or mental impairment have suffered the loss of the healthy body they once knew as their own. The original loss may bring on further losses of self-esteem and self-confidence, of friends and playmates, of school and career goals, and so on. These people may also be deprived of later life experiences they might otherwise have enjoyed. If the condition is progressive, their losses may be further compounded. This is an example of loss resulting in further losses as well as in deprivations. In dealing with these people, we need to be aware not only of their grief reactions but also of gaps in their experiences that even the working through of grief cannot restore.

The Fear of Loss

Because from early infancy we face the threat of loss in the innumerable experiences of union and separation from the mothering person and later from other valued people, it is understandable that the fear of loss should lie deeply buried in all of us. A loss is never forgotten. It remains in the unconscious, ever ready to surge up anew as a later loss occurs or as a new threat of loss hovers.

The fear of loss arouses in each of us the infantile, deep-rooted fear of abandonment. Abandonment to the infant would mean death. Thus, a feeling of anxiety or intense fear accompanies the fear of loss. We may fear danger from outside forces or even fear our own destructive impulses.

Probably the most powerful fear is the fear of death. This fear incorporates fear of the unknown, of punishment in the hereafter, of loneliness, and of the ultimate separation from significant people.

The fear of abandonment (death) is so overpowering that the infant, the child, and even the adult will go to any lengths to avoid feeling unwanted or rejected—being unwanted implies that one is deserving of abandonment or death. Children will erect powerful defenses against the recognition of rejection by parents. Experts believe that the fear of death is woven into the major conflicts underlying many emotional and mental disorders.[9]

The fear of loss through impending death is found in reactions to catastrophic illness, as well as in such ordinary behavior as parental worry about children riding bicycles in traffic, starting to drive a car, or even in the rebellion of adolescents, which constitutes a symbolic killing off of parents by rejection of their values. Fear of loss through death can unconsciously underlie fear of the loss of a loved one through separation, of a part of the body or body function, of material objects, or of losses synonymous with growth and development.

Folklore and customs attest to the deep-seated awareness of our fear of loss. The amulet worn around the neck is a protection against injury or misfortune (loss). Belief in the evil eye—the power attributed to some people of being able to harm others by merely looking at them—is cross-cultural. It goes hand-in-hand with the belief that the gods, too, will look with envy upon anyone who is too fortunate. Thus, happiness and good fortune should not be too openly displayed lest they arouse envy in the gods or our fellow human beings. "Laugh in the morning; cry at night," is one admonition children are taught to minimize displays of pleasure and thus avoid envy.

This fear of misfortune is seen in the tendency we have to shun the bereaved (whether it be the widowed, the divorced, the physically maimed) as if their fate were catching. It is probably likely that every woman during pregnancy has fears of giving birth to a defective child. These fears are often traceable to unconscious expectations of punishment for past sexual sins or for sins such as ingratitude toward parents. Similar unconscious fears are also found in those with psychosomatic disorders and other psychiatric problems.

One loss not only can set off further losses but can also set off fears of further loss. The child who loses one parent worries about losing the other. The physically maimed can fear economic loss because of prejudicial hiring policies; they can worry about keeping up appearances, about rejection from people because of their handicap, about being clumsy, unclean, or making other social errors. The elderly worry with each succeeding loss about what the next loss will be. The cancer patient waits for the next outbreak of the disease. Political refugees fear political instability in the new land.

The Merging of Losses

Although loss was outlined earlier in this chapter as having four distinct categories, loss cannot be understood if each loss is seen as separate and discrete. Loss cannot be viewed as a single, total, unitary experience. Rather, it must be seen in all of its complexities and partial aspects. This point is made by one expert on blindness, who lists twenty losses that make up the total handicap of blindness. These are as follows, and even these, he maintains, do not cover all the possible losses involved:

Basic losses to psychological security
    Loss of physical integrity
    Loss of confidence in the remaining senses
    Loss of reality contact with the environment
    Loss of visual background
    Loss of light security

Losses of basic skills
    Loss of mobility
    Loss of techniques of daily living

Losses in communication
    Loss of the ease of written communication
    Loss of the ease of spoken communication
    Loss of informational progress

Losses in appreciation
    Loss of the visual perception of the pleasurable
    Loss of the visual perception of the beautiful

Losses concerning occupation and financial status
    Loss of recreation
    Loss of career, vocational goal, job opportunity
    Loss of financial security

Resulting losses to the whole personality
    Loss of personal independence
    Loss of social adequacy
    Loss of obscurity
    Loss of self-esteem
    Loss of total personality organization[10]

It is important to point out that these losses occur in the once-sighted person, not in a person blind from birth. This refers to the point made earlier in this chapter about the distinction between never having had and having had and lost something of value, that is, between original deprivation and a gap in experience and loss.

A loss remains forever alive in the unconscious, in which there is no sense of time such as we think of when we consider past, present, and future events. Thus, past losses are aroused when set off by a current loss or even a reminder of the loss, just as current losses or the memory of past losses evoke fear of further loss in the future. Past and present losses determine our defensiveness in warding off the threats of further loss, the extent to which the fear of loss operates in our lives, and our general openness to life and new experiences.

"I want so to get married and to have someone to love and who will love me," reflected one thirty-year-old man. "But the memory of the pain I felt when my girlfriend walked out on me is so great that it is all I can think of when I meet a woman I like. I worry that if I get involved, the same thing will happen again. And I couldn't stand it. I'd rather have superficial relationships than suffer like that. Frankly, I'd rather be dead than go through that kind of pain again."

This merging of past and present losses is readily seen in aging. In visiting a home for the aged, a therapist saw a number of examples of this. One old woman, well into her nineties, wandered from room to room, telling everyone she met in the hallway that she was looking for her mother. "Have you seen my mother?" She asked. Another older woman wept for the infant she had lost in childbirth sixty years before. Still another mourned for her husband, dead for over a quarter of a century. And finally, a woman grieved for her sister who had been dead for thirty years.

It seems reasonable to believe that these women had not spent all the intervening years grieving for their lost loved ones. Why the revival of grief in old age? It is clear that the daily lives of these elderly women are filled with loss—of vitality, health, status, independence, mobility, memory, and loved ones—the inevitable fate in the aging process. In these elderly people, where mental functions such as orientation to time and place and people diminish with the loss of the organic supports to such mental processes (due to poor blood supply to the brain or even the loss of brain cells with aging), all losses over the lifetime are merged in the unconscious and expressed as if they are occurring in the present.

The merging of loss and the fear of loss is also seen in clinical work. An attractive woman of fifty-seven came into treatment with the presenting problem of a personality change which had been taking place over the preceding two years. From a warm, mothering, interesting, involved person she had watched herself become angry, hateful, and jealous. One by one she had terminated friendships so that her telephone now seldom rang with social calls. At work people hardly spoke to her because she was so "bitchy."

The woman dated her personality change from the time when a new employee entered her office and began to compete with her for the "mother hen" position with younger female employees. Slowly she felt herself rejected and isolated, until finally she felt she could no longer stand it. She requested and was granted a transfer to another office of the company. With this move she went from a large, busy office where she had attained some prestige over the years to a new, smaller office where she was an unknown newcomer. She felt the loss of importance keenly and realized that by the move she had actually made matters worse rather than better. In her unhappiness she withdrew into herself even further. Her interests narrowed, her concern for others decreased; she hated the younger workers who were speedier and more efficient than she was; she detested their lunchtime chatter and went off to eat by herself.

The history revealed that her two married children and their families, with whom she was close, had moved to the other side of the country during the past year. Thus, she could no longer visit with them on weekends. She had been divorced for about fifteen years and had a good, long-standing relationship with a male friend. He was giving to her both emotionally and financially, but did not seek marriage, and he reserved his weekends for visiting with his grown children and grandchildren. Thus, she found herself isolated during the work week and suddenly alone during her free time. She further revealed that this male friend had, over the years, encouraged her alienation from her aunts, uncles, and cousins following dissension at the time of her mother's funeral. In spite of reassurance from her friend, she felt very guilty over her lack of attention to her elderly father and stepmother in their final years. She had cared for them out of a sense of duty, not love. Now she feared her own aging, yet knew it was inevitable, and wondered if she too would be left lonely and cared for out of duty, as punishment for her own lack of love of her parents.

She knew nothing of psychotherapy but she knew things could not continue as they were. She had to do something because she did not like herself the way she was.

It was a revelation to this patient in therapy to discover during the course of history-giving how many losses she had encountered, some that had happened to her and others that she herself had brought about. She was encouraged to try to correct some of the latter. She was urged to begin by finding something positive to say to one of her co-workers. It was with great difficulty that she struggled to find something kind and sincere to say. With great effort—and trepidation —she was able to tell one of her young co-workers that she seemed to be a very warm and loving mother. To her surprise, the response was such gratitude that before long she was invited to eat with the younger girls, and eventually she became more and more included in the office life. She was also encouraged, despite her friend's advice to the contrary, to reestablish contact and relationships with her elderly relatives. To her delight she found them warm and accepting, and as her contacts with people broadened, her unhappiness and "bitchiness" diminished. The warmth and interest in people returned.

We need to be cognizant of the wide range of loss experiences that confront all of us as we move through life. When the person who has suffered a loss is aware that a loss has occurred, the task confronting him is that of going through the grief and mourning processes to the point of healthy restitution. The components of this task are described in later chapters.

However, many of the experiences described earlier as losses are not recognized as such by either the bereaved or those close to them. People may go through the physical, emotional, and mental distress of grief without knowing the cause of their pain. Many medical and mental health professionals to whom they may turn are not yet adequately trained to associate various physical or emotional symptoms, interpersonal problems, or disturbances of behavior ranging from the mild to the extremely destructive with past, current, or anticipated loss.

It can be helpful merely to identify an experience as a loss. For example, a client telephoned for an emergency appointment while her regular therapist was on vacation (experienced as a loss of a supportive relationship). She had that day been confronted by her high school students, who told her she was disappointing as a teacher; they had expected more from her from what former classmates had told them. The students said they found her dull, her examples uninteresting, and they just wanted her to know how they felt. The client was devastated by their attack. Despite her hurt, she kept wondering why her daughter's recent mental breakdown kept coming to her mind during all the time the confrontation was taking place. When asked gently what she thought the connection might be, she pondered for a moment, then replied, "In both cases I feel like a failure." The feeling of failure was the loss experience connecting the two traumas.

It should be clear from all that has been said that losses cannot be understood if viewed singly, because past losses emerge from the unconscious to mingle with current losses and with the fear of future loss.

To summarize, we need to be able to identify a loss, to view it in all the complexity of the myriad sub-losses that make up its totality, and to connect it to past losses and the fear of loss in the future. All this has to do with the perception of the loss itself. One might conceive of a model as follows:

Past losses and separations
have an impact on
current losses and separations and attachments
and all these factors bear on
fear of future loss and separations and
capacity to make future attachments.

Notes

1. David Peretz, "Development, Object-Relationships, and Loss," in *Loss and Grief: Psychological Management in Medical Practice,* ed. Bernard Schoenberg et al. (New York: Columbia University Press, 1970), p. 4.

2. Peter Marris, *Loss and Change* (New York: Pantheon Books, 1974).

3. See for example Henry Grayson, "Grief Reactions to the Relinquishing of Unfulfilled Wishes," *American Journal of Psychotherapy* 24 (April 1970): 288, and Otto Rank, *The Trauma of Birth* (New York: R. Brunner, 1952).

4. Marris, *Loss and Change,* pp. 20-21.

5. Myrna M. Weissman and Eugene S. Paykel, *The Depressed Woman* (Chicago: University of Chicago Press, 1974).

6. Grayson, "Grief Reactions."

7. Gregory Rochlin, *Griefs and Discontents: The Forces of Change* (Boston: Little, Brown and Co., 1965).

8. Michael Rutter, *The Qualities of Mothering: Maternal Deprivation Reassessed* (New York: Jason Aronson, 1974).

9. Rochlin, *Griefs and Discontents.*

10. Thomas J. Carroll, *Blindness: What It Is, What It Does, and How to Live with It* (Boston: Little, Brown and Co., 1961).

3/
Duration of Grief and Mourning

Definitions

The magnitude of the task of attempting to set forth a framework for understanding grief is enormous, but the task must be attempted. Life does not await our understanding. It moves on and carries us with it toward joy or suffering, but not necessarily in direct proportion to our understanding of it. The person who falls from a height does not escape harm because he is ignorant of the laws of gravity. However, although ignorance was no guarantee against hurt, knowledge could have helped protect him. Because loss and grief are all about us daily, we are liable to do repeated harm to ourselves and others by our lack of knowledge. A beginning attempt at filling some of the gaps in our knowledge is, therefore, justified, even though it cannot be all-inclusive.

Bereavement has been defined by some as the act of separation or loss that results in the experience of grief. This locates it at a point in time, thus making it a precipitant event rather than a process.[1] Others disagree and consider bereavement the complex series of responses that follow a loss and divide it into two components—grief and mourning.[2]

Grief is a state defined by Webster as "intense emotional suffering caused by loss, disaster, misfortune, etc., acute sorrow; deep sadness." *Anticipatory grief* is the term applied to grief expressed in advance of a loss when the loss is perceived as inevitable. The intense grief which follows a loss has been given the label *acute grief.* Although the grief preceding a loss may be intensely painful, as with the dying patient and his family, pre-loss grief continues to be classified as anticipatory grief despite its acuteness. As will be seen below, there is considerable similarity in the reactions to the stages of anticipatory and acute grief.

Mourning is another ambiguous term, one that has been used interchangeably with grief. It is also regarded as the lengthy process following loss, of which grief is a part, but extending beyond the first reactions into the period of reorganization of the new identity and reattachment to new interests and people.[3] Perhaps the most helpful definition of mourning is the one offered by James R. Averill, a psychologist, who regards it as the conventional behavior determined by the mores and customs of a given society, dictating the way in which a person should conduct himself following the death of an individual.[4] This prescribed behavior may or may not coincide with the actual feelings of the bereaved, but they risk incurring censure if they disobey these social dictates.

The reactions to grief are physiological and psychological rather than cultural, as in mourning, and there is even evidence that there is a biological base to grief.[5] Support for this assertion comes from John Bowlby's study of the behavior of animals following loss, behavior that parallels that of human beings in grief—the attempt to recover the lost member, the upsetting of all bodily functions, hostility, misery, bad temper, a proneness to infections, a picking at the flesh, and even death.[6] It has also been hypothesized that grief has an adaptive function "to insure group cohesiveness in species where a social form of existence is necessary for survival."[7] We will see later how each of the components of grief serves this purpose.

Grief and mourning may occur simultaneously in situations where feelings are supported by social customs such as funeral rites. These rites not only give structure to the bereaved at a time of disorganization but also help to reinforce social and religious behavior, thus strengthening group cohesiveness at the same time. Mourning can also take place when death has, in fact, produced little or no grief and the feelings of the bereaved do not match the intensity of the cultural expectations centered on the loss. The rites help the bereaved save face where the disclosure of true feelings might bring criticism. Mourning without grief can also take place where grief is inhibited, aborted, or denied, and again protect the bereaved from criticism. These situations will be discussed fully in later chapters.

When one considers the numerous situations that can be considered as losses, it is clear that Western society, at least, has very few mourning rituals to cover them. The basic ritual has attended death, but with the move toward secularism during the twentieth century this ritual is also in decline and even being eliminated. Cremation, which is replacing the traditional burial, eliminates even the evidence of death for later reality testing. Clearly, urban growth has contributed to the decline of the funeral service; families are scattered, with little if any tie to a religious group; a clergyman is called upon to speak about a deceased person he did not even know; a nonreligious memorial service is substituted. Increasingly, the funeral service can become a matter of form without meaning or substance.

Of more frequent occurrence, however, is the matter of grief following losses that go unrecognized as such and are, therefore, unsupported by mourning rituals. What rituals do we have for divorce, for rape, for a mastectomy, for the loss of a job? One might consider the retirement party as a mourning ritual for the end of the work life, but the popular complaint hidden by humor, "Thirty years with the company and all I get is a gold watch!" is, perhaps, an indication of the way in which this ceremony fails to meet the emotional needs of the retiree.

Because this book deals with losses of many kinds, most of which have no mourning rituals attached to them, the focus herein will be on grief rather than on mourning. It is the psychological, personal, painful aspect of the reactions to loss rather than the cultural, social behaviors that will concern us here.

Grief, although a normal life process, involves such profound physical, emotional, and mental changes that its symptoms often resemble those found in physical, mental, and emotional disorders. Thus, normal grief has often been misdiagnosed as maladjustment. It is this similarity to emotional disorder that often brings the bereaved to the attention of people in the helping professions.

As has already been stated, grief has been compared to a physical illness. Both states take time for healing. Both include emotional and physical aspects. Both may be self-limiting or require intervention by others. And in both, recovery can range from a complete return to the preexisting state of health and well-being, to partial recovery, to improved growth and creativity, or both can inflict permanent damage, progressive decline, and even death.

Even the most common and trivial disorder can touch off emotional conflicts in illness similar to grief. The person with a cold, for example, blames self-neglect for bringing on the cold. He voices his guilt, shows wishes for exceptional treatment and special care, magnifies the significance of his aches and pains, and shows increased preoccupation with the self.[8] He may also exhibit hostile behavior by insisting that he is not spreading infection and by going out to do precisely that.

Phases of anticipatory grief

Elisabeth Kübler-Ross's classification of the stages of anticipatory grief in the dying patient are by now well known. The stages are:

1. Denial and shock—"Not me."

2. Anger and irritability—"Why me?"

3. Bargaining—"If I promise this, or do that, I'll get better," "Perhaps me, but. . . ."

4. Depression and beginning acceptance—"It is me."

5. True acceptance—"Okay."[9]

Other researchers stress the importance of distinguishing between the anticipatory grief of the dying patient and that of the patient where death is a possibility but not a certainty. These stages are:

1. Shock.

2. Anger.

3. Grief and anticipatory grief.

4. Bargaining or "promissory note" behavior.

5. The period of uncertainty.

6. If the outcome is favorable:
   Renewal and rebuilding—
   Integration of the experience.
   If the outcome is unfavorable:
   Stages then follow those of Kübler-Ross detailed above.[10]

This outline would apply to situations other than illness where a catastrophic loss is a possibility but not a certainty. Examples are loved ones missing in war, kidnappings, loved ones disappearing because of other reasons, impending political crises, or rumors of job loss.

Avery D. Weisman, a psychoanalyst, has a different outline for stages of adaptation to a serious illness that does not necessarily lead to death. This outline is also applicable to other types of anticipated losses and is as follows:

1. Recognition of the painful reality of the pending loss.

2. Repudiation of a threatening portion of that reality (denial).

3. Replacement with a more acceptable or tolerable meaning of the reality.

4. Obligatory yielding or capitulation to some aspect of the loss.

5. Resolution of the conflict by a process of repudiation and yielding (intermittent denial).

6. Resolution of the conflict.

7. Reorientation to the changes through reconstitution of the new reality.[11]

By definition anticipatory grief would end at the time the actual loss takes place, at which point it would merge into acute grief. Thus, in contrast to the dying patient who undergoes only anticipatory grief, his family, friends, caretakers, and others concerned with him undergo both anticipatory and acute grief.

Anticipatory grief may accelerate or decelerate in intensity up to the point of loss depending on a number of factors, such as the extent of the denial of the loss, the length of time the loss is anticipated, the hopes aroused for the loss not to take place, and the timing of the grief work to the actual loss itself. Grief work that is not completed by the time the loss actually takes place should be continued after the loss in acute grief. Grief work that is completed too early in advance of the actual loss can lead to a withdrawal of emotional investment in the endangered object. In this event, if the loss does not occur after all or if it takes too long to happen, it is often difficult, if not impossible, for the person so threatened to reattach feeling to that which he feared losing—the job one struggled to keep now has no appeal. This phenomenon accounts for some of the tragedies that have made headlines following the release of American prisoners of war. Wives who had already worked through their grief over their missing husbands had invested emotionally elsewhere and, therefore, could not become reattached to their spouses.

Because many of the components outlined above for anticipatory grief are also found in post-loss grief, they will be discussed in detail later in the chapters on denial, anger, and depression. Bargaining will be mentioned in the chapter on initial responses to loss; acceptance will be covered in the chapter on restitution and depletion.

Phases of post-loss grief

Acute grief following loss has been described by various terms, terms that tend to fall into three major phases distinguished by their focus on the past, the present, and the future. Despite great variation in possible responses, it is possible to trace a sequence in both behavior and feeling states. The sequence, according to Bowlby's research, "begins with anxiety and anger, proceeds through pain and despair, and, if fortune smiles, ends with hope."[12]

The components of acute grief and mourning can be outlined as follows:

PHASE 1. Shock, alarm, and denial.
PHASE 2. Acute grief, consisting of:
Continuing, intermittent, and lessening denial.
Physical and psychological pain and distress.
Contradictory pulls, emotions, and impulses.
Searching behavior, composed of:
preoccupation with thoughts of the loss, a compulsion to speak of the loss, a compulsion to retrieve that which was lost, a sense of waiting for something to happen, aimless wandering and restlessness, a feeling of being lost, of not knowing what to do, inability to initiate any activity, a feeling that time is suspended, a feeling of disorganization, and a feeling that life can never be worthwhile again, confusion and feelings that things are not real, fear that all the above indicate mental illness.
Crying, anger, guilt, shame.
Identifying with traits, values, symptoms, tastes, or other characteristics of the lost person.
Regression or return to behaviors and feelings of an earlier age or connected with a previous loss or reactions thereto.
Helplessness and depression, hope or hopelessness, relief.
Decrease in pain and increasing capacity to cope over time.
A compulsion to find meaning in the loss.
Beginning thoughts of a new life without the lost object.
PHASE 3. Integration of the loss and grief.
If the outcome is favorable:
Acceptance of the reality of the loss and return to physical and psychological well-being, diminished frequency and intensity of crying, restored self-esteem, focus on the present and future, ability to enjoy life again, pleasure at awareness of growth from the experience, reorganization of a new identity with restitution for the loss, and loss remembered with poignancy and caring instead of pain.
If the outcome is unfavorable:
Acceptance of the reality of the loss with lingering sense of depression and physical aches and pains, diminished sense of self-esteem, reorganization of a new identity with constriction of personality and involvement, and vulnerability to other separations and losses.

There is general agreement among the experts on acute post-loss grief that these phases are not discrete and sequential. They do not follow each other in any prescribed order. They tend, rather, to overlap and to proceed in a jagged pattern of a forward thrust, then retreat to an earlier phase, then a forward movement again. No two people will react alike, and the same person will not react in the same way to every loss. Although loss is a necessary precursor to grief, not every loss must result in grief. Losses that are experienced as mild, benign parts of development can, while the person is protected by sufficient external supports, be integrated into the personality without grief. The experience then becomes part of the adaptive behavior of the individual. The painless loss of a baby tooth, aided by parental praise for growing up and monetary reward (cultural recognition of the need for restitution for the loss), represents such a benign loss.

"When you reach twenty-one," remarked one young man on his birthday, "it is too late to be a child prodigy." For him this was a nostalgic, benign loss. For another, with aspirations or parental pressure for early achievement, it might well have had more tragic overtones. Therefore, although not all the bereaved manifest the same psychological and physiological reactions to a loss, certain features of bereavement are sufficiently alike to constitute a definable syndrome. Despite the lack of a definite sequence, each phase has identifiable characteristics that are predominant, even though they may appear to a lesser degree in the other phases. Each phase must be experienced to a peak of intensity before it can be resolved. In our society, it is easy for the bereaved without appropriate help to become bogged down at any stage of the process and thus preclude its completion.

Unquestionably, grief is most acute in response to the death of a loved one or to the loss of a major part of one's own body. The same type of reactions can, however, be set off by other losses. For example, experts in adoption report that unwed mothers who try to keep their babies, and later find they cannot provide for them as they had hoped to, plead for the right to maintain some contact with their children after the adoption. They equate the traditional complete relinquishment without access to their children "with amputation of a part of their bodies, or with the loss of a close relative through death."[13]

A minor loss can set off repercussions of an earlier major loss. A loss regarded as minor by others can have devastating symbolic or unconscious meaning for the people concerned, for example, the would-be parent who is infertile, the couple unable to conceive. Many bereaved people, regardless of the loss, feel that nobody even understands, much less cares.

Some form or degree of grief may be expected whenever any loss occurs, although the intensity, duration, and expression of the grief vary from individual to individual, from culture to culture, and in the same individual at different times of life. It is the operation of the common dynamics of grief, set off by losses ranging from the most fleeting wish or disappointment to a major catastrophe, that enables us to conceptualize a model for understanding grief. Normal grief, despite its pathological appearance, is healthy and should, under favorable environmental conditions, lead not only to recovery but also to growth and healthy change.

Grief Work with Adults

It has often been said that if something does not kill you it will make you stronger; this statement applies to loss and grief. Freud termed the business of what goes on during mourning "grief work." It is a painful process that requires a great deal of effort.

The bereaved look about themselves and see that that which they loved no longer exists. Living demands that they detach their emotional investment from that which no longer exists so that they will have energy for living in the present. But people do not willingly or readily abandon something or someone in which they have invested emotion. They are thus thrown into a state of confusion and feel a pull back toward the lost object as well as a pull toward the current reality. They are torn in two directions and keep going back and forth in their minds between the past and the present.

Eventually, in a healthy person with enough opportunities for restitution, reality wins. But it wins only bit by bit, after a great expenditure of time, energy, and suffering, leaving little interest or energy for other concerns while the process is going on. The bereaved are immersed in their grief as much as the sick are in their illness; an investment of energy is necessary if one is to recover from either condition. Bereavement represents a moratorium in living. During bereavement each of the memories and expectations having to do with the lost object is brought up and lived through anew. It is a painful process, because each memory comes into conflict with present reality, reminding the bereaved that that part of their life is no more. It is the sum of the accumulated satisfactions one has derived from being alive that finally persuades the bereaved to sever the attachment to that which has been lost and to find pleasure in new attachments.

Kate Holliday, a veteran magazine reporter, described movingly the individual memories and expectations involved in her grief following an injury to her shoulder and the muscle deterioration which followed:

> I shall never ever be whole again. The mishap has affected the way I make a living, the way I sleep, the way I hug my grandchildren, the way I shake hands, the way I drive a car, the way I write my name and, perhaps worst of all, my entire way of thinking.
>
> The fall broke my right shoulder so badly that, even after two years, the

fracture has not healed. For more than four months, I sat immobile, my arm in an orthopedic sling. I have twice undergone surgery, and my doctors talk of more. For now, there is the pain.

There are also challenges to the mind, and countless new situations to which I must adjust. For the first time in my life I am forced to say, "I cannot do that. I will never be able to do that again." It is tough to accept, all this without self-pity; to accept, and still keep my confidence, to accept, and get on with my job as a professional writer. . . . A handicap is always "there," creating its own traps. Shyness is one. When you have been isolated for months and finally go out, you find yourself talking too much about your problems and are mortified later.[14]

Holliday has here described an ongoing process following loss. Even when the acute grief is over, a new surge of grief can be set off by a reminder of the loss. For her it was the pain and disability that required her to reorganize her life.

Grief in Infancy and Childhood

If as a society we have used denial in regard to adult losses and griefs, even more have we disallowed grief experiences of children. How often do we hear it said that a child in the midst of tragedy is lucky because he is too young to understand? Even many professionals do not as yet fully appreciate the impact loss has on infants and young children. Nor do they understand the differences in reactions between the younger child and older child or adolescent. The subject is complicated and cannot be adequately covered in this book. However, some mention must be made of childhood grief because of its profound effect on later life experiences. Adults are, after all, people who once were children, and they carry with them the impact of experiences from those years.

Children are able to withstand a range of frightening experiences provided they have the assurance of a positive and durable tie to a nurturing figure. (For the sake of clarity that figure will hereinafter be referred to as the mother.) Evidence points to a causal relationship between the loss or interruption of the early nurturing tie or deficiencies in the quality of care from the mother and disturbances in the life of the child.

During infancy the baby and mother are in a symbiotic state of oneness, which reaches its peak of intensity at about four or five months of age. This continues on in varying degrees of intensity until the child is about age three. There is considerable controversy and disagreement on technical issues over the age at which the infant or child first becomes capable of grieving.[15] Space does not permit an exploration in detail of these varying points of view. For our purposes it is sufficient to note that there is increasing agreement among experts that loss of the mother figure between about six months and three or four years of age places the child at risk emotionally.[16] It cannot be emphasized enough that healthy development in the human being requires a long phase of good attachment of the young child to the mother. When negative experiences with the mother outweigh positive, and when lengthy or permanent disruptions in the mother-child unit occur, the seeds are sown for future emotional disturbances—psychoses, neuroses, character disorders, borderline disorders, psychosomatic disturbances, addictions, depressions, anxieties, and delinquencies. Common to all of these disorders is the persistence of separation anxiety and a tendency toward abandonment depression.[17]

Another source of vulnerability to loss in the child's development has been described as having to do with the infant's "drive toward progressive self-differentiation as an object separate from the mother and the latter's complementary facilitating responses in relation to it."[18] The mother needs to accept both the toddler's moves away from her and his return to her to enable him to tolerate the anxiety of his venturing into the larger world. Should she reward his dependency and punish his exploratory attempts instead, he is again left with a proneness to anxiety and depression, now around any attempt at autonomy or self-directedness. His vulnerability then is not only to loss and separation but to growth itself, which activates the fear of loss.

Up to about age three years, the child is closely attached to his mother physically, content in her presence, distressed when she is out of sight. Even momentary separations are protested. Permanent loss or prolonged separation from the caretaking figure from the second half of the first year up to age three brings a grief reaction which has been classified into three phases: protest, despair, and detachment, a sequence of responses considered characteristic of all forms of mourning.[19]

The child's yearning for and anger toward the mother for leaving may be held in abeyance during her absence, with feelings bursting forth following reunion. First, however, there is a period during which the child seems to not recognize her and remains detached and unresponsive to her overtures. The determination of whether the separation has been traumatic to the child can be made on the basis of his ability to reattach emotionally to the mother. The young child does not perceive time sufficiently well to grasp the distinction between a temporary and a permanent separation and, if the separation goes on so long that the child truly detaches or if it is a permanent separation or loss, the groundwork is laid for future pathology.

The Duration of Normal Grief and Mourning

The need for time

Time is a very important aspect of grief work, and for this reason the word is part of the title of this book. The recovery to creative, healthy living is through the painful process of grief itself. There are no shortcuts. How little this is understood was indicated recently in an advertisement by professionals in the mental health field. The advertisement was an offer to ease the pain of grief after divorce or break-up with a lover through the use of an electric shock applied every time the bereaved thought of the lost lover! Thus is the pain of loss to be overcome speedily and efficiently.

Because of the multitude of factors that affect the way an individual will react to grief, there can be no cookbook approach to helping the bereaved nor can there be a set timetable for the grief process. Broad principles need to be applied and modified for each person, each family, and every loss situation.

It is a mistake, however, to think that time alone will heal the pain of grief. It is how time is used that will be a factor in determining how long the pain remains acute, whether it is even fully experienced, and how long it will take for recovery. The course of normal grief depends on the ability of the bereaved to do the grief work necessary to separate themselves from that which was lost and reinvest themselves elsewhere.

As has been stated, there are thousands of memories associated with the lost person, body part, house, homeland, or other object that has been valued and lost. The feeling must be accurately perceived, experienced, identified by its right name (for example, shame and guilt are not the same), endured, and finally mastered through sufficient expression and discharge. Healing comes from immersion in the pain, actually a reattachment through memory to the valued object, the ability to endure the pain of grief, eventual relinquishment of the attachment, and finally reattachment to new people, values, and goals.

Grief is an active, not a passive, process; Freud rightfully labeled it "work." It is mental and emotional labor. It is exhaustive and exhausting, not only for the bereaved but also for those about them and those who would be of comfort to them. Ideally, it should allow for an emotional return to the helplessness of a safe infancy, a kind of symbolic rebirth from which a new chapter of life can be woven out of the fabric of the old, the pain and struggle of the grief process itself, and the hopes for the future.

Grief is so painful that people will attempt to flee from it by any means possible. Some of these are discussed in the chapters that follow, to show the forms such flight from feeling can take. Flight from the pain of grief, however, can offer only temporary relief; eventually the price is costly.

The process of grief cannot be directed from outside, although the style and length of grieving is definitely culture-related, with religious and social customs giving structure to the course of grieving. In our grief-denying culture, the helper needs to be sensitive to how and when to bring the bereaved back to the painful task of grieving so that all feelings can be discharged. The ability to grieve is also the ability to enjoy life, as eloquently expressed by Kahlil Gibran:

Then a woman said, Speak to us of Joy and Sorrow.
And he answered:
Your joy is your sorrow unmasked.
And the self-same well from which your laughter
rises was oftentimes filled with your tears.[20]

The expressions "it will take time" and "time heals all wounds" do have a sound basis in reality. In most instances of normal loss the pain of grief does lessen with time, and the open wound heals, but a permanent imprint is left in the memory, and the person is changed by the experience.

Mourning ends with the detachment of emotional investment in the lost object and reinvestment of that emotion in a new object. This is made possible through restoring a good image of the lost object to the inner world of the bereaved. By retaining the object in one's inner life it remains forever a part of us, and thus it is possible to let go of it in the outer world.

Recovery from grief and mourning is judged to be the return to normal activities with full capacity for pleasure in the present without guilt, shame, or remorse, or the need to be overtly or covertly destructive to oneself or others. There is a renewed confidence, self-respect, spontaneity, and pride, renewed energy and initiative, organization and planning replacing the disorganization of the grief period, and a search for new objects, roles, or interests. There is a feeling of peace and an acceptance of pain as a necessary part of living.

Despite this optimistic picture, that which is lost is never forgotten. Freud stated it thus:

Although we know that after such a loss the acute state of mourning will subside, we also know we shall remain inconsolable and will never find a substitute. No matter what may fill the gap, even if it be filled completely, it nevertheless remains something else. And actually this is how it should be. It is the only way of perpetuating that love which we do not want to relinquish.[21]

The duration of grief in adults

There is considerable confusion in the literature and in the public mind regarding the duration of normal grief. Professionals tend to underestimate its length and intensity. Research studies have been primarily concerned with death and widowhood. There appears to be no systematic research on other kinds of losses. Information derived from clinical observations exists but it is difficult to draw conclusions from these data because populations and the variables studied are not comparable.

In 1909, Freud stated that "a normal period of mourning would last from one to two years."[22] How much impact this statement had is not known. The modern view of duration of grief was more directly influenced by Erich Lindemann's work of the 1940s, in which it is stated: "With eight to ten interviews in which the psychiatrist shares the grief work, and with a period of from four to six weeks, it was ordinarily possible to settle an uncomplicated and undistorted grief reaction."[23]

Lindemann's subjects were adults experiencing grief following the sudden death of loved ones. The group consisted of both neurotics and people not in treatment and, therefore, assumed to be free of neurosis. Subjects were followed only through the first year of bereavement. The criterion of good adjustment appeared to be the ability to leave the hospital psychiatric service and return home; thus it is not known how these people fared during the months that followed. Yet, while working with some of these bereaved individuals, researchers found evidence of old unresolved losses going back ten and twenty or more years. It is difficult, therefore, to understand the basis of Lindemann's conclusion.

Another point that needs further examination is that the Lindemann research was on sudden catastrophic death from the Cocoanut Grove nightclub fire in Boston, which claimed 492 victims and touched many lives. It has been postulated that an anticipation of loss, no matter how brief, tends to prolong the grief period, and that where group factors exist, such as in situations of shared mourning and widespread sympathy over a disaster, these factors tend to facilitate an earlier working through of grief.[24] This hypothesis, however, needs to be tested. We do not have sufficient information on the later adjustment of people bereaved by disasters that would indicate anything other than that these massive disasters leave long-lasting scars on survivors. For example, survivors of the Holocaust who seemed to function adequately during the decades following their trauma are now, with the losses of the later years, beginning to show pathology related to the earlier losses. Furthermore, it is coming to the attention of social workers and other mental health workers that the children of survivors, born after the events, carry within them the scars of their parents' ordeal.

It is unfortunate that the timing of grief set forth by Lindemann's research prevailed in professional thinking for three decades. Anyone who took more than the prescribed number of weeks to get over a loss was considered maladjusted and treated as emotionally disturbed. Thus, the helping professionals themselves became deterrents to the proper working through of grief. Coincidentally, it was during those same years that Western society was moving from a religious to a secular orientation, so that valuable religious guidelines which would have supported Freud's lengthier grief period were lacking.

Only in recent years, in research primarily concerned with widowhood, is Freud's earlier statement that normal grief can go on for years, not weeks or months, being validated. In some of the subphases of grief, it has been observed that the initial phase of shock can last from a few hours or days to a week or more, merging gradually into the phase of denial and acute grief. It has also been found that acute grief in widowhood began within a few hours or days of bereavement and usually reached a peak of intensity between the second and fifth weeks of bereavement. Experts now tend to agree that for most people it takes six to ten or twelve weeks for the worst of the pain of intense grief to begin to diminish.[25]

Regardless of how effectively grieving is done, it cannot be collapsed in time. Events such as birthdays, anniversaries, and other important dates are associated with that which has been lost and these calendar events must be experienced at least once after the loss before the bereaved can feel the pain of living through the event without that which he has lost. It takes, therefore, at least a year before each of these calendar-related events can be lived through. The first anniversary of the loss is a critical time for the bereaved.

Grief is normal in the widowed even after a year, and often only during the second year following bereavement can the bereaved admit to hope about the future. The second year arouses memories not only of the lost object but also of the pain of the first post-bereavement year. But there is value in experiencing the pain of recalling the emptiness and suffering of the early months of grief. Only after this process is there room for new attachments, with objects sought not solely as replacements of the old but also as replacements of the vacuum occasioned by the loss. After the acute grief period has passed, however, reminders such as a photograph, a piece of clothing, a familiar tune, or a new loss can set off a grief reaction anew.

Studies show that widows take three or four years to stabilize their lives. Only then are they found to be happily engaged in a rich and full life, no longer depressed, remembering their earlier marriages and the grief of bereavement, but moving toward recovery, different as a result of their losses but stronger for having passed through a successful grieving period. However, the studies tended to support Freud's earlier observation that the loved one is never forgotten:

> For none among the bereaved does recovery mean forgetting. Even after they have established new lives and regained their energy and capacity for happiness, the loss and their reaction to it will not only have been a major determinant of the people they have become, but will emerge, again and again, in their thoughts and feelings.[26]

In some instances of losses without closure, or where no restitution appears possible, mourning may never be completed, for example, in families who have lost a child through murder or kidnapping, or in situations in which a loss has started a downward spiral of further losses and deprivations; also, in the young, where the ego is not fully developed and integrated, and the old, where losses pile up one on another and opportunities for restitution are diminished.

The duration of grief in children

Whereas the task in adult grief is that of eventually relinquishing the tie to the lost object so as to free energy for investment in new and available objects, the problem in the child is that this detachment takes place too soon.

Some of the major defenses in childhood loss are repression, fixation, and splitting of the ego. In the latter, one part of the personality acknowledges the loss and another part, conscious but secret, denies the loss, believes that it will be recovered; the two parts can coexist over many years. In these defenses, and in the speed with which they set in following bereavement, "lies a main explanation . . . of why and how it is that experiences of loss in early childhood lead to faulty personality development and proneness to psychiatric illness."[27]

Particularly in the case of the child who has suffered the loss of a parent, one of life's greatest assaults on personality development, it is not really possible to speak of a duration of grief. It is generally postulated that the child, because of the immaturity and weakness of the ego and the cognitive inability to grasp the meaning of the event, as well as the inability of adults to tolerate the pain of the child's distress, is unable to complete the task of mourning. Thus, the surface adjustment we note in children is a form of self-protection and the real task of completing the mourning process awaits the child in later life.

The fact of death or other reason for the loss of the parent should not be kept from the child. Explanations should be kept at the age-appropriate level for the child and as free from contamination by the feelings of other family members as is humanly to be expected. Religious explanations regarding death are of little help to the young child and can often be confusing.

If the terminally ill or dying parent can explain the situation to the child, it is much better for the child than his having to experience the death as an event that comes out of the blue, that is, one minute the parent is there, the next he is not. Disappearance hinders reality testing. The child also needs the security of continued caretaking. Premature independence as a result of parent loss or parent absence may appear precocious on the surface but augers ill for the mental health of the child. The child should be allowed to express his feelings of anger at abandonment. Regardless of the reason for parent loss, to the child it means abandonment. For some children psychotherapy may be indicated.

It is generally agreed that it is important:

> ... That a child have available a single and permanent substitute to whom he can gradually become attached. Only in such circumstances can we expect a child ultimately to accept the loss as irremediable and then to reorganize his inner life accordingly.[28]

Failing the availability of an appropriate substitute for the child during childhood, we need to be alert to the potential for future pathology in the child who has lost a parent. The implications of this statement for the child reared in a single-parent home are profound in view of the increase in the number of such homes in American society during recent years. The younger the child at the time of parent loss, the more severe the potential pathology. The depth of therapeutic intervention needed by such a child is as yet beyond the comprehension of many in the helping professions.

Margaret Clark, an anthropologist, notes a "perversity in human affairs," at least in Western cultures, "which decrees that one group of people in a society shall be guarded, rewarded, and enriched only at the expense of another group."[29] How tragic, indeed, it would be if the parents of today find their enrichment at the expense of the children of tomorrow.

Implications for Intervention

When loss is recognized and grief proceeds normally the bereaved need people who will encourage the process. This means encourage-

ment to recognize not only the major loss but also all the separate sub-
losses that constitute the major loss, much as was described regarding
blindness in chapter two.

If there are physical complaints, medical attention is indicated.
Once physical illness has been ruled out, attention can be focused on
the emotional aspects of the complaints. However, caution is needed
because the grief-stricken can also have physical problems that must
not be overlooked on the premise that all pain is due to grief.

The bereaved also need gentle encouragement to endure the pain
of grief. This does not mean being pushed to face reality. Grief is a
time when the insistence on a realistic approach to life is erroneous.
Rather, there should be someone willing to tolerate repetition without
becoming bored, or without needing to cut off the expression of feeling by advice to "shape up," or to "consider how lucky you are to have
lost only an arm instead of your life," or "you're better off than I am,
at least you have children to take care of." The bereaved need someone who can listen to their confusion and help them make sense out
of what has happened to them—without reliance on religious beliefs
if they are nonreligious and without reliance on platitudes or false
gaiety to relieve the listener's discomfort. They also need to be assured of their sanity where this is appropriate, to be helped to accept
psychiatric care if they do break down emotionally, to be relieved of
the routine chores of housekeeping, child-care, handling finances,
and other decision-making responsibilities, if possible, to be protected
against their own impulse to get rid of possessions painfully associated
with the loss, and ultimately to be encouraged to find healthy forms of
restitution for that which has been lost. Throughout they need someone who can be constantly "pushed away" without leaving or feeling
rejected.

Bereavement is a family matter. The family of the dying patient,
for example, needs support from outsiders during the crisis of the
final illness and death. They cannot share all their pain with each
other when their pain comes from the same source. Grief demands
help from a person of strength, and one cannot be both bereaved and
strong at the same time without suppressing grief. Family members
also need help after the death of a member. Some seek comfort from
persons who had come to know the deceased, such as hospital personnel; others want nothing to do with the scene of their despair and loss.
The same principles hold for families bereaved by other losses: rape,
physical disability, aging, imprisonment, and so on are all family, not
individual, crises.

It is not always possible to determine easily whether a person is
experiencing an acute, normal grief reaction or one of the dysfunctional forms such as a severe depression, delayed or absent grief,

hostility, inappropriate sexual behavior, and so on. Denial, physical complaints, depression, guilt, and anger occur in both normal and dysfunctional grief. In some cases only time, provided the bereaved are given the opportunity to grieve appropriately, can reveal whether reactions are normal or pathological. The problem may be compared to one in physical illness, where a temperature may be part of a temporary, self-limiting condition or an early symptom of a serious disease process.

Where any of the behaviors described in this chapter as part of normal grief are present, we need to look for a loss which has already taken place or one which is feared or ongoing. Connecting the behavior to loss puts it into the category of the normal rather than pathological. When a significant loss takes place which should normally be followed by grief and there is no grief, we need to be on the alert for one of the dysfunctional substitutes for grief to be discussed below.

The task of mourning is completed when a personality reorganization takes place, through which the old self and the new self, now without that which has been lost, are integrated. This is different from the attempt at retrieval of the loss that characterizes the first phase of grief. That which has been lost is now retained in memory. A new sense of identity, a new stability, a hopeful and positive interest in the present and future mark the end of grief and mourning. The search for new avenues of gratification lead to restitution for the loss through new relationships, new interests, new values, and new goals. With restitution comes a restoration of the sense of self-esteem damaged by the loss. The new self is enriched by the memories of that which has been lost as well as by the growth through suffering and the mastery of grief. Healthy grieving should end with new avenues for creative living.

Grief work, a normal part of living, has been called nature's exercise in loss and restitution.[30] Bereavement is among us at all times. In most instances, grief becomes a self-healing process if proper supports are provided to the bereaved. Most people do not need or seek professional help in times of acute grief. However, self-healing, proper supports from others, and adequate grieving time are not common elements in our society; they are rather the ideal.

Various reasons have been given by experts on grief for the development of pathological grief reactions. The helper must be on the alert for signs of these. Some of the clues to pathological reaction are given below:

- Does the bereaved avoid grieving out of a wish to avoid the pain?

- Has the bereaved become fixated on an attempt to retrieve the lost object or at some point in acute grief?

- Has a pre-existing instability of personality reasserted itself? (The lost object has been loved on an immature level as a provider of narcissistic supplies rather than on a mature level.)
- Was the relationship to the lost object extremely ambivalent or hostile?
- Is the bereaved fixated on an oral or symbiotic level?
- Have there been sudden, traumatic forms of loss?
- Are there personality problems prohibiting expression of one or more of the feelings needing expression in grief?
- Are there important reality demands making it impossible for the bereaved to grieve?
- Are there social supports to grieving?
- Can the bereaved tolerate the pain of grieving?
- Is there a history of past unresolved losses?
- Is there a major defensive system based on stoicism, competence, and independence and an inability to tolerate a position of weakness and taking help?

The task in working with pathological grief is to help convert the problem into normal grief and then facilitate the grief work necessary to a healthy outcome. This task is not for the novice, well-intentioned, untrained volunteer helper. At best, irresponsible pushing may only solidify the pathological grief and the person continues on as before. More seriously, however, is the danger of provoking psychosis or suicide. Pathological grief reactions are best left to skilled practitioners.

Notes

1. S. Sunder Das, "Grief and the Imminent Threat of Non-Being," *British Journal of Psychiatry* 118 (1971): 467–68.
2. See for example James R. Averill, "Grief: Its Nature and Significance," in *Grief: Selected Readings,* ed. Arthur C. Carr et al. (New York: Health Sciences Publishing, 1975), pp. 232–60.
3. Das, "Grief and the Imminent Threat."
4. Averill, "Grief: Its Nature and Significance," p. 232.
5. See for example Charles Darwin, *The Expression of the Emotions in Man and*

Animals (London: Murray, 1872); Averill, "Grief: Its Nature and Significance"; and John Bowlby, "Processes of Mourning," *International Journal of Psychoanalysis* 42 (1961): 317–40.

6. Bowlby, "Processes of Mourning."

7. Averill, "Grief: Its Nature and Significance," p. 232.

8. Gregory Rochlin, *Griefs and Discontents: The Forces of Change* (Boston: Little, Brown and Co., 1965).

9. Elisabeth Kübler-Ross, *On Death and Dying* (New York: Macmillan Co., 1969).

10. See Stephen V. Gullo, Daniel J. Cherico, and Robert Shadick, "Suggested States and Response Styles in Life-Threatening Illness: A Focus on the Cancer Patient," in *Anticipatory Grief*, ed. Bernard Schoenberg et al. (New York: Columbia University Press, 1974), p. 64.

11. Avery D. Weisman, *On Dying and Denying: A Psychiatric Study of Terminality* (New York: Behavioral Publications, 1972), p. 96.

12. Bowlby, "Processes of Mourning," p. 317.

13. See Annette Baran, Reuben Pannor, and Arthur D. Sorosky, "Open Adoption," *Social Work* 21 (March 1976): 99.

14. Kate Holliday, "The Sudden Handicap: A Special Curse," *Los Angeles Times*, 5 February 1976, p. 5.

15. John Bowlby, "Grief and Mourning in Infancy and Early Childhood," *Grief: Selected Readings*, ed. Arthur C. Carr et al. (New York: Health Sciences Publishing), pp. 137–80.

16. Ibid., p. 138.

17. James F. Masterson cited in Donald B. Rinsley, "Object-Relations View of Borderline," *Borderline Personality Disorders: The Concept, the Syndrome, the Patient*, ed. Peter Hartocollis (New York: International Universities Press, 1977), p. 56.

18. Margaret S. Mahler quoted in Rinsley, "Object-Relations View," p. 55.

19. John Bowlby, "Childhood Mourning and Its Implications for Psychiatry: The Adolf Meyer Lecture," *American Journal of Psychiatry* 118 (1961): 481–98.

20. Kahlil Gibran, *The Prophet* (New York: Alfred A. Knopf, 1946), p. 35.

21. Sigmund Freud, "Letter to L. Binswanger: No. 239," in *Letters of Sigmund Freud*, ed. E.L. Freud (London: Hogarth Press, 1961).

22. Sigmund Freud quoted in George H. Pollock, "Mourning and Adaptation," *International Journal of Psycho-Analysis* 42 (1961): 344.

23. Erich Lindemann, "The Symptomatology and Management of Acute Grief," *American Journal of Psychiatry* 101 (1944): 144.

24. See C. Knight Aldrich, "Some Dynamics of Anticipatory Grief," in *Anticipatory Grief*, ed. Schoenberg et al., pp. 7–8.

25. See Paula Clayton, Lynn Desmarais, and George Winokur, "A Study of Normal Bereavement," *American Journal of Psychiatry* 125 (1968): 168–78; May E. Romm, "Loss of Sexual Function in the Female," in *Loss and Grief: Psychological Management in Medical Practice*, ed. Bernard Schoenberg et al.

(New York: Columbia University Press, 1970), p. 178; Geoffrey Gorer, *Death, Grief and Mourning* (New York: Arno Press, 1965), p. 83; and Peter Marris, *Loss and Change* (New York: Pantheon Books, 1974), p. 27.

26. Ira O. Glick, Robert S. Weiss, and C. Murray Parkes, *The First Year of Bereavement* (New York: John Wiley and Sons, 1974), p. 15.

27. Bowlby, "Childhood Mourning and Its Implications for Psychiatry," p. 487.

28. John Bowlby and C. Murray Parkes, "Separation and Loss Within the Family," in *The Child and His Family*, ed. E. James Anthony and Cyrille Koupernik (New York: Wiley—Interscience, 1970), p. 207.

29. Margaret Clark and Monique Mendelson, "Mexican-American Aged in San Francisco: A Case Description," *The Gerontologist* 9 (1969): 90–95.

30. Vamik Volkan, "A Study of a Patient's 'Re-grief Work,' Through Dreams, Psychological Tests and Psychoanalysis," *Psychiatric Quarterly* 45 (1971): 255–73.

4/
Initial Responses
to Loss

Shock

When a loss comes entirely without warning, the element of shock is experienced. Shock is defined as a sudden, violent, or upsetting disturbance. Even when a loss is expected, its coming about can still result in shock; this is often true in regard to a death. We have not yet reached the point of being able to predict the exact moment of a death. As one physician remarked, "I have been wrong so often in predicting death that I have stopped doing so. Some people who seem to have nothing going for them keep on living far beyond anything one would expect. And others, who seem to have everything in their favor, just slip away."

So often one hears from a newly bereaved widow: "They told me he was resting, that he would certainly rest through the night. They insisted I go home and get some rest. I had been at the hospital for days and hardly slept. I did go home, and no sooner did I get to bed than the telephone rang. I knew what it was even before I answered. He had died in his sleep, and I wasn't even with him. No one expected he would die that night. . . ."

People who expect or who have just undergone major surgery also experience shock. The element of danger can be found in the physical dependency and helplessness set off by the anesthetic and the surgery, as well as in the fear of death itself from the conditions necessitating and surrounding the surgery. Other physical illnesses and conditions which evoke a feeling of helplessness can arouse similar reactions. Some of these are stroke, heart attack, diabetes, incapacitating arthritis, severe burns, and cancer. The initial reaction of a woman who has been told she has a lump in her breast is anxiety, even if she is assured that it is benign. If she undergoes surgery for a breast nodule, having given permission for the removal of the breast should it prove to be cancerous, she is also subject to shock on awakening from the anesthetic. Does she or does she not have the breast?

The shock of learning of a major loss can remain as a seedbed for future pathology. For example, a woman recounting in therapy the many losses she had experienced remembered keenly the way in which she had learned of the death of her father when she was eight. He had developed pneumonia and was taken to the hospital. As far as everyone knew, he was recovering. One afternoon on her way home from school, she saw a group of children gathered on the sidewalk in front of her apartment house. As she came near, one of them ran up to her with great excitement and said, "Mr. Mike is dead!" It was her father.

Another example shows how long the moment of shock is remembered: A mother, mourning the suicide of her adult daughter, recalled the way in which she had learned the fatal prognosis on her husband some thirty years earlier. She had taken her baby to the pediatrician because of a minor illness. "Did anyone tell you what's wrong with your husband?" she was asked. She repeated the diagnosis, which meant nothing to her but a medical term. "That's fatal!" she was told. "He'll never recover." As she recalled the trauma three decades later, she said, "I'll always hate him for the way he told me that!"

Bad news always comes as a shock and it should be broken as gently as possible, preferably when the bereaved person is in the presence of others with whom feelings can be shared. The moment of the shock of bad news is remembered for years.

Alarm and Anxiety

The reaction to shock is alarm. Alarm is defined as fear or anxiety caused by the sudden realization of danger. Alarm can be set off by any unfamiliar or unexpected situation, exposure to danger, loss of security, isolation from other human beings, or the loss of a child or child substitute.

During a Los Angeles earthquake in 1971, for example, it was found that people who were alone at the time of the earthquake were much more likely to react with greater panic and alarm than did those who were in the presence of another person, even though everyone was equally helpless.

Alarm sets off autonomic physical reactions consistent with an organism that is in a state of arousal. It is only the fully aroused organism, be it human or animal, that is prepared to defend itself by fight, flight, or immobilization.

Physiological reactions characteristic of the state of alarm—increased heart rate, rapid breathing, increased muscular tension, sweating, dryness of the mouth, bowel and bladder relaxation—are usually found in the initial response to loss or the threat of loss. They reveal the insecurity set off by the loss and the organism's autonomic preparation to defend itself against danger.

When the loss is a major one, such as the death of a spouse around whom one's lifestyle and security systems have been built, episodes of arousal, alertness, or even panic can occur well beyond the early phase of loss and, in fact, can be set off anew whenever security is threatened. The insomnia which is common during the first year of a major bereavement may be explained as part of this alertness to danger. To sleep means to be able to trust that all will go well while one is off guard. Once a major loss has befallen an individual, the ability to trust that the world will be a benign place has been severely shaken. Insomnia may also be a way to avoid the unconscious guilt that can surface in the dreams of the bereaved.

Widows have reported anxiety in regard to carrying on life alone, to their children having to face the future without a father, to financial problems, household responsibilities, and moral and personal dangers.

Rape or burglary victims also lose their trust in the goodness of the world and remain apprehensive of further invasion. People who have lived under conditions of a police state can, despite changed circumstances, remain subject to panic at the ring of a doorbell, or the sight of a shadow, or a policeman in uniform:

> Although systematic studies of the physiological processes of bereaved people have not yet been carried out, there are indications from many sources that the grieving person is in a state of high arousal during much of the time and that this occasionally approaches panic.[1]

The physiological symptoms reported by the bereaved are similar to those which occur in many different types of stressful situations; that is, they are not unique to bereavement but may be considered evidence that bereavement can be classified as stress.

Although most pronounced in the early stage of bereavement,

alarm reactions can last up to one year or longer (these physiological symptoms will be discussed at greater length in chapter six). Physiological alarm symptoms need to be given careful attention by both medical and mental health personnel. It is easy to dismiss such symptoms as part of a grief reaction and thereby overlook physical malady.

Alarm may be experienced directly or may take other forms. In surgical cases, for example, anxiety regarding death, or the anesthesia which represents a forced passivity symbolizing death, can be so massive that it cannot be dealt with directly. Instead, it may be displaced to some minor aspect of the surgery, such as obsession with the tube in gall-bladder surgery, or with the stitches rather than the tumor underneath that proved to be inoperable. Massive anxiety may also be hidden by a patient in order to please the doctor, who prefers patients to be calm. For example, research has shown that most patients appear almost casual on the day preceding surgery. Yet psychological tests administered at the time show their control to be only surface level, with severe underlying trends approaching psychotic proportions. The hidden anxiety usually disappears after surgery, although some patients continue to hide their fears, admitting to them only after recovery. These are people who consider it infantile to be frightened.[2]

Learning theorists have found that mild to moderate anxiety is conducive to learning, while excessive stress or strain paralyzes the organism and inhibits learning. It would appear, therefore, that the task of the helper is to evaluate, from the physiological symptoms as one measure, the degree of stress with which the bereaved are struggling.

There is a limit to the amount of anxiety or stress an organism can tolerate. When that limit is reached, the individual will defend himself by removing himself emotionally from the stressful situation. The state of alarm provides such removal on a temporary basis, allowing him to muster resources for problem solving. If the anxiety continues over time, for example, as in a concentration camp experience, emotional withdrawal may take on more permanent features to enable the individual to survive physically. Thus, shock, alarm, and anxiety can serve a protective function in keeping away a flood of emotion with which the person may be unable to cope.

Bargaining

Bargaining, which is part of anticipatory grief, entails an attempt to postpone the inevitable. It is a form of magical thinking wherein a person hopes to influence a higher power through making a promise of certain behavior or sacrifice if he gets his wish.

The importance of bargaining was brought into focus by Elisabeth Kübler-Ross in regard to her work with the terminal patient.[3] She considered it the third stage in anticipatory grief, following that of anger. The terminal patient may bargain for an extension of life, for relief from pain, for a final pleasure before succumbing to death, and for acceptance into Heaven. She equates bargaining with the little child's attempt to get parents to change their minds after they have once said "no." When temper tantrums fail, the child may turn to ingratiating promises to try to manipulate the parents.

This analogy is perhaps too simple for the range of feelings expressed in bargaining, which experts have called the last refuge of the desperate. Bargaining can be done in secret, as in the terminal patient's promise to God to forsake homosexuality, or marital infidelity, if only the impending fate were lifted. It can be open, as in a promise to contribute to a religious or other charitable cause if only one is spared.

Bargaining is not confined to the terminal patient. It is a part of everyday life. Bargaining maneuvers are made when facing examinations, job interviews, and other desired or feared pending goals or outcomes. It is a reflection of the awareness that often our best efforts are not enough to insure success and that slim chance does play a part in life. Bargaining serves to decrease anxiety through resting our case in the care of a higher power. A fifty-year-old woman in a good marriage suddenly found herself unable to respond sexually to her husband. In tracing the problem back to the time of its origin, it became clear that her problem began when she first learned that her daughter was to undergo a biopsy for a lump in her breast. The problem was an attempt at unconsciously bargaining with God through her sacrifice of sexual pleasure in return for a diagnosis of nonmalignancy in her daughter.

Kübler-Ross makes the point that in bargaining there is an implicit promise that the patient will not ask for another favor if the original one is granted, but that these promises, to her knowledge, are never kept. The patient always asked for more.[4] A story from World War II exemplifies this point. The soldiers at the front begged to be saved and promised that if only God would spare their lives, they would never ask for another thing. Once the danger to life was over and they were removed from the front lines, they became aware of their wet feet. Now all they wanted were dry socks and boots, and they would ask for nothing more. When that problem was solved, they noticed they had been living on K rations for weeks on end and the idea of a juicy steak became their next obsession. Eventually, that wish too was gratified, and they realized they had been without female companionship for longer than they had realized. As one desire after another was met, another emerged.

One can see from the above example the range of intensity in feelings contained in the bargaining process. At its most intense degree bargaining might be compared not only to the child begging for a parental favor but also to the child pleading with a parent of whom he is terrified. The abused child is one such example. "If I died, Mommy, will you then love me?" is a pathetic example of a child bargaining for that which he desires most, the affection of the parent, from a parent whose fury he cannot understand. All religions contain elements of bargaining, from the primitive sacrifice to the god of fertility as a magical way of insuring a bountiful crop to the modern fasting and praying. Bargaining takes over when human powers are exhausted.

Ambivalence and Catharsis

In acute grief the bereaved are torn between the past and the future. The result is a painful period characterized by many overt and subtle ambivalences or contradictory pulls. Ambivalence has been called the keynote to grief in both individual loss and community changes which are experienced as losses:

> Whether the change is sought or resisted, and happens by chance or design; whether we look at it from the standpoint of reformers or those they manipulate, of individuals or institutions, the response is characteristically ambivalent. The will to adapt to change has to overcome an impulse to restore the past which is equally universal. What becomes of a widow, a displaced family, a new organization or a new way of business depends on how these conflicting impulses work themselves out, within each person and the relationships of which he is part.[5]

The process that goes on during normal grief is one of working out of the ambivalence through identifying the conflicting impulses, suffering the pain of the awareness, and eventually mastering the feelings. It is this struggle and pain that drain the bereaved of energy for other routine tasks of living. In the dysfunctional conditions that substitute for normal grief and mourning, the conflict may never be admitted, or the process of going through the pain may be avoided, so that the conflict is never resolved.[6]

For example, a divorced woman of thirty, pulling out of a depression, reported that she had had a good week except that on Tuesday, for no apparent reason, she had been nervous all day. She had, in fact, wanted to telephone her therapist but managed to get through the day at work, then went directly home and to bed. In being asked to describe what she meant by nervous she gave a classic description of a mild grief reaction—stomach distress, inability to go about the tasks of the day without extra effort, a wish to withdraw, feelings of helplessness, crying for no apparent reason, and irritability. Her therapist commented that it sounded like a mild grief reaction. For what could she have been grieving? She then recounted a series of events preceding that Tuesday—seeing a former lover the previous Friday, spending the weekend as part of a group that included a number of happy, intact families, remembering her own unhappy marriage, subsequent divorce, and relinquishment of her daughter, a telephone call from another male friend with whom marriage was not a possibility, and a telephone call from her mother who had promised to send her money toward therapy expenses but had neglected to do so. This meant cutting her visits from twice to once a week. It became clear, therefore, that her nervousness was a reaction to a series of loss experiences.

The ambivalences of grief take many forms. The bereaved show both a desire to be alone and a craving for companionship. There is an attempt to avoid reminders of the past, yet a compulsion or urgency to talk and dwell on the loss exists. There is a conflict between being passive and active, dependent and independent, regressive and moving forward, and between being supersensitive to the least slight from others and rebuffing overtures of help and sympathy when offered. The conflict shows in the insistence that life has lost all meaning coupled with the simultaneous competent attention to the daily routines of living. The bereaved alternate between despair and hope, between anger at the deceased for dying and guilt at failing to keep him alive. They are torn between wanting to be helpless and to be exploitative of others and the fear that they will lose all their friends if they are. They may compulsively seek distractions only to discover they have no interest in these very distractions. They may be curious about some aspect of the loss (the disposition of an amputated limb, for example) and at the same time not wish to know the answer.

Resolution of acute grief and its ambivalence is through the recognition of feelings, thoughts, and ambiguities, and the release of feelings appropriate to each. This release or emptying out of feelings is known as catharsis.

Implications for Intervention

There is no sequence or set order to the feelings in grief. They vary in intensity and in the stimuli which set them off. No one can predict which feeling will be uppermost from one minute to the next. In addition, particular feelings associated with a loss will vary with the meaning of the loss to the individual, the personality of the individual, and the cultural and family sanctions or taboos relating to the expression of a particular feeling (for example, the open expression of anger), or to the expression of feelings generally.

Not all feelings will be found in every loss. However, whatever feelings are aroused by the loss or are appropriate to a particular loss need to be expressed and validated if grief is to be overcome and catharsis effected.

Feelings are subjective. They occur within an individual and can only be inferred from outside by facial, body, and verbal cues. The same behavior can signify different feelings. Crying, for example, can signify sadness, anger, guilt, helplessness, hopelessness, relief, gratitude, or pleasure. Feelings exist—they cannot be changed by edicts, scoldings, criticisms, or disapproval. A person cannot be told by someone else what to feel or what not to feel, nor can he tell himself what to feel. Dictates and criticism can, however, add another layer to feelings —shame, guilt, self-doubt, repression—and thereby delay the expression of the original feeling and the completion of grief work. It is the recognition, acceptance, and validation of each emotion as it arises that enables the bereaved to move from one feeling state to another so that grief can be completed.

Mental health workers are faced by people in all their complexities and must deal with those complexities to the best of their ability. The researcher can afford to isolate parts of experience for close inspection. Colin Murray Parkes, a leading researcher on widowhood, rejects this holistic approach because of the difficulty in understanding feelings:

> We may not know, until after it has occurred, whether a given life-event is to be construed as a loss or a gain. . . . [A major change such as a wedding of a child] may be regarded as a net profit or a net loss. She [the bride's mother] may grieve or she may rejoice, or, with the typical human ability to split herself, she may oscillate between tears and delight. The hard-headed research worker may well find it hard to classify such life-events as the marriage of a daughter as losses or gains.[7]

It is at just this point that the researcher and clinician part company. Clinicians do not have the luxury of isolating the data with which they work. They are confronted by troubled people, with all their ambivalences, ambiguities, "splits," oscillations, tears, and delights. It is this very attempt on the part of the bereaved to add and subtract positive and negative feelings, to average out love and anger, relief and sorrow, that can obscure the recognition and expression of feelings and create an obstacle to the working through of grief. This attempt reflects the struggle to keep certain feelings from awareness, thus buried but still alive. "I can't be angry at her. She has been so good to me. How can I possibly be critical of her?" is an example of such an attempt.

Leftover feelings can be compared to pus in a wound. The scar may form, cover the wound, but the pus festers from below and eventually must create trouble. Residual feelings surrounding loss, if repressed and unacknowledged, remain as potential sources of future emotional disruption. Feelings are not quantitative. They are qualitative and discrete. Each feeling must be expressed separately, and identified and validated. Only then are the bereaved free to relinquish the feeling without a further sense of additional loss.

The grief process must include a period of intense distress and pain associated with the release of feelings connected with the loss, a going with or yielding to the grief process rather than resistance to it.

The therapist needs to face the onslaught of intense emotion without withdrawing, flinching, or offering comfort as a way of turning off the emotional torrent. The pain of the bereaved must be met with empathy not pity, their fears without panic, their aimless wanderings without the urge to structure their energy, their helplessness with the strength of understanding, and their guilt, shame, and anger with respect. The following case example illustrates this kind of situation.

Mrs. West suffered a series of losses within a short period of time. After twenty-five years of marriage her husband left their home. Within a few months she underwent a mastectomy, and shortly thereafter her last of three children left home for college. From a busy household full of people she suddenly found herself alone. In her search for new companions she met a man and the ensuing relationship turned out to be not only disappointing but destructive, as his professed interest slowly emerged as an intense hatred of women. By the time she was brought for psychotherapy she appeared almost psychotic in her panic at the destructiveness of outside forces. Most important to her was that the therapist believe her as she described experiences that sounded unrealistic. This belief was her tie to another human being and her protection from what she called "losing my grip." Slowly, with gentle help, she was able to begin to express her anger at the situation in which she found herself. At home she wandered around aimlessly through empty days, but during the therapy sessions she moved rapidly from panic to tearless anger to bitter tears, then helpless crying. Throughout, however, she depended on the therapist to assure her that she would work again, that her aimlessness was normal, that others had been in the same place and come out of it, that crying did not mean weakness, that there was no joy in life because it was a time for tears, and that the future was black because she saw it with eyes clouded by the bleakness of the present moment.

The therapist needs to help facilitate the catharsis of feelings, recognize the forces operating against the expression of emotion, respect denial as a necessary defense against overwhelming emotions, tolerate the emotions as they are expressed, and be able to wait without rushing the process.

Grief work must be shared. In sharing, however, there must be no impatience, censure, or boredom with the repetition, because repetition is necessary for catharsis and internalization and eventual unconscious acceptance of the reality of the loss. The bereaved are sensitive to the feelings of others and will often not only refrain from revealing feelings to those they consider unequal to the burden of sharing the grief but may even try to comfort the helper. For example, a nurse, changing the bedding of a terminal cancer patient, went about her task with tears flowing down her cheeks at the pain she knew the patient was undergoing as a result of this simple and routine process. The patient reached up and patted her on the back, as if assuring her that everything was all right.

The helper needs to walk a tight rope between encouraging the expression of emotions and respecting denial. Group situations are particularly likely to break into denial unless the group leader is alert to the dangers of pressure on a vulnerable group member (and the bereaved are highly vulnerable) to reveal emotions out of the needs of others rather than his own. Several instances have occurred where people have suffered psychotic breaks as the result of such group pressure.

The bereaved tend to worry about the normalcy of their reactions. Glick found widows worrying whether their feelings of grief were too strong or too mild:

> [It is] a generally held belief in our society that painful feelings are best dealt with by being fully expressed, at which point they are done with. This model assumes that sorrow can be treated as an entity that exists in a certain quantity, and that expressing sorrow uses it up or expels it. Therefore, it should be possible for the individual to "get it all out," to fully externalize or discharge it. It is consistent with this model to believe that crying should continue until sorrow is fully expressed but that once this is done further crying is self-indulgent. Thus some of our widows experienced disappointment and self-blame when their grief lingered despite their attempts to get it all out.[8]

Parkes found that people seeking psychiatric treatment after a major loss tended to experience immediate overwhelming grief, lasting an unusually long time, or an absence or diminished degree of grief at the time of the loss, with a severe reaction in subsequent weeks.[9]

The healthy reaction is perhaps to be able to express grief and yet not be overcome by it. It is at this point that the sharing of grief protects the bereaved from being overwhelmed. Despite catharsis, grief will not be emptied out as a container might be emptied of a certain circumscribed content. Although it may decline in intensity, it will recur with later reminders, and needs to be expressed whenever it arises.

Notes

1. Colin Murray Parkes, *Bereavement: Studies of Grief in Adult Life* (New York: International Universities Press, 1972).

2. Richard S. Blacher, "Loss of Internal Organs," in *Loss and Grief: Psychological Management in Medical Practice,* ed. Bernard Schoenberg et al. (New York: Columbia University Press, 1970), pp. 132–39.

3. Elisabeth Kübler-Ross, *On Death and Dying* (New York: Macmillan Co., 1969), pp. 82–84.

4. Ibid.

5. Peter Marris, *Loss and Change* (New York: Pantheon Books, 1974), p. 5.

6. Ibid., p. 28.

7. Colin Murray Parkes, *Bereavement,* pp. 192–93.

8. Ira O. Glick, Robert S. Weiss, and Colin Murray Parkes, *The First Year of Bereavement* (New York: John Wiley and Sons, 1974), pp. 58–59.

9. Colin Murray Parkes, "Bereavement and Mental Illness," *British Journal of Medical Psychology* 38 (1965): 1–26.

5/
Denial in
Grief

Psychodynamics of Denial

When a loss occurs, two conflicting forces become operative. One is the realistic need to relinquish that which has been lost; the other is the wish to hold on to what was lost in order to avoid the pain set off by the loss. Mourning, a time- and energy-consuming process, is the period involved in this struggle between holding on and letting go. Denial serves in the interests of holding on.

According to psychoanalytic theory, denial is an unconscious defense used to reduce, avoid, or prevent anxiety which arises from an objective danger. It is the earliest defense to emerge in psychic development, the most persistent of all defenses, and a normal part of ego development. Some denial is necessary at every stage of life to make life bearable for all of us.

Denial operates by shutting out of awareness that which would be too disturbing. The infant does it by closing his eyes and turning his head away. We speak of people who hide their heads in the sand, or sweep their worries under the rug. A person who takes the defense of denial to an extreme fails to develop more sophisticated defenses or effective ways of dealing with reality.

In loss, denial goes on at one level of awareness, while acknowledgment of the loss goes on at another.

Denial of the loss, accompanied by a simultaneous acknowledgment of the loss, was explained psychodynamically by Freud as a splitting of the ego. It is considered to be a normal, not uncommon, albeit incomplete stage of the grieving process. It needs to give way gradually through the process of active grieving.

Otto Fenichel saw the task of the mourning process as twofold: "the first being the establishment of an introjection [of the lost object], the second the loosening of the binding to the introjected object."[1]

Introjection, the taking in of the object and thereby retaining it within the psychic makeup, allows the individual to relinquish the object in reality without damage to the self from the loss. However, introjection cannot take place until the loss is completely acknowledged. Denial of the loss, necessary for the preservation of mental health by protection against a reality that needs to be integrated in bits rather than in one overwhelming indigestible lump, delays the introjection necessary for the working through and integrating of the loss.[2]

In the course of normal grieving, daily reminders of the lost object confront the person repeatedly, and in small doses, with the reality of the loss and the pain of that realization. Each confrontation enables the person to make a partial introjection of the object and at the same time a partial detachment from it. To make use of the confrontation with the reality of the loss, however, the bereaved must allow himself to experience the pain of the realization. With the expression of the pain and the passage of time, pain subsides and energy is released for new tasks of living.

The new widow or divorcee needs to sign a check. Is she still Mrs. John Smith, or is she now Mary Smith, or Mrs. Mary Smith? It does not matter that books of etiquette address themselves to this point. The question arises and with it a memory of the loss, and the pain that goes with the memory. Countless experiences such as these bring home the reality of the loss.

If denial is the shutting out of an unbearable reality, what then is its counterpart? Hope and the acceptance of death have been postulated as the opposite side of the coin of denial. Hope does not mean survival for its own sake, but rather the desirability of survival arising from a healthy self-image and self-esteem, and the belief in one's ability to exert even a small degree of influence on one's own fate, surroundings, and other people.[3]

Hope is an accompaniment of significant survival, not mere animal survival determined by artificial stimulation of vital organs.

Hope and acceptance of death are natural accompaniments of each other.

The inescapable fact of death belongs to the incomprehensible act of being alive. The living need the dying as the dying need the living, for the same reasons. If we accept being alive, then we must accept the fact of death.[4]

Translated into everyday experiences, hope and the acceptance of death as a reality mean that the individual can accept tension and anxiety as a part of living. This would imply the ability to bear the discomfort and pain of loss as part of the human condition, carrying with it normal, transient feelings of sadness and an existential depression as a consequence of the realization that life has its pain as well as its joy.

Denial of the reality of the loss itself

The most easily recognized form of denial is that of disbelief in the recognition of the loss itself. This can take place in words, actions, feelings, thoughts, fantasies, daydreams, nighttime dreams, and wishes. It can be seen in the total range of losses—of a significant person, of a part of the self, of good health, of material objects, values, beliefs, hopes, and in developmental loss. Such denial of the reality of the loss can take a variety of healthy or dysfunctional forms. As the first reaction in every major loss, denial serves to provide a moratorium in time to protect the individual from a flood of emotions and a new reality. Here denial is appropriate and healthy—it serves as a cushion against psychic trauma which might otherwise be overwhelming. As an unhealthy response, denial impedes the process of grief and, therefore, restitution.

Denial of the fact of illness itself tends to be found in the early stages of illness. Miss Hartford, a fifty-one-year-old single woman, was told she had myasthenia gravis. The disease was described to her in terms of the symptoms and their expected course. Double vision was her most troublesome symptom, particularly because she worked as a typist. She was told to rest her eyes for five minutes of every hour at work. She was advised to do no extra reading as recreation, nor strain at watching television, but to find substitutes such as listening to the radio or other nonvisual activities to allow her eyes to rest as much as possible.

Miss Hartford "forgot" to follow the doctor's advice about curtailing her visual activities and taking the prescribed medication. She insisted she had always been well. She always knew when she was sick before. She had no pain, so how could she possibly be sick? Maybe the symptoms would go away. Maybe vitamins would help. Maybe she needed psychotherapy (something she had always laughed at before). She did not own a car, so the danger of her driving with her double vision was not an issue. With increasing care at street crossings she managed to get around on buses as she always had. Here denial worked strongly to defend against an unbearable reality.

Denial of the reality of a loss can go beyond denial of the loss itself. Some of the disorientation and disturbances of attention in patients with a delirious syndrome has been attributed to the defense of denial. Patients are so alarmed by their illness and threat of dysfunction that they have to shut out awareness of their immediate surroundings, of time, of people, and of conditions that led up to their disturbance.[5]

Mrs. James, a seventy-six-year-old widow, had a successful mastectomy. The two widowed daughters with whom she made her home were devoted to her welfare and supportive of her throughout the necessary chemotherapy and follow-up care. Gradually, the daughters began to notice strange behavior which the doctor said could not be explained either by the reactions to chemotherapy or by aging alone. At times Mrs. James was rational, at times disoriented as to place, time, and people. The family was able to trace the beginning of the disorientation to the day the mother, while being helped with her bath, stared at her body as if noticing for the first time the absence of her breast. From then on she stared at the bodies of her daughters, rambled on about there no longer being "two of them," mourned for the twin sister who had died four years earlier, and asked on one occasion, "Why are there no Daddies in this house?" All her thoughts seemed to focus on past relationships and losses, yet she never spoke of her changed body. Often she would ask "What place is this?" or "Who are you?" of the daughters with whom she had lived for years.

If an illness progresses to a chronic state, denial is found in regard to the inferences the patient draws or fails to draw about the implications of the illness.

Miss Ilse, aged thirty-three, had an inoperable brain tumor. Out of his own sense of helplessness, the neurosurgeon insisted on announcing to her each time she came for an appointment that the statistics for her condition gave a life expectancy of from three to five years. "Why are you telling me this?" she demanded to know. "You are driving me crazy." Finally, she confronted him with the statistics themselves until he admitted that it was 60 percent of the patients who tended to have a life expectancy within that range. She did not ask what happened to the other 40 percent (who may have died even sooner) but concluded triumphantly, "Well, then I'll be among the other 40 percent and outlive that prediction!" As the months went by she did show signs of an awareness that her life might be limited, but she quickly returned to a stance of denial with such remarks as "I'll show the old sadist! I'll outlive him for spite!"

The final denial is that of death itself. The role of denial in the terminally ill is one of Elisabeth Kübler-Ross's major themes. In her work with dying patients she found that a temporary use of denial in cases of impending death was present in every patient. In most patients it was usually soon supplanted by a "partial acceptance" of death. Where previous defensive patterns of the particular person included a consistent use of denial, the patient tended to use more denial than others in facing death as well.[6]

Although Kübler-Ross outlines stages of denial, anger, bargaining, depression, and acceptance in the terminally ill, these stages are by no means distinct, orderly, and progressive. Denial persists on some level throughout, as does hope. The focus of hope may shift from hope for a cure, a miracle, a spontaneous remission, to hope for a painless ending, for reunion with loved ones after death. Hope may be indistinguishable from denial and the patient carries hope to the very end.[7]

Any uncertainty about the finality of a loss increases denial. For example, when people disappear, are kidnapped, or are missing in action, denial persists. The parents of leukemic children are especially vulnerable in this area. A decade ago a child with leukemia was faced with certain death. Today, new methods of treatment have made remissions quite common. Parents, therefore, need to be prepared both to lose the child and to have him live. Denial is increased during remissions. Each setback brings grief anew.

Another form of denial through disbelief is found in impending loss through normal developmental crises where the growth of a family member makes demands on family equilibrium. This is particularly common with children on the threshold of leaving home and with parents in regard to their own aging.

The emancipation of children is looked forward to with mixed feelings by both the child and parents. Adolescents both desire and fear growing up. It is not uncommon for youngsters to recognize their wish to grow up while denying the fear of leaving the safety of the parental home. One way in which many youngsters resolve this internal conflict is to manipulate the parents into setting limits and then complain that they want to keep them babies! This fear can remain safely unconscious, thus protecting their self-esteem, while they also make a conscious thrust toward emancipation. The ensuing delay allows a period of time for an adolescent and his or her family to work through their mixed feelings about the impending separation and loss.

Parents too often act out their denial of a youngster's leaving home. One family bought expensive patio furniture when their first child left home. It was rarely used as it did not fit their usual form of entertaining. It had been merely a symbolic gesture of attempting to reinstate family togetherness.

It has been said that although most of us are eager to grow up and to take our place in the world as adults, aging is also universally resisted. This resistance can take the form of denial.

Physical aging can be felt as a catastrophic bodily assault, with death the distant inevitability. The elderly may try to "save face" by denying decreasing physical strength or sensory losses. Some blame their problems on others. They complain of objects lying in their path rather than admit to decreasing vision. They accuse people of stealing from them rather than admit that they can't remember where they placed their eyeglasses or false teeth. They accuse people of speaking too softly or may pretend to hear a conversation when they in fact do not, so that their comment may be completely unrelated to the topic under discussion. This may appear to the onlooker as mental confusion or even senility unless the hearing loss is known.

One form of denial among the elderly that can be particularly trying to adult children or other caretakers is the resistance to the dependency which is a requirement for comfortable aging: for example, disallowing household help when they are no longer physically able to do their own work or resisting living with others when living alone may be dangerous.

Denial focused on aging is also seen in retirement issues, particularly where the work life has constituted a major source of self-esteem to the individual involved. One man miscalculated the date of his compulsory retirement by one year, with resulting confusion over finances that had been computed on the basis of a full salary continuing for another twelve months. Denial is seen in resistance to preretirement planning programs, as well as to programs geared toward preparing women for widowhood.

Denial of loss can take the form of refusing to believe that those we trust may let us down; examples are often seen in clinical work.

Mrs. Lane, a woman of fifty, sought treatment because of depression following the loss of her job. She had worked for her brother for fifteen years and one day, without provocation or warning, he had told her to go! For months she mourned the loss, not only of the job itself, the loss of income, the shame of being fired, and the shock regarding the way in which the dismissal took place, but most of all of the warm relationship she had always had with her brother. She could not reconcile his behavior toward her with her image of him as a loving brother. Only when in anger he told her some months later that he would have given her the severance pay due her had she not "talked back" to him, and that he had found someone who could do the work as well as she had for half the salary did the veneer of her disbelief begin to crack. Slowly, from week to week, she began to remember aspects of her brother's behavior that were in contradiction to the picture she had had of him. Now it appeared that he had always been self-serving, lashing out in anger at anyone who opposed him. Bit by bit, as Mrs. Lane allowed herself to acknowledge the reality of her brother's true character, her depression began to lift and her anger emerged. Not until her brother's blatant further attack, too obvious to ignore, brought home fully the reality of his character could she begin to make sense out of the loss and begin to express the feelings appropriate to that loss.

Denial of the reality of a loss is commonly seen in psychotherapeutic work, which is in itself a growth process. Patients who dwell on the past interminably are unconsciously trying to remake the past to their liking. Their compulsive repetition is their attempt to hold on to unfulfilled wishes that can never be realized and their persistence in denying the reality of what the past actually was.[8]

Denial as isolation of feelings

Denial can take the form of cognitive recognition of a loss, but without the appropriate feelings to accompany that recognition. This form of denial is really the defense of isolation. If it occurs for a short time it may be considered a normal postponement of the pain of grieving. For example, Mrs. Miller sought help following the suicide of her adult daughter. In talking of the way in which the police came to tell her of the death, she said: "I heard every word they said but I felt like I was turning to stone." Isolation of feelings that would prove overwhelming can preserve sanity in times of such shock and loss.

Denial through isolation may also occur when the bereaved, faced by reality tasks that must be solved, cannot afford to let down emotionally. The widow left with young children who must be cared for, faced with moving, getting resettled, finding a way to make a living, may need to resort to isolation. Isolation may occur later on out of the exhaustion of mourning to allow a respite from the pain of suffering. If it continues without interruption for any length of time, however, it may symbolize identification with the deceased, a pathological reaction to the loss.

Belief in the reality of the loss but separation of feelings from the facts can be seen in such typical remarks as: "I have cancer but it doesn't bother me; the doctor has it all under control." "My marriage may be ending but it is all for the best." "Everyone loses hearing, vision, and memory with age."

The pain of loss can also be defended against by denial of the importance of the lost object through depreciation, contempt, and devaluation of it: "I don't miss him, really. He wasn't much good as a husband. He was gone more than he was home." "He wasn't much of a lover." "I don't miss the job. I got one with more money anyway." "Status? I stuck around long enough to see what was underneath all that status—backbiting, envy, climbing at the expense of others."

Isolation of feelings is referred to in the substantial literature on the reaction of patients to very severe burns and the resulting disfigurement:[9]

> R. P. was a thirty-year-old married male lineman who sustained severe electrical burns when he accidentally came in contact with a hot line while at work. His injuries required complete amputation of his left arm and leg two days after admission. He was a tall, good-looking man who had been happily married for eleven years and who enjoyed such sports as swimming, boating, and water-skiing. He had been a lineman for thirteen years. During the course of hospitalization, he remained consistently cheerful and optimistic, making realistic plans for obtaining prosthetic limbs and eventually obtaining a desk job with his company. Denial was a prominent adjustment mechanism: he avoided discussing his disability and when asked about it he made replies such as, "I'll just have to get used to it . . . it'll work out . . . I've known others with artificial limbs and they have done okay." Discussing how he would manage the steps in his two-story home prior to obtaining a leg prosthesis, which could not be fitted for several months, he smiled wryly and drawled, "I dunno . . . I guess I'll just have to slither up and down." His wife remained with him almost continually and also remained cheerful and optimistic. He wept only once, when he voiced concern about how his young daughters might react to his injury and at no time showed any symptoms of depression or even grief about his loss. An MMPI showed a 6-9-3 profile with the 6 and K scales greater than 70, indicating that he was quite a sensitive person, prone to keep his feelings and thoughts well-hidden, with a high level of energy and a superficial air of optimism. He was seen about one month after discharge and at this time he and his wife indicated that he was doing quite well.[10]

The above example shows the discrepancy among the surface cheerfulness, character structure, and underlying unresolved feelings about loss. In such a case, grief work might well be delayed until after the prosthesis has provided some measure of restitution, to avoid possible catastrophic impact of the full extent of the loss. The report of R.P.'s good adjustment a month after discharge should not lead the helper to believe that adjustment to loss has been completed. Unfortunately, this is too often exactly what does happen.

Denial has even been classified as a good adjustment reaction to major loss by psychiatric researchers contrasting good and poor reactions among burn patients during hospitalization. The absence of highly charged emotional reactions was considered as positive because it facilitated the patient's cooperation with hospital procedures and routines, thereby making the life of the hospital personnel much easier.

The same dilemma faces dialysis and kidney transplant patients. Renal dialysis centers tend to expect that patients should be engaged in productive work, should not complain excessively about their restricted lives or physical conditions, and should adhere to their medical regimens. All too often, when patients fail to meet these expectations and give way to feelings of grief over their losses, they are called uncooperative by hospital staff.

Isolation of feelings can serve as a valuable defense in instances of catastrophic personal and material losses from fires, floods, war, or other cataclysmic events, which may have been the case for survivors of an earthquake in Guatemala in 1976 that left an estimated 22,419 dead, 74,105 injured, and one million homeless. Newspaper reports described the survivors as looking about them at the scene of death and destruction and speaking of how lucky they felt to have survived as they set about the grisly task of hunting for loved ones and possessions among the ruins.

This focus on what is left rather than on what is lost is also seen in individual catastrophes. Following a colostomy, a man spoke of his operation not in terms of loss but as a way of saving his life. This is isolation of feelings and may be a problem, particularly for men who are afraid of breaking down and appearing unmanly. There is fear of the discomfort, the pain, the helplessness of the grief process: isolation of feelings serves as a defense against all of these elements.

Isolation of feelings also occurs in losses that are much less than catastrophic. One woman noticed a reaction that is not uncommon. Whenever she made a major change of address, in her case moving from one city to another—her work demanded such changes at least every two years—she went through a period of "feeling almost dead" at the time of the change. This feeling lasted until she "got used to the new place." There was no confusion. There was competent functioning in the face of new tasks. The feelings of the loss of the old attachments were repressed rather than dealt with and lived through. Here confusion would have been a healthier reaction indicative of normal grief over the loss.

Denial in other manifestations

The syndrome of the "phantom limb," which occurs after amputation, may be considered another form of denial.[11] This is a complicated phenomenon in which amputees continue to experience sensations from a lost part of their bodies. It is a reaction of the central nervous system "to the sudden interruption of a very complex and sustained set of stimuli."[12] One must be careful, however, to avoid attributing all of this phenomenon to psychological factors because of a possible neurological basis in the central nervous system for the condition. In fact, a patient immediately fitted for a prosthesis may experience the phantom limb phenomenon for a shorter period of time: nevertheless, this phenomenon can be seen as a reaction to body image loss and its impact on emotional adjustment.

"Phantom limb" is a term usually associated with people who have lost a part of or an entire arm or leg and still experience sensations from it, but the same term has been applied to other types of physical disorders where people attempt to ignore severe physical disabilities. Among these cases are people who have lost the sense of sight but insist they experience seeing. Others have lost the sense of hearing but claim they hear. Still others try to function as normal with paralyzed limbs, and some people with central or peripheral nervous system damage insist they have not lost the functions served thereby.[13]

Denial in illness can take a number of other forms as well. Henry Krystal and Thomas A. Petty organize denial of illness into four categories: the "quack-seeker," the "compensator," the "crusader," and the "paranoid denier."[14]

The *quack-seeker* dismisses authoritative opinions and seeks relief through faith healers, cultists, and quack remedies in a persistent search for the good mother with the miraculous cure. The time lost in treatment of a catastrophic illness by people who seek medical miracles has long been a concern of the helping professions. It is not only time that is lost but energy and money as well. The process may have begun, however, by the patients having been given conflicting diagnoses: when does one accept that a situation is hopeless when the medical experts themselves disagree?

The *compensator* acts out the denial of the feared mutilation by aggressive or sexual overactivity. He rushes into action as an outlet for anxiety. For example, a physician recalled that when he was an intern he suffered a severe pain in his chest. In panic he ran the four blocks from his rooming house to the hospital to see a doctor. Only afterwards did he realize his behavior was really denial of the possibility that the pain might be symptomatic of a heart attack. Had he really been having a heart attack instead of the gastrointestinal disturbance it turned out to be, his behavior could have been fatal.

The *crusader* compulsively fights the threatening illness itself. This behavior is seen, for example, in advertisements where cancer victims warn others how to avoid the fate which overtook them—these crusaders believe they are making a valuable contribution to society with such warnings. Unless some of the anger and hostility inherent in the grief process intrude, this form of reacting to catastrophic illness can be considered an acceptable form of sublimation or restitution. The observer, however, sees only the behavior and does not have access to the thoughts and emotions of the bereaved. One cannot say for certain, therefore, that the crusader has fully accepted his own impending fate. There might well be an element of bargaining in crusading—the hope that the loss may still magically be prevented.

The *paranoid denier* becomes the litigious patient prone to sue for the slightest imagined cause. Certainly, medical negligence does occur, but even the very best of patient care cannot guarantee a successful outcome and there are areas where medical practice verges on the borders of the unknown. In the case of a mastectomy, for example, the surgeon is often faced with a possible dilemma because of the existence of the paranoid denier. If he performs a radical, he can be sued for mutilation. If instead he chooses the newer nonradical procedure and the patient later shows evidence of further cancer, he can be sued for negligence. Obviously, the fear of encountering the paranoid denier has serious implications for both physician and patient.

Denial may start out as a normal safeguard against unbearable anxiety but go on to dysfunctional extremes. This can be seen in the denial that does not give way to reality testing within a reasonable length of time. One example of such denial is what has been found recently among concentration camp survivors, some of whom seemed to have experienced lengthy symptom-free intervals of some ten to twenty years. This period may instead have been one of denial of illness by both patients and doctors, with the latter denying it out of identification with their patients despite the evidence of gross emotional disturbance.[15]

Denial may also take the form of a hectic search for replacement of the lost object in order to avoid the pain and recognition of the loss. This is easily seen in the urgency to date or even remarry on the part of the newly divorced or widowed. Mrs. Queens, a recent widow of thirty-five, found herself driven to begin dating with almost frantic haste following the death of her husband. The death occurred after a prolonged illness during which they had been able to grieve over his impending death together with openness and tenderness. It had been a particularly happy marriage of shared interests, values, and intimacies. Even granting that some of the grief had been worked through in anticipation of the death, there was a premature and driven quality to the dating. Only after her first sexual experience with another man did Mrs. Queens realize that what she had really been seeking was a relationship with a man in bed. It had been in bed that the final months of relationship with her husband had taken place because of his limited mobility. Suddenly she realized the new man was not her husband, and her need to date ended abruptly. She then went on to a more normal process of completing the grief work.

The same search for replacement can take place in fantasy rather than in action. It is not unusual that a new widower, for example, will become obsessed with a complete stranger, or with someone he had known while married but never thought of as a romantic figure. Although there is preoccupation with the individual there is no attempt to make contact in reality; the obsession remains on a fantasy level. The fantasies serve as a denial of loss by the substitution of thoughts of another. They are a defense against a grief that would be overwhelming at the time.

Denial is also the defense used in the syndrome of the "replacement child." In this situation, a new baby is used by the parents as a substitute for a child who has died. A child may be conceived for this purpose or may be sought through adoption to fulfill this assigned role. Such children are expected to develop into the idealized image of the dead child and are thus deprived of the right to develop their own identity. Myron, the second of three brothers, one older by four years, another younger by two years, was one of these children. The family myth centered on the mother's miscarriage of a child conceived subsequent to the birth of her first son. Although the miscarriage occurred too early in the pregnancy for the sex of the child to be known, the mother had it fixed in her mind that she had lost a girl. Myron was the replacement child for the fantasied dead sister. He was dressed daintily, his hair was kept in long curls until he was old enough to rebel against it, and so on. As an adult he entered psychotherapy with problems regarding his possible homosexual preferences. As treatment progressed, however, he discovered that he was, in fact, attracted to women and he gradually began to integrate a sense of his own sexual identity.

The replacement child syndrome can pose a serious problem in adoption if it is not understood by adoption workers. Where the parents are unable to work through their grief at the loss of the dead child, the adopted child is in psychic danger. A crisis can occur around the anniversary date of the child's death, when the replacement child becomes the target for the unresolved grief feelings of the parents.

The denial of mourning parents who insist on keeping the room of a dead child intact is seen as an example of chronic grief and was the case with Mr. and Mrs. Roberts who said that people told them that it was not right to keep their son's room intact. Their home was small and their two daughters were forced to share a bedroom despite pleas for separate rooms because space was now available. The parents were torn between their daughters' anger and their own inability to make the necessary change. It would have been as if the girls and the whole family were benefiting from the son's death. Without reassigning the rooms it was as if he were just off to college as before and would be home for vacation.

Denial is considered the foremost defense in the psychoses, demanding the expenditure of energy and depleting resources available to deal with reality.[16] Denial is also found in the wide range of dysfunctional physical and emotional disorders that serve as substitutes for grief.

Implications for Intervention

Denial is best dealt with by the supportive presence of an understanding person. Words are often not needed and may even serve as an intrusion. It is particularly important not to argue with the bereaved or try to talk them out of denial. Denial, found in both normal and pathological grief reactions, is the defense against an unbearable reality and should be respected as such. Gradually, given enough time and the opportunity to talk, the normally grieving person will slowly begin to take in the loss he has been avoiding. But talking about feelings is not enough; it is still denial through isolation. Talking must be accompanied by an expression of the feelings themselves. The inexperienced helping person can be easily trapped into being satisfied with a bereaved person who seems to have an intellectual understanding of his situation. Grief is a painful experience from which everyone wants to escape. For this reason denial is often reinforced by the very people in the environment who mean to be helpful.

In psychotherapy, when the therapist must ward off material with which he cannot deal, a tacit collusion through denial can develop between the therapist and patient. The patient can talk at length of details about his life but carefully avoid painful areas, which the therapist does not see. Conversely, if the helper's anxiety is as great as that of the bereaved patient, he can be of little help because anxiety is contagious and will only increase the patient's need for denial.

Denial is one of the most difficult defenses with which to work. It must be remembered that the breaking of a defense is in itself a loss, and a person will resist one loss following another. On the surface denial appears as an affront to common sense and so illogical that one is tempted to attack it head on. In some cases such an approach does nothing more than leave the would-be helper feeling frustrated and useless. Because the bereaved are so emotionally vulnerable, however, there can be danger in such an approach. Premature attack on this defense of denial can be risky to the mental health of the bereaved. The bereaved need no further attack. At best, they may simply "turn off" the would-be helper or avoid further contact with that particular person.

Mr. Nathan, aged twenty-eight, sought psychotherapy because of a diagnosis of colitis. His illness was a catastrophic loss as it cut into his work toward a doctorate degree. He had seen five specialists and was confused by the contradictory medical opinions. He kept making the rounds from one doctor to another, taking what he wanted out of their recommendations, with the result that he was, in effect, prescribing his own regimen. To make matters even more confusing, he was told five different things regarding psychotherapy. One doctor said psychotherapy was urgently needed if he expected to recover. Another cautioned that psychotherapy might make him worse because it would arouse conflicts which would exacerbate his illness. A third said psychotherapy could neither help nor harm him as his illness was strictly physical. A fourth said psychotherapy would not be harmful if it remained at a superficial level. And the fifth wanted to see him five times a week at fifty dollars a session for intensive psychoanalysis. Mr. Nathan finally decided that, regardless of what the doctors said, if he had to be ill he would rather that it be without "hang-ups" than with them. He therefore committed himself to psychotherapy.

One of the first tasks of the therapist was to help Mr. Nathan commit himself to one physician and abide by his regimen. Although too ill physically to even drive himself to appointments, Mr. Nathan maintained a bland, nonchalant attitude toward his illness which masked his underlying panic. He knew that the choice of physician could be a life-or-death decision. The more anxious he became, the more he stalled. Any sign of urgency on the part of the therapist aroused anxiety in the patient and increased his denial. After many weeks he was able to select a physician through a slow-moving process which kept pace with his own readiness to proceed to the ultimate decision. The therapist compared the experience to that of a tight-rope walker in a circus.

Therapists must also be alert to their own need to deny—particularly when professionally responsible to personal friends. Because of their reluctance to see the tragedy facing a friend, physicians can make serious diagnostic errors. One physician failed to see signs of a malignant brain tumor in an intern who was his student. Another failed to recognize a beginning cancer of the colon in a colleague, thereby allowing the condition to progress until it was almost too late to save the patient's life.

In dealing with survivors of concentration camps, for example, doctors and other helpers entered into collusion with the survivors to help them gloss over that experience. A study of a twelve-page report on a survivor is full of details of the man's childhood and young family life, but only one line refers to the trauma of his concentration camp experience. He was the sole survivor out of a family of ninety-one people. The man had been in Auschwitz for five years. The doctor writing the original report was as hesitant as the patient to bring out material describing how the patient had been forced to stand by helplessly, held by guards, knowing he would be killed for trying to resist cruelty, while watching one of his children and other family members being "transformed into lumps of flesh and blood." The conclusion of the psychoanalytic experts was that such an experience reached levels beyond mere denial. Denial would mean it could not be true; here the feeling was that to maintain any kind of belief about life itself such a thing *must not* be true.[17]

The position has been taken that the personality and countertransference feelings of the therapist are more important in cases of traumatic neuroses, such as with survivors of assault, concentration camps, or other catastrophic traumas, than in cases of psychotherapy of a more conventional nature. People suffering from such traumas are particularly sensitive to any signs, verbal or nonverbal, that the therapist is not ready to stay with the outpourings of feelings. A lapse of attention, meaningless would-be supportive remarks, or an indication of discomfort can squelch the outpouring of emotions rapidly. Unless the initial sessions show evidence of the patient's expression of appropriate affect, the treatment should not be undertaken by that particular therapist with that particular individual.[18]

Certainly, it is a safe principle to follow that unless the helper is prepared to deal with the feelings aroused when denial gives way, it is better not to work toward a break in denial, because to uncover pain and then flee from it psychologically is to do the bereaved a great injustice; in grieving over a loss it can, in fact, feel like a loss compounded.

When attempting to help the compensator—who acts out his denial of impending damage to himself by aggressive or sexual overactivity —the therapist must deal with the situation on the basis of the individual's overt activity. Compensators need the attention of skilled professionals who can help them to face their panic regarding their helplessness in the hands of powerful, hurtful figures.

Janet, age thirteen, handled her fears by aggressive behavior. She had been placed in a residential treatment center because her parents, although loving, were unable to provide adequate care for her. As the social worker drove her to the dentist for root canal work, she screamed at the top of her lungs: "You are crazy! You are crazy!" She would not address any possible fear about the forthcoming dental procedure. Finally, the social worker said, "You keep calling me crazy —I wonder if it is something you wonder about yourself?" Janet then, with relief and sobbing, revealed that a year previously she had been given an electroencephalogram. It was part of the diagnostic work-up before admission to the institution. She had not been prepared for the experience, nor had it been explained to her what it meant or what the results had been. (It may even be possible that these things had been told her but in her high state of anxiety she had not been able to hear them at the time.) For a year she had kept her fears to herself. Her behavior in the institution had often appeared psychotic. The social worker now had an opportunity to allay her fears and assure her that she was not crazy. As her panic subsided, she was then able to reveal her fear of the coming dental procedure wherein she saw herself helpless in the hands of powerful, hurtful adults. The social worker was able to offer her support, explain what she knew of the procedure, and suggest to the dentist that he take time to prepare Janet step by step for the experience. Not only did she do well throughout the necessary dental work, her behavior in the institution improved also.

Mental health practitioners must be sensitive to the timing of interventions in getting the bereaved to express their grief. Denial, nature's protection against an intolerable reality, can often be confused with lack of motivation or lack of anxiety. This is treacherous ground for the novice or the insensitive, or for one who has himself not experienced grief following initial denial. It is an area where fools can rush in where angels fear to tread! There are no statistical guides, no rules of timing. The bereaved need listeners who follow closely as they approach the pain of grief, the fear of the future, and the full impact of their loss. In addition, acceptance of the behavior of the bereaved must be genuine as an aid to the restoration of self-esteem and the ability to face future losses.

Therapists must never be lulled into thinking that denial is a stage that ends at a certain point. In some form and at some level denial remains. When it is temporarily cast off the bereaved can, that moment, deal with the reality of the loss. The next moment, however, denial may be back and needs to be respected. Or, rather than there being an alternating between reality testing and denial, there can be through an ego-split denial at one level and reality testing at another, both going on at the same time.

A young woman who had lost her father through cancer when she was five years of age remembered that following the loss, although she knew her father was dead, she at the same time maintained the fantasy that he was really a spy in the service of the United States government, off on a secret and important mission. Some day he would return. "I believed that for years," she recalled, "until I could bear to know he was dead."

Intervention in denial also requires an understanding of the risks that would be taken if the denial is allowed to work itself out or is maintained.

The daughter of Mrs. Olds, an elderly woman of seventy-six, bombarded her therapist with demands that she confront her mother with the seriousness of her many illnesses—diabetes, high blood pressure, glaucoma, and so on. Mrs. Olds had always denied unpleasant realities concerning marital difficulties, disappointments with her children, and financial problems. Her total security was built on the defense of denial and keeping up appearances. The therapist questioned the wisdom of attacking this defense during Mrs Olds's final months of life and decided against a confrontation. Mrs. Olds's life's work was done, her children grown and independent, and her house, so to speak, was in order. She went on to a peaceful death, maintaining her facade that all was well. Her personality remained intact to the very end with the defenses she had used over a lifetime.

Where life has been fulfilling and rich, retrospective memories can be truly rewarding during the depletion of the end of life. Where memories might be too painful, denial and fabrication can serve to enhance self-esteem. If denial helps one approach the end of life with less pain and guilt, does it then really matter?

Notes

1. Otto Fenichel, *The Psychoanalytic Theory of Neurosis* (New York: W.W. Norton, 1945), p. 394.

2. Channing T. Lipson, "Denial and Mourning," in *The Interpretation of Death,* ed. Hendrik N. Ruitenbeek (New York: Jason Aronson, 1973), pp. 268–75.

3. Avery D. Weisman, *On Dying and Denying: A Psychiatric Study of Terminality* (New York: Behavioral Publications, 1972), pp. 20–21.

4. Ibid., p. 22.

5. Edwin A. Weinstein and Robert L. Kahn, *Denial of Illness* (Springfield, Ill.: Charles C Thomas, 1955).

6. Elisabeth Kübler-Ross, *On Death and Dying* (New York: Macmillan Co., 1969), pp. 32, 40.

7. Ibid., p. 138.

8. Henry Grayson, "Grief Reactions to the Relinquishing of Unfulfilled Wishes," *American Journal of Psychotherapy* 24 (1970): 287–95.

9. See for example David A. Hamburg et al., "Clinical Importance of Emotional Problems in the Care of Burn Patients," *New England Journal of Medicine* 248 (1953): 356.

10. N.J.C. Andreasen, Russell Noyes, Jr., and C.E. Hartford, "Factors Influencing Adjustment of Burn Patients During Hospitalization," *Psychosomatic Medicine* 34 (1972): 518–19.

11. Frederick C. Redlich and Daniel X. Freedman, *The Theory and Practice of Psychiatry* (New York: Basic Books, 1966), p. 107.

12. Victor S. Nehama, "Grief and the Imminent Threat of Non-Being," *British Journal of Psychiatry* 120 (1972): 121.

13. Gregory Rochlin, *Griefs and Discontents: The Forces of Change* (Boston: Little, Brown and Co., 1965), p. 336.

14. Henry Krystal and Thomas A. Petty, "Rehabilitation in Trauma Following Illness, Physical Injury, and Massive Personality Change," in *Massive Psychic Trauma*, ed. Henry Krystal (New York: International Universities Press, 1968), pp. 293–94.

15. Emanuel Tanay, "Dynamics of Post-Traumatic Symptomatology and Character Changes," *Massive Psychic Trauma*, p. 92.

16. Robert Waelder, *Basic Theory of Psychoanalysis* (New York: International Universities Press, 1960).

17. William G. Niederland, "An Interpretation of the Psychological Stresses and Defenses in Concentration-Camp Life and the Late Aftereffects," in *Massive Psychic Trauma*, p. 62.

18. Emanuel Tanay, "Initiation of Psychotherapy with Survivors of Nazi Persecution," in *Massive Psychic Trauma*, pp. 219–33.

6/
Somatic Distress, Crying, and Yearning

Physical Distress

When an object is lost, the bereaved tend to withdraw emotional investment from outside the self in order to avoid further pain from further loss. This unconscious withdrawal of emotion back toward the self might be seen as nature's way of centering all energy on survival, the basic task of any living creature. Somatic distress, or increased awareness of bodily pain and discomfort, can be regarded as part of the process of investing in the self. To the unsympathetic onlooker this might appear as self-centeredness on the part of the bereaved. It is a necessary and natural focus of attention and needs to be regarded as part of the armor of survival in the face of a severe blow. Somatic distress during grief can be expressed in any of the physical systems of body organs—cardiovascular, sensory, kinesthetic, muscular, gastrointestinal, respiratory, or reproductive.

One of the most common complaints of the bereaved is an inability to sleep. There may be difficulty either in falling asleep or, more frequently, waking in the early hours of the morning and remaining awake for the rest of the night. This is normal during acute grief and can go on for as long as a year following a major loss. Sleep is a complicated function which is only recently beginning to be understood. A number of important dynamics need to be considered in understanding sleep. The prayer "Now I lay me down to sleep" has in it the implicit trust in a higher power to take care of the sleeper while he is off guard. The ability to sleep is associated with the ability to let go of control and trust that all will go well without the person needing to direct the order of events. Bereavement is an experience of loss of control, in which one is often a passive victim of an external event. The need to maintain control can be a defense against the fear of further loss; thus, one remains aroused, wakeful, and ready for action. Sleeplessness can also be a result of a reluctance to let go in sleep for fear of being overwhelmed by unconscious thoughts and feelings. This can be expressed as fear of nightmares, fear of loneliness in bed, and out of the very fear of not sleeping itself.

The bereaved need to be told that problems with sleep are normal after a loss, and that they will subside as time goes on. What is strange about these sleep disorders is that the person is often not groggy the next day as he would be if he really did go without sleep, but seems to function quite adequately. This raises the question as to whether the bereaved sleep more than they think they do but at a shallow level rather than at a deeply satisfying one.

Somatic distress can also represent the physiological reactions set off by the emotional pining after the lost object; pangs of grief, aimless restlessness, inability to concentrate, compulsion to talk about the loss, crying, sobbing, feelings of weakness, fluctuations in sexual desire, or a feeling of exhaustion. Other physical symptoms include dizziness, menstrual irregularities, muscular pain, and exacerbation of old ailments. Symptoms similar to those of the deceased may occur, and feelings of numbness or coldness can represent identification with the deceased, the final illness, or the condition of death.

Another major complaint in grief is disorder of the gastrointestinal system. Symptoms may occur at any place in the digestive system and have various symbolic as well as autonomic nervous system meanings. One widow recalled reacting to the news of her husband's sudden death with an urge to vomit and the thought "This I cannot swallow."

Weight loss can be a normal reaction following a major loss providing it does not continue too long, and anorexia is not uncommon. Other complaints may be that food is tasteless, that one lacks appetite, that there is a failure of saliva to flow, that eating is impossible. Problems of ingestion can reflect resistance to taking in the reality of the loss. Complaints can also be of a feeling of tightness in the throat, a choking sensation, gagging, and nausea.

A feeling of emptiness in the stomach can be another reaction representing the feeling of emptiness from loss. Hunger, which can cause the bereaved to eat excessively and put on weight, can reflect the physiological counterpart of the subjective emotional state of pining after the lost object. Diarrhea, part of the alarm syndrome, and constipation, symbolizing an unconscious attempt to hold on to the lost object, are not uncommon gastrointestinal disorders in bereavement and normal if not prolonged.

It is of interest to note that sleep disturbances and gastrointestinal disorders, the most common somatic disorders in grief, are also the same disorders found in psychological disturbances in infancy, in psychosomatic emotional disorders, and in the physiological disorders of aging. This similarity would tend to confirm that grief strikes at a most fundamental psychological or even physiological level.

Respiratory complaints are also a normal part of grief reactions. Among these are complaints of shortness of breath, deep sighing, rapid breathing, especially when discussing the loss, a feeling of weakness, lack of strength and exhaustion, as if it is too much effort to go on, and above all an acute feeling of distress. These feelings may come in waves lasting from minutes to hours. They can be set off by expressions of sympathy, by a reminder of the loss through something in the environment, a remark, or a thought or memory of the lost object. They may be tied in with the alarm reaction or pining aspect of the loss.

Physical distress arouses further anxiety and often leads the bereaved to seek medical attention. The physician who takes a purely physical view of illness may put the patient through exhaustive and expensive laboratory tests, often with no organic findings, and may then dismiss the patient with medication for nervousness and reassurance that all is well without any awareness on the part of either the physician or the patient that a grief reaction is in process.

Mrs. Tyler interrupted therapy when her husband was hospitalized because of a heart attack. Shortly thereafter she too was hospitalized with stomach complaints. She was put through extensive diagnostic tests with no organic findings. Her physician could not account for her complaints. When she finally returned to therapy she herself pinpointed the cause of her difficulties. "My husband's heart attack was too much for me. It was just like my first husband's—hospitalized two weeks, me running to the hospital every day—I couldn't take it a second time. Only this time he lived." Her symptoms had been part of a grief reaction set off by fear of loss, unrecognized by her physician and not mentioned by the patient because she felt it would not be understood.

Loss can, however, precipitate physical diseases and it is of first

importance to have all symptoms medically investigated so that organic disease can be ruled out. If no such findings appear, the complaints can then be dealt with as part of grief with confidence that the
individual is in good physical health and that the problem is functional in nature.The bereaved should be told and helped to understand that their physical complaints are a normal part of their grief
and will ease with time. One of the important ego-supportive techniques is to help identify feelings, make sense of what patients are
experiencing, and, wherever possible, to identify that which is normal
in the behavior of the bereaved. They need to know that others have
felt as bad as they do now and that they have recovered.

It must be remembered, however, that physical symptoms and
complaints in the bereaved can also be indicative of hypochondriasis,
an abnormal grief reaction used as a defense against grieving, of
psychosomatic disorders where emotional factors are important contributory aspects of physical illness, and of serious physical ailments
which begin or are exacerbated by the helplessness set off by grief.

When a patient comes into therapy with functional complaints, it is
necessary, after establishing that no physical illness has been diagnosed, to consider that the patient may be reacting with grief to a loss
without knowing it. Questions helping to bring out such feelings need
to be initiated by the therapist in order to help the patient identify
what factors set off the grief reaction that emerged as somatic
complaints.

Crying and Yearning

Contrary to popular opinion, the most characteristic feature of
grief "is not prolonged depression but acute and episodic 'pangs.'" A
pang of grief may be defined as "an episode of severe anxiety and
psychological pain" during which time "the lost person is strongly
missed and the survivor sobs or cries aloud for him."[1] The same
dynamics apply to pangs of grief following many of the other losses
enumerated in chapter one.

Psychodynamics of crying

To better understand the cry in grieving, Colin Murray Parkes
compares the grief of adults, children, and animals and postulates a
phylogenetic basis to crying. Although it has been noted that, aside
from the human, the dog is the only animal that cries,[2] John Bowlby,
in his attachment theory, believes that the cry is an important behavioral trait contributing to the survival of both individual and species.
The cry makes it more likely that any stray or lost individual will be
recovered before he is overtaken by predators.[3] Sobbing is seen as an

aborted form of weeping; although the cry itself is muted, the spasmodic inspiratory movement remains. This is easily seen in the young child before and after a weeping spell.[4] Similar to this is the deep sighing of the bereaved which represents the inspiratory spasms of the cry. The facial expression of the grieving adult reflects a compromise between the urge to cry and the urge to suppress such "unadult" behavior.[5]

Child development theorists tend to agree that the normal child becomes capable of experiencing and expressing longing sometime during the second part of the first year of life. It is at this time that the child reaches the beginning of what is known as the stage of object constancy. At this stage the mental image of the mother is retained not only at times when the infant has need for her attention but even at times when tensions from unfulfilled needs are not present. The infant is able to regard her as a person in her own right and not someone who exists solely to meet his needs.

The ability to tolerate painful inner tensions such as yearning depends on the child's experiences in having an opportunity to build up a tolerance for separation and disappointment through experiences that did not surpass the limits of his endurance. If such limits are exceeded, the child may become overwhelmed by feelings or will resort to defenses enabling him to ward off the intolerable feelings. In the latter instance his capacity for recognizing, tolerating, and expressing sadness and anger may be temporarily or permanently impaired.[6] For example, children who have lost a parent rarely have an opportunity to work through grief until adulthood. Frequently, the grief remains bottled up until some later problem brings the adult into psychotherapy. Invariably, the problem is related to the unresolved grief. On the other hand, the child who is not allowed to experience tolerable separations, such as being left with a baby sitter, is deprived of the opportunity to develop the capacity to cope with longing.

Freud struggled to explain the emotional pain set off by loss and compared it to the pain of physical injury arising from the same condition: "the cumulative effect of a continuing stimulus that cannot be escaped." In the case of loss this stimulus is the mounting yearning for the lost object.[7]

The attachment theory postulates that the task of grief, based on the biological mother-child tie, is to bring about reunion through the mutual signaling between attachment figures. "Only in the rare event of a permanent separation do the most obvious features of acute grief, pining and yearning become gradually extinguished without reunion occurring."[8]

Barriers and supports to crying

The ability of the bereaved to let go in tears is determined by societal, cultural, familial, and personal factors:

Grief seems to be a universal human response to loss, and though we cannot be sure that it provokes the same reactions everywhere, irrespective of a society's culture, the mourning rituals described by social anthropologists in widely different societies seem to reflect similar underlying tensions. The bereaved may be expected to show violent distress, and be formally restrained.[9]

The various reactions of Israeli women following the deaths of their husbands in the 1967 Six-Day War exemplify these cultural and social differences:

Women with oriental ethnic backgrounds found relief and comfort by observing the overt mourning rituals and customs sanctioned and followed by their community: tearing their hair and clothes, scratching their cheeks, rocking back and forth rhythmically, and indulging in periodic *crisot* with symptoms of faintness, nausea, and even blackouts. Not only did these rituals serve to demonstrate the intensity of grief, but they enabled the women to slip more easily into their new role of widow. Visits to the cemetery became absorbing and ritualistic in their intensity.

Women from a restrained western background and those who were not religious found it harder to cope with the initial threat to past security. Many reported being given tranquilizers to "ease the pain of suffering" and said it took weeks to take in fully what had happened. In some cases, they confessed they would have liked to weep and wail but felt restricted by well-meaning relatives, who resolutely changed the subject when they tried to talk openly about their husbands or were inhibited by the common *sabra* (native-born Israeli) ethic of denial, stoicism, and inarticulateness.

The widow in the kibbutz, for example, experiences a special problem. In some kibbutzim, although the death of a member is keenly felt and mourned by all members, the absence of meaningful mourning rituals and the tendency to shield the widow from outside contacts or worries usually leaves her roleless and bottled up, unable to find a socially sanctioned way to grieve. She may be relieved of her work and child-caring responsibilities and often spends her time in loneliness or in putting up a facade.[10]

Family members and friends can be influential in inhibiting the tears of the bereaved. Some families laud stoicism as a virtue, condemn the crybaby, and teach the belief that crying implies weakness. A person raised in such an atmosphere will find it difficult to cry in grief.

This inhibition of tears can be passed on from one generation to the next, as was the case with a young girl named Patty. Her first encounter with death came when she was thirteen years of age and her beloved paternal grandfather was killed in an automobile accident. At the funeral she was shocked at the display of grief by the grown-ups because she knew many of them had been unkind to her grandfather during his lifetime. Her mother was not one of these. She had been welcomed as a daughter-in-law and had responded with respect and love. "I believe in treating people well while they are alive and crying less when they die," she said to Patty at the funeral. This then became Patty's model for grieving. Little did she know that her mother's lack of grief, despite the rationalization, was a dysfunctional grief reaction: Patty's maternal grandfather had died when her mother was five years of age, locking her into the absent grief reaction characteristic of children so young. Years later in therapy Patty had to undo her mother's teachings.

Families and friends can also, out of the wish to avoid the pain of seeing a loved one suffer, depreciate the value of the lost object, as if to convince the bereaved there is no reason to suffer as the loss was not great anyway.

Mrs. Reed, a young mother of two small children, came into treatment because of a depressive reaction following the separation from her husband. Although she efficiently cared for her young children and held down a part-time job, she felt unable to get organized, to clean her house, to plan activities for the weekend, and, most of all, to take any definitive action toward filing for divorce. She had a male friend who was devoted to her and the children, but she could mobilize little interest or energy in the relationship. She did not cry. When threatened with sadness or tears, she gave a nervous laugh and smiled broadly. When asked why she smiled when she felt so unhappy, she said crying had been sneered at in her childhood home. Her older brother used to tease her, and outfight and outtalk her. When she cried in helpless frustration, she was called a crybaby. Now, people could not understand why she would want to cry about someone like her husband. He had been little good as a husband or father, they insisted. Yet she cried because he was the father of her children, and they had spent some years together. True, he did have problems, but she knew what a difficult childhood he had had. Perhaps had he had help as a child things might have been different for them. Although she could not live with him, she nevertheless could feel sorry that the marriage had not worked. Slowly, with validation that she truly had a loss for which she was entitled to mourn, the tears started and the depression began to lift.

People often brag of their refusal to cry in front of friends, for fear of "wearing out my friendship." Popular sayings unfortunately support this view: "Laugh and the world laughs with you; cry and you cry alone." It is true that some friends can be worn out by the grief of the bereaved, particularly those who have not known and overcome grief themselves. The bereaved not only fear losing friendships. They fear losing dignity through open crying, embarrassing others, or inviting criticism. It is not unusual to hear remarks such as: "She makes no attempt to pull herself together. She's just feeling sorry for herself. It's been a month already." The bereaved, in turn, fear feeling sorry for themselves. Some feel guilty at their own grief in the face of what they feel are larger tragedies in the world.

People, whether out of ignorance, embarrassment, or even hostility, can be intrusive as well. One widow reported receiving a condolence letter which read: "I am so sorry to hear about your husband's death. He was a wonderful man. Everything is fine with us here. My husband was just promoted on his job. . . ."

A woman who was dying of cancer commented on the parade of visitors who passed through her house. "I haven't seen some of these people in twenty years. They are just curious to see me because I am dying. So I'll give them a good show." In her case there were no tears. People spoke of her stoicism in the face of her physically draining illness, of her cleverness in hiding her emaciated body with long-sleeved blouses and high necklines. At times she even served refreshments to her visitors: here she was continuing to shoulder the burden of responsibility, as she had throughout her lifetime.

Envy from the listener, or fears of the listener's destructive power, can also stop the flow of tears. Bereavement is a time of vulnerability, leaving the grieving person open to attack.

A young mother of two children was widowed within a few months after the family moved to a new city where the father had taken an important position. To her great surprise, a casual acquaintance from the former community suddenly appeared. This seemed somewhat strange to the widow, who remembered, however, that the woman had on a few occasions spoken of her unhappy marriage. She kept urging the widow to cry, to give way to tears, but the widow felt on guard and the tears refused to flow. Finally, in exasperation, the visitor telephoned to ask her husband to come for her, making a point of stressing that he would come in their private airplane. She departed, never to be heard from again.

Crying and the exhibition of strong feelings can be equated by some with psychosis, particularly if an immediate family member had a psychotic break with violent expression of raw emotions. The awareness of strong emotions at the time of a loss can set off fears of such a break.

The searing pain of sorrow can be defended against by the bereaved themselves in many ways. One way is to disparage the value of what was lost. "Why should I miss her? She was never happy with me anyway." The "I'll leave you before you leave me" maneuver is another way of attempting to avoid the pain of loss. And feelings and thoughts can focus on one minute aspect of the loss as a defense against more overwhelming feelings.

Jenny was eight years old when her mother died. As an adult she could not remember grieving; many of her memories around the time of the death were blocked off. She was left to the care of a devoted and competent father and two loving older brothers. But she remembered a persistent worry following her mother's death. She looked about her and knew that little girls were flat chested and women had large breasts, but she could not figure out how the little girl changed from flat to curved! In this worry was condensed the larger concern—how does a little girl (I) grow up without a mother?

Tears may be held back because of fear of attack from the listener, including the helping person.

A woman revealed her reluctance to disclose her pain at the loss of the lover who withdrew because of her attacks and control. "I was afraid to cry in front of you because I thought you would say what my friends are telling me: 'Why are you crying when you are the one who drove him away?'" Because one has contributed to the creation of a loss does not make the loss any less mourned for; it may, in fact, increase the pain.

Would-be helpers can demand greater expression of emotion than the bereaved is ready to reveal or even feel. Arthur, aged thirty-five, began to mourn the break-up of a long-standing relationship with a woman friend. He spoke with feeling of the good times they had had and mourned the fact that the neurotic elements in their relationship made it imperative that, for the time being, at least, they separate.

As Arthur spoke he remembered a past loss and his experience in group therapy at that time. He had been torn with grief, he said, but added "I had not fallen apart."

"It is not necessary to fall apart," commented the therapist, and was about to continue when Arthur interrupted:

"Stop right there, please. You just said something and I do not even think you realize what you said." The tears came to his eyes as he went on. "I want to thank you for that remark. In my previous therapy they kept pushing at me in the group to fall apart, and I couldn't. I kept saying, 'What do you want from me, my guts? I'm bleeding and hurting and telling you so. What kind of a show do you want?' You have just validated me beyond anything you can imagine. I was right. I hurt and knew it but did not fall apart. They were pushing me out of their need." With this validation he was free to release the tears as he saw fit; they were not something to be dragged from him. It was noted too that he had felt his mother always demanded greater performance from him than he had ever been able to give.

How can one describe the pain of yearning? The bereaved can be picturesque in their description. People speak of feeling "torn apart" with "searing pain," which may, at the same time, be experienced as a relief.

A young man who had lost his father in infancy became aware of a pain in his chest, in the region of his heart, which eventually he was able to connect with thoughts or feelings about the father of whom he had no conscious memory. In describing the pain he said, "It is as if there is a hole in the center of my heart. The hole expands, as if pushing against the walls of my heart. If the pushing went on long enough, it is as if my heart would burst under the pressure. So something pushes from the outside, and there is a counterforce that seems to cause the pain." It was at this point that for the first time in his life he began to cry with the sadness of an adult, not with the tears of childhood when he could not have his way. He welcomed the tears as a release of the tension and of the feeling of pressure within his chest.

Implications for Intervention

The question might well be asked whether the resolution of grief is ever possible without weeping taking place in the presence of another. Although there is no doubt that crying by oneself can be helpful in releasing feelings, this is only a part of the grief process. If Bowlby's theory about crying is correct, that it is biologically centered in the evolution of the species as a signal for retrieval of the individual who strays from the group and is in danger from predators, then the cry of the bereaved should be used also for reconnection to another.

The deepest form of connection with another is through the feeling of being understood; even a casual acquaintance showing empathy can provide comfort. A widow related that the two hundred condolence letters she received following her husband's death could be divided into two categories—those from people who had themselves experienced a major loss and those from others who obviously had not. One letter puzzled her. It was from a single woman whom the widow had always regarded as being entirely lacking in empathy, and yet it revealed a capacity which did not fit this image. Curious about this discrepancy, the widow inquired further about the woman. She learned that this woman had had a thirty-year romance with a man whom she deeply loved who was unable to live with her. At the time of his death she had not even been free to express her sorrow openly, yet she knew the pain of the loss of a loved partner and was able to communicate her awareness to another in pain.

Reconnection to another is possible when the bereaved can feel safe in their vulnerability. For this they need to feel that crying is normal and healthy, that it does not necessarily mean weakness or inadequacy. Before such reassurance is possible, however, the helper must be aware of the pitfalls of releasing emotions. Some people may, in fact, "come apart at the seams" as grief overwhelms them. The helper must be prepared to stand by the bereaved if feelings are released. Standing by means being prepared to see the bereaved more frequently than in traditional therapy. Frequency should be determined by the length of time the grieving person can tolerate between appointments. Weekends, holidays, and free time are particularly painful for people who feel abandoned and without inner strengths. Frequent contacts encourage the outpouring of emotions. The bereaved need to share in the decision regarding the frequency of appointments so as to experience some control at a time when they feel helpless and powerless. Some may need the therapist's encouragement when the pain of grieving tempts them to dilute the process or to terminate treatment.

In an agency setting, where one worker does the evaluation and the case is assigned to another worker for treatment, one must be careful at intake to avoid uncovering too much material because the bereaved person may want to continue with the helper who, in his mind, is associated with the release of emotion. Keeping the bereaved waiting for reassignment is contraindicated if emotions are released. The bereaved cannot tolerate their pain alone and the helper or helping agency has the responsibility of following through once the process is begun.

Some people may need help in crying. An appropriate remark can help release tears. Others need to know they will not be shamed if they cry in the presence of another. A young woman in therapy because of depression berated herself for being unable to stop crying. "I'm sick of it," she exclaimed. "I want to go on with the business of living. How long can I go on crying? I've been crying for years."

"Have you been crying alone or with another?" she was asked.

"I've always cried alone. Who is there to cry with?"

"I wonder if anyone can overcome grief by crying alone," was the response.

The first hour she cried copiously, using countless tissues, but she kept sniffing back the nasal mucous, a physical expression of the inability to externalize feeling.

"Do you think today you could just let your nose drain instead of trying to hold things back?" she was asked gently.

"I'm afraid it will look so awful," she answered. But by the end of the hour she was blowing her nose freely. Gradually, from session to session her crying tapered off, and within a short time she was ready to move on to other aspects of the therapeutic work.

Merely crying, however, is not enough. The bereaved need help in identifying the meaning of the tears, and the meaning will change from moment to moment as the grief work progresses. In the recognition of the meaning of the cry lies further understanding and thus connection to another. The ability to weep freely in the presence of another is a clue to the working through of grief.

Notes

1. Colin Murray Parkes, *Bereavement: Studies of Grief in Adult Life* (New York: International Universities Press, 1972), p. 39.

2. Louis Paul, "Crisis Intervention," *Mental Hygiene* 30 (1966): 141–45.

3. John Bowlby, quoted in Parkes, *Bereavement,* p. 41.

4. Ibid.

5. Ibid., p. 42.

6. Erna Furman, *A Child's Parent Dies: Studies in Childhood Bereavement* (New Haven, Conn.: Yale University Press, 1974), p. 15.

7. Sigmund Freud quoted in Channing T. Lipson, "Denial and Mourning," in the *Interpretation of Death,* ed. Hendrik M. Ruitenbeek (New York: Jason Aronson, 1973), p. 269.

8. Ira O. Glick, Robert S. Weiss, and C. Murray Parkes, *The First Year of Bereavement* (New York: John Wiley and Sons, 1974), p. 8.

9. Peter Marris, *Loss and Change* (New York: Pantheon Books, 1974), p. 30.

10. Naomi Golan, "Wife to Widow to Woman," *Social Work* 20 (1975): 371–72.

7/
Searching and Attempts at Retrieval

One of the most perplexing aspects of loss and grief is the compulsive need to go after and retrieve that which has been lost, behavior that Colin Murray Parkes has most appropriately given the name of *searching*. Although *searching* is the term that describes the behavior, the terms *pining* or *yearning* are used to describe the emotional accompaniments of the searching behavior. Parkes states:

> In order to get the search for a lost person into perspective we have to bear in mind that a great deal of human and animal behaviour contains elements of searching. Searching fills the gap between aim and object. Traditional psychology has paid little attention to this category of behaviour and it is only with the advent of ethology that the significance of searching has been recognized. . . .
>
> In the griever the only happening that seems important is the return of the one who is lost. And in social animals, from their earliest years, the principal behaviour pattern evoked by loss is searching.[1]

Searching can be understood in terms of the theory of attachment behavior—the tendency of members of the species to stay within proximity of one another as a defense against predators. Among animals, then, searching and crying serve in the interests of recovery of the stray and thus ultimately in survival of the species.

Although catastrophic loss brings deep sorrow, searching behavior, by contrast, can be found in losses ranging from the most severe to the most trivial. In the latter, it can occur without the emotional accompaniments of pain and yearning. An example of searching in trivial loss is the compulsivity with which one goes after the discrepancy of a few cents between the monthly bank statement and one's own checking account. Were the discrepancy sizable, the urgency to find the error would be understandable. Where the discrepancy is of a trifling amount, however, in a private checking account (a business account which needs to be audited is another matter), the time spent in the search is out of proportion to the importance of the few pennies missing.

Searching is fascinating behavior to observe in oneself as well as in others. It may be conscious or unconscious. In either case it represents a compulsion that is irresistible despite one's understanding of the phenomenon. "When I lose something," people say, "I know there is no point in looking for it. I never find it when I look for it. But later, when I least expect it, there it is and usually in a place I have searched over and over again."

Novelist William Armstrong's intuitive understanding of searching is poignantly reflected in a son's search for his father sent off to work on a chain gang:

"Time is passing" the woman would say. "I wish you wouldn't go lookin', child." But when one of the field hands had heard something or when somebody said that a road camp was moving, she would wrap a piece of bread and meat for the boy to eat on the way and say nothing. Looking back from far down the road, the boy would see her watching at the edge of the porch. She seemed to understand the compulsion that started him on each long, fruitless journey with new hope.[2]

The Components of Searching Behavior

The major components of searching behavior were described by Erich Lindemann in the early 1940s as part of the symptomatology of normal grief.[3] Each piece of the behavior, however, was viewed as a separate entity. It was not until three decades later that Parkes made the dynamic connection between these separate components in his conceptualization of searching behavior.[4]

The behavior associated with searching as seen in acute grief is as follows:

Preoccupation with thoughts and images of the lost object.
A compulsion to speak of the loss.
A compulsion to retrieve the lost object.
Aimless wandering, restlessness, marking time.
A feeling that time is suspended.

Disorganization.
Inability to initiate any activity.
Lack of zest or interest in daily activities.
A feeling of going through the motions of living.
Effort required to accomplish previously routine tasks.
Confusion, feelings of unreality.
Fears that any of the above may denote mental illness.

Parkes views grief as a gradual process whereby the real event of loss that has taken place in reality is gradually made real inside the self, a modification of internal representation that takes place only over time. The grief process that facilitates this appropriate modification of the internal world involves the pain of repeated awareness of the discrepancies between what is and what once was, and, thus, repeated frustration. Because the repeated frustration of any behavior, according to learning theory, eventually leads to its extinction, grief too is a process of learning. Eventually, through extinction, the pining and searching lessen and energy is released for new interests.[5]

A poem by Edna St. Vincent Millay eloquently describes this repeated awareness of discrepancies and repeated frustrations:

Time does not bring relief; you all have lied
Who told me time would ease me of my pain!
I miss him in the weeping of the rain;
I want him at the shrinking of the tide;
The old snows melt from every mountain-side,
And last year's leaves are smoke in every lane;
But last year's bitter loving must remain
Heaped on my heart, and my old thoughts abide.
There are a hundred places where I fear
To go,—so with his memory they brim.
And entering with relief some quiet place
Where never fell his foot or shone his face
I say, "There is no memory of him here!"
And so stand stricken, so remembering him.[6]

Preoccupation with Thoughts, Image, and Speech about the Loss

Preoccupation with the loss is in the forefront of consciousness in bereavement. The newly widowed, for example, have their deceased spouse constantly in mind, regardless of what else they might be doing. Phylogenetically this preoccupation with the lost object serves a useful purpose in creating a perceptual set that prepares the bereaved to recognize the lost object should it appear. Thus, among social animals, the stray animal is more likely to be recognized and, where possible, retrieved by the operation of this perceptual set.[7]

However, psychologically a preconceived set makes it easy to mis-perceive what one sees; one often tends to see that which one wishes or is preset to see. These hallucinations wherein the bereaved believe they see the lost object are normal but very upsetting if not under-stood. For example, the back of the head of someone walking alone on the street can appear to the bereaved as the back of the head of the lost object. He hastens his steps, only to find to his great disappoint-ment and embarrassment that the person is a complete stranger. Once more he has experienced the pain of awareness of discrepancy between what is and what once was.

The bereaved are compelled to ruminate and to speak of various themes surrounding the loss. Often uppermost is the theme of how the end finally came about, the tendency of the bereaved to engage in "obsessional review" concerning the loss.[8]

Repeatedly, the bereaved go over each step that led to the inevita-ble loss. Was it the right choice of doctor? of hospital? Should they have taken the advice of the consultant who had disagreed with the surgeon? Or, concerning the death of a child: Why didn't I take note of his complaints earlier? He said he had a pain but I thought he was just trying to get out of school. Why did I wait weeks until he finally said, "Mother, I think I should see a doctor." Or, in divorce: What if I hadn't gone on that trip when he wanted me around? Would he have left me? Was I too bossy? Or too easygoing? Did I put the children first? Did I allow my parents to be too intrusive? Or, about the loss of health: Why didn't I check for warning signs earlier? We all know to watch out for unexplained bleeding or lumps. Or about a robbery: I shouldn't have gone out that night. I had a feeling I hadn't checked the back window. I knew the lock was temperamental and always meant to have it fixed. And on and on.

When in death a loved one seems particularly disfigured, the be-reaved may be haunted by memories of the final trauma of suffering. A widower was obsessed with the image of the face of his wife on her deathbed. "Her eyes just stared at me, as if pleading to help her, although I knew she wasn't even aware of me anymore. She looked shrunken from her former robust self. I can't get her eyes out of my mind. They haunt me." As the months went by his talk slowly turned to other memories of his wife and his life with her.

Conversely, the look of repose on the face of the deceased can offer solace to the bereaved. One young widow took great comfort from the fact that her husband after years of suffering looked in his coffin as young and carefree as he had at his confirmation. To her, despite her own grief and sorrow, his struggles were over and he was at peace.

To add to the confusion of the bereaved, there can be, at the same time that there is preoccupation with the lost object, an inability to recall the face of the deceased as he appeared in normal life. This can lead to feelings of guilt if interpreted by the bereaved to mean lack of love. Because most often people suffer the loss of loved ones singly, there is usually no one to talk to who can validate the normalcy of this lack of recall. The bereaved may, therefore, not mention this and carry the distress alone.

The bereaved are preoccupied with memories of the entire lifetime with the lost object. This too is a form of searching. It serves a dual purpose in acute grief. It serves as a means of holding on to the lost object and thereby delaying the pain of accepting the inevitability of the loss. At the same time, the experience of facing each memory, thought, and feeling associated with the lost object, to the extent that one is able to bear the pain, helps to integrate the reality of the loss gradually.

Going to bed alone, a toothbrush in the holder, disposing of the clothes of the deceased, the smell of familiar food, a song of special significance, one's favorite television program, walking through a department store and seeing clothes for men, women, children, infants —all can set off memories of the loss.

Some reminders of the loss may be too painful to bear and thus may be avoided entirely. One family who had invested money and energy into building a home and farm could not bear to see their land after a disastrous fire in the area destroyed hundreds of acres. After a few halfhearted attempts at clearing the scorched land, they gave up, never returned, and eventually put the land up for sale. Reactions do differ, however, and other families with equal losses could rebuild on the same site. Similarly, some women raped in their homes must move elsewhere; others fight the urge to do so.

The ruminations and obsessional talking of the bereaved may be considered a kind of searching. Some theorists hold that the talking represents the search for some point in the decision-making process where a different decision may have led to other consequences; they are engaging in the avoidance of loss. How far back can one go? To the final illness? To the previous lifestyle? To the beginning of the relationship itself? Obviously, if there had been no tie, there would have been no loss.

The same kind of searching through rumination goes on with losses other than the loss of a loved one. Victims of rape, robbery, fire, flood, or other catastrophic losses need to ruminate and talk about the events leading up to the loss. Eventually comes the realization that what was had to be, that the past cannot be altered, and that the loss did occur and cannot be undone.

Compulsion to retrieve the lost object

Another important component of searching is the drive to retrieve that which has been lost. Where the loss is of a person or thing still in existence, such as loss through divorce or separation, a stolen object, and so on, this drive to retrieve is understandable.

A young woman who broke off the relationship with her lover found herself going past his home no matter where her own daily routine took her. "I have radar which directs me there," she quipped.

Searching in instances of divorce serves the interest of reality testing. Each confrontation brings the hope of remaking the past and either motivates the partners toward the kind of changes necessary to make a better relationship or, failing that, breaks the fantasy of reunion and reaffirms the inevitability of the decision to separate. The concept of searching also explains the many attempts at reconciliation, the sleeping together at night while fighting during the day, the reluctance to let go of someone or something one once had and valued.

Although the search for an absent figure is understandable, the search for one lost through death seems irrational. Yet even here the urge for retrieval of what was lost goes on. Researchers at the University of Minnesota found in a study of bereavement in sixty-six cultures that in almost every case people tend to perceive something like the ghost of the person who has died. These experiences, depending on the culture, can be found gratifying and reassuring or, as in the American culture, may be frightening because people think it means they are losing their minds.[9] Retrieval of the lost object can also be sought through dreams, some of which can bring back the lost object almost in ghostlike form.

In addition, searching can take place through displacement. Here the attempt at retrieval is not directed toward the lost object but toward a substitute. This can be seen in the way in which some who have sustained a loss of a loved one develop a fantasy that they are in love with someone and, in some cases, even that the feelings are reciprocated.

Searching can also occur through substitution, such as in hasty remarriage. It can also be seen in the search for gratification from others of that which was once received from the deceased. This happens frequently when an elderly parent dies and the remaining parent transfers to adult children a dependency formerly centered on the spouse.

Searching is common in physical losses—from the compulsion to touch the tongue to the empty place where a tooth had once been to the phantom limb phenomenon. One man, who had been disfigured by cancer, spent hours looking at old snapshots of himself and friends; it was a way of searching for the intact body of former years. In developmental loss, searching can be seen in the child's renewed attachment and holding on to a toy or piece of clothing about to be discarded. It is found in the holding on to old possessions that symbolize significant ties of past years. It is rampant in the search for eternal youth.

Searching for the lost parent

Searching is observable in children who have lost a parent, particularly through death or permanent separation. A woman whose father, an architect, died when she was six years of age recalled that she and her younger sister and brother were obsessed with watching houses being built. Another woman remembered searching for her deceased father in another form when she was about ten. Every evening at suppertime she would go to the corner lamp-post where she could search the faces of men coming home from work. She was sure that one night it would be her father's face she would see.

Children who have lost a parent through death can also become fixated on the aspect of burial. A film that won the grand prize at the Venice Film Festival in 1952 deals with this theme of burial. It begins with the Luftwaffe strafing panic-stricken refugees fleeing from Paris along a country road in 1940. A man and his wife are killed, leaving their five-year-old daughter with her dying dog in her arms. The girl finds refuge with a peasant family. The eleven-year-old son of the family joins the girl in conducting a sad little funeral for the dog and creating a cemetery of their own in an abandoned mill. The children continue to bury dead insects and animals—a mole, a beetle, a chick—until their compulsive night raids on the adjacent churchyard for crosses to place on these symbolic graves bring them into conflict with the country people of the village.

One expression of the compulsive search for the lost parent is found in the growing movement of adult adoptees to locate their birth parents. Formerly seen as a neurotic need for love, this urge is gradually coming to be regarded as a combination of a need to know one's ethnic background and medical history, simple curiosity, and as a part of the consolidation of a sense of identity. Contrary to the fears of adoptive parents and the stereotyped attitudes of social workers, this need does not arise from a need for love and affection denied by adoptive parents.[10] As part of completion of the task of identity formation, this search, which may begin in late adolescence, becomes more intense when the adoptee plans to marry and have children.

Thus, while searching is a normal part of acute grief, it can continue on and become part of permanent character structure. One form this can take is sublimation into career choices such as archeology, anthropology, and history—the search into the past of cultures rather than a direct search for one's own past losses.

Searching through creating "false" losses

It is a well-known fact in mental health work that the turning of a passive into an active experience helps reestablish emotional equilibrium. This phenomenon can also be seen in searching behavior. Because loss is an experience one usually suffers passively, the creating of a second loss can turn the passive experience into an active one. Results can range from the most trivial and even humorous to potentially dangerous ones.

A sixty-five-year-old widower, on the first Mother's Day following the death of his wife, did something that made him sure he was losing his mind. He had shopped the evening before at a nearby supermarket and, because the weather was lovely, he decided to walk home. Sunday morning he awakened, went to the garage to get his car, found it was not there. He panicked, certain it had been stolen. Gradually he remembered he had left it in the parking lot of the supermarket the day before. He ran all the way to the market, sure it would either be missing or broken into and damaged. In his frantic state of mind he failed at first to see the car, even though it was the only one parked there at that early morning hour. Finally he located it and to his relief he found it was safe and undamaged. With relief he drove off, wondering how he could have done such a "stupid" thing. Was he losing his mind? Not at all. What he had done, since his original loss of his wife was not retrievable, was to create a secondary loss that was. His retrieval of one lost object somehow provided comfort around the loss that could not be undone.

In another example, an elderly widow had spent the winter months with her children in California. As she packed for the return home she remarked, "I can't find my address book. I seem to be losing things lately. I must be getting senile." The daughter answered, "No, Mother, you are not getting senile. You are just losing things because you are going through an experience of loss in leaving us. You had a wonderful time. You will miss us. You have not lost your address book; you just think so. It is us you feel you are losing." Within a few minutes the address book had been found, lying within sight all the time.

It appears as if experiences associated with a loss take on meaning associated with the lost object. Thus, the retrieval of an article connected with the lost object can symbolize some aspect of retrieval of the lost object itself.

Restlessness, marking time

Because the search for the object lost through death would appear irrational to both the bereaved and others, it is often not recognized as searching but appears to be aimless wandering, restlessness, and the search for something to do. Time seems to be in limbo—something to be endured. The bereaved seem to be waiting. But waiting for what? It has been conjectured that the unconscious expectation of the bereaved is that something will happen to make things the way they were before the loss. Time drags by as each activity of the day, formerly routine, is now performed laboriously, with great expenditure of energy and thought. Every activity that impinges on the loss has to be lived through without the lost object.

Disorganization, loss of initiative

Another normal, misunderstood, and highly disturbing aspect of bereavement is the loss of initiative. External demands can alleviate and camouflage some of this behavior. For a homemaker, the demands of children needing care, laundry, shopping, cooking, and cleaning provide some of the structure needed. Even here there are blocks of free time that can loom as gigantic obstacles to overcome. For the worker outside the home the job can prove a blessing. But then there is the free time of evenings, weekends, and, most painful of all, holidays. The unemployed, the retired, and the elderly can have great difficulty filling the hours of bereavement.

"What will I do with the rest of today?" wailed a new divorcee. "Yesterday I sat all alone in my house. The children were in school. The telephone did not ring all day. How can I go on like this day after day?" A telephone call would have provided external structure; for her to have initiated a call demanded an ability she did not possess. This endless stretching out of time can frighten the bereaved. Some associate it with mental patients sitting around in back wards of hospitals. Others compare it to the elderly, sitting in nursing homes waiting for death.

Disorganization may also take the form of starting a task and failing to follow through as the mind drifts off to other thoughts, often about the loss. This ambivalence is typical of searching behavior, as is the waiting for something to happen. With such apparent lethargy and emotional investment in the loss, it is not surprising that the bereaved have little relish for living in the present. The pain of the loss is so overwhelming that normal pleasures seem inconsequential by comparison.

The lack of zest of the bereaved usually extends to their sexual and social life. The bereaved are often exposed to blatant attack by both the lay person and the professional who seem to feel that grief can be healed by replacement with a sexual object. Also, some bereaved women, whether widowed, divorced, or separated, complain that if they are not involved sexually they seem to arouse anger in some of the men with whom they come into contact. They are given the feeling that by their abstinence they are causing needless sexual deprivation. They feel vulnerable to exploitation and unprotected by the presence of a partner.

In addition, because of the confusing of sex with intimacy so prevalent today, the bereaved can be upset by advice coming from well-meaning friends who are struggling with this conflict themselves. Such advice can add additional hardship to the bereaved by encouraging their involvement in activities that may run counter to their value system, as well as exposing them to disturbed and destructive people seeking their own relief through using others.

Implications for Intervention

Because normal behavior in grief is so different from what is considered normal behavior generally, it is not surprising to find that the grieving person does not know whether his behavior is normal or pathological. Family and friends are often of little help because they too are confused over this issue. The bereaved thus suffer double trauma—the loss itself, and the bewilderment over whether their reaction is normal or an indication that they are "losing their minds." Whenever possible, the bereaved need to be reassured that their behavior is typical of acute grief. (See again "The Components of Searching Behavior" on page 91.) Nightmares are also common in acute grief as well as hypnogogic hallucinations. The latter can be particularly alarming because one tends to associate hallucinations with mental illness; in grief, however, they are normal. All of this behavior needs to be validated as it appears.

Previously adequate and active people who find themselves unable to work, sitting around aimlessly, feeling that time is suspended, unable to initiate an activity or organize their day, need to be told their behavior is a normal part of grief. Without proper knowledge of this component of grief, the bereaved can become frightened by their own inactivity. They need to hear that this stage will pass in time, but that the passage of time alone is not sufficient and that recovery lies in the expression of feelings. Active grief work will enable them to move on to renewed interest and to restitution.

The pathway from searching to restitution is through the expression of feeling and through talking. This requires that the bereaved have people with whom they can talk themselves out. The helper must recognize roadblocks to the expression of different kinds of feelings and must know how to recognize and facilitate the small steps a person may need to take in order to experience the full expression of each of the emotions necessary to work through grief. Release does not happen as a one-time matter. Feelings surge and need to be expressed, there is then a period of quiescence, and then feelings surge anew. The bereaved need to be helped through each new resurgence and need to be reassured constantly that such resurgence does not mean regression but is a normal part of the process of grief work.

Impatience on the part of the listener with any aspect of searching can delay rather than facilitate grief work. A curt remark such as "Let's not dwell on the past," or "Let's stay in the present," can cut off the flow of speech and make the bereaved feel misunderstood. Mental health professionals commonly make this error when they fail to understand that past and present losses and griefs merge in the unconscious. Grief is a self-draining process. Insistence by the helper on a problem-solving approach or a here-and-now approach can thus be counterproductive in grief work.

The grief therapist may need to be openly critical of other helpers, whether family, friends, or professionals, in order to provide the bereaved with a healthy view of the grief process and their own place in it.

"My daughter tells me I was more lucky than most women. I had twenty-five years of a happy marriage and should be grateful for that," remarked one widow.

"Your daughter may think she is being helpful," the therapist replied. "But her remark is more likely to cut off your grief than to allow you to experience it. Maybe you need to talk to someone besides her, because your suffering is obviously getting to her."

One of the areas where therapists frequently err is in the advice they give about ambivalence. Although ambivalence has already been covered in chapter four, it bears some repetition here because it ties in with the inactivity of searching behavior. Rather than urging people to act in the face of ambivalence, which occurs normally in grief, it is important that the newly bereaved be discouraged from making important decisions about moving, disposing of possessions, and so on, while in a state of acute grief. The danger of their creating secondary losses at such a time is great and direct intervention on the part of the helper may sometimes be needed to prevent traumatic losses. Major decisions, such as the sale of a home for practical reasons, should be delayed. The practical may not always meet emotional needs of holding on to beloved possessions until the first pangs of bereavement are over. Destructive actions are less likely to occur when feelings surrounding loss are recognized and verbalized.

Of course, even the most patient listener can become weary at the repetition necessary for the bereaved to integrate the loss. Thus, it is helpful if there can be more than one listener. Highly skilled professionals are needed for complicated grief reactions, but where the bereaved is able to express emotion openly in the presence of another, the helper can be anyone who understands from his own past experiences with loss what is needed.

Not all grief, however, is resolvable. Where losses have been as massive as those suffered by the victims of concentration camp atrocities and atomic bomb warfare, researchers have found that survivors are often unable to talk about their experiences because words are inadequate for them to express the massive psychic trauma that was endured. Even when talking was in the interest of their receiving financial compensation for their losses, many found it difficult to speak up—the horrors they had witnessed aroused feelings too overwhelming to be allowed into full awareness.[11]

In most instances, however, education focused on grief and emotional support through the process are the most helpful interventions. "The biggest thing I get out of coming here," said one bereaved mother to her therapist, "is learning that everything I feel, think, and say is normal. At least I have that. With your support I can bear the pain and hope some day to move on to joy again. I do have much to live for."

Notes

1. Colin Murray Parkes, *Bereavement: Studies of Grief in Adult Life* (New York: International Universities Press, 1972), pp. 40, 54, 56.

2. William H. Armstrong, *Sounder* (New York: Harper and Row, 1969), p. 86.

3. Erich Lindemann, "The Symptomatology and Management of Acute Grief," *American Journal of Psychiatry* 101 (1944): 141–48.

4. Parkes, *Bereavement*.

5. Ira O. Glick, Robert S. Weiss, and C. Murray Parkes, *The First Year of Bereavement* (New York: John Wiley and Sons, 1974), pp. 8–9.

6. Edna St. Vincent Millay, *"Renascence ii,"* in *Collected Sonnets* (New York: Harper and Brothers, 1941), p. 2.

7. Parkes, *Bereavement.*

8. Glick, Weiss, and Parkes, *The First Year of Bereavement,* p. 128.

9. Jackie Roedler, "Ghost Experiences 'Real,' Natural Part of Mourning," *The Dispatch* (Minnesota), 21 January 1976, p. 3.

10. Annette Baran, Arthur Sorosky, and Reuben Pannor, "The Dilemma of Our Adoptees," *Psychology Today,* December 1975, p. 38.

11. William G. Niederland, "An Interpretation of the Psychological Stresses and Defenses in Concentration-Camp Life and the Late Aftereffects," in *Massive Psychic Trauma,* ed. Henry Krystal (New York: International Universities Press, 1968), p. 62.

8/
Anger and Its Manifestations

Most people think that grief is primarily sorrow. It comes as a surprise to many, therefore, to find that anger is a prominent aspect of grief.

Theoretical Considerations

There is controversy in the literature over the place of anger in healthy and pathological grief. The controversy goes back to Freud and his followers, who believe that ambivalence—love and hate—is absent in normal mourning and that its presence denotes pathological mourning.[1]

John Bowlby, who has done extensive research on loss, disagrees. He considers anger an integral part of all grief in both children and adults. It occurs regardless of whether the loss is temporary or permanent, and it is found in both normal and dysfunctional grief. However, Bowlby does agree that the ratio of anger to sadness is significant—too much anger can indicate a pathological reaction.[2] In this his position is close to that of Erich Lindemann, who regards hostility as the main feature of intense grief where the previous relationship to the lost object was mainly negative.[3]

According to Bowlby's attachment theory, mentioned in chapter six, anger at the object that is lost can be considered a biological response in man with roots deeply set in prehuman group life:

> This requires that every separation, however brief, should be responded to by an immediate, automatic and strong effort both to recover the family, especially the member to whom attachment is closest, and to discourage that member from going away again. For this reason, it is suggested, the inherited determinants of behavior (often termed instinctual) have evolved in such a way that the standard responses to loss of a loved object are always urges first to recover it and then to scold it. If, however, the urges to recover and scold are automatic responses built into the organism, it follows that they will come into action in response to *any* and *every* loss and without discriminating between those that are really retrievable and those, statistically rare, that are not. It is an hypothesis of this kind, I believe, that explains why a bereaved person commonly experiences a compelling urge to recover the object even when he knows the attempt to be hopeless and to reproach it even when he knows reproach to be irrational.[4]

Bowlby supports his study of animals with data from anthropology, where there is evidence that in all societies provision is made for either the direct expression of anger following loss or for special social sanctions against its expression, indicating thereby the importance of the affect. This anger at the lost object is seen clearly in the child's protest at his mother's leaving, his demand that she return, and his scolding and reproaching of her for leaving him to try to make sure that she does not do it again. Anger can also be useful in adult relationships because the individual who protests vigorously and with rage is less likely to be abandoned than the one who submits passively to the wishes of another.

Psychoanalytic theoretician Melanie Klein takes yet another view of anger in relation to loss. She states that the mourner's anger toward the lost object is:

> Increased by the fear that by dying the loved one was seeking to inflict punishment and deprivation upon him, just as in the past he felt that his mother, whenever she was away from him and he wanted her, had died in order to inflict punishment and deprivation on him. . . . In mourning as well as in infantile development, inner security comes about not by a straightforward movement but in waves. . . . If the mourner has people whom he loves and who share his grief, and if he can accept their sympathy, the restoration of the harmony in his inner world is promoted, and his fears and distresses are more quickly reduced. . . .
>
> Feeling incapable of saving and securely reinstating their loved objects inside themselves, they [people who fail to experience mourning] must turn away from them more than hitherto and therefore they deny their

love for them. This may mean that their emotions in general become more inhibited; in other cases it is mainly feelings of love which become stifled and hatred is increased.[5]

Most of the literature on mourning comes from studies weighted toward premature and unexpected losses; the work of Lindemann and Marris are examples.[6] Death without warning, such as from a fatal heart attack or accident, may result in reactions of diffuse anger which may be absent or mild where the death is expected.[7]

The fact that the lost object does not return despite the mourner's angry protest is the reality testing needed for the eventual relinquishment of the object. This happens because, with repeated disappointments and frustrated attempts at getting it back, the urge is gradually extinguished. Only then can the person accept the fact that the loss is irretrievable and eventually move on to face a life without the object lost to him.

Anger Directed Outward

Anger basically has two directions—outward or inward. Turned outward in healthy grief it is universally and inevitably directed against the lost object itself, even when the object is lost through death. Anger toward the lost object stems from two sources: previous hostility present in the relationship, and hostility at the object for dying or going away and leaving the bereaved person helpless and deprived. For example, one widow remarked, "Oh, he was the smart one. Never admitted how much he smoked. Just a half a pack or so a day, he'd say, but it was more like three packs. He always checked out his doctors to see if they smoked because then they would never tell him not to. 'I'm not interested in statistics,' he'd say. 'I'm only one person, not a statistic.' So now he's gone, and he is a statistic, and I'm left by myself. That's how smart he was."

Anger can also be directed against those believed responsible for the loss or those who seem to be preventing reunion with the lost object. This can take the form of blame of doctors, medical personnel, relatives, the other man or woman, the suspected rapist, burglar, arsonist, and so on. Fire and flood victims berate the police and fire departments for failure to save their homes. Such anger is the basis for the vendetta or other acts of revenge. Child placement workers are often the targets of anger from the mother of a child being removed from a home she feels has been adequate but which society has decreed is not so.

Anger toward the physician who last attended the deceased is not uncommon. "You might have done something more" is a typical accusation. Kidney donors often express anger toward the medical staff who encouraged their sacrifice. The prospective kidney donor is told that his decision is entirely voluntary, but feels he has no real choice. How can anyone refuse to be a donor for a loved one? The donor is thus put in an impossible bind—to refuse possible life to a loved one or to relinquish a part of his own healthy body in a procedure that is still experimental. Anger can be directed against anyone who is not suffering in the same way as the bereaved. A woman spoke of her envy of intact families. Tears of anger came to her eyes at the injustice she still felt at being left to raise her children alone after her husband's desertion. Anger can also be directed toward people who attempt to be comforting or to offer condolences, because to accept such comfort would be a reminder or admission of the loss and set off the pain of grief. Acute grief is a time of supersensitivity, so what might in the ordinary course of events be a normal remark is taken as a severe slight.

In addition, anger can also be directed against institutions, agencies, bureaucracies, aging, death itself, religion, and God. A Catholic woman said: "I stopped going to church when my mother died. She was such a religious woman, and so good. She never hurt anyone. If God could let her suffer so, then I don't believe in all that stuff." And a Jewish woman remarked: "I stopped keeping kosher when my mother died. What's the good of all that religion when she is gone? All the heart went out of me for ritual."

The bereaved can also feel bitter about the expense of psychotherapy: "Have you ever noticed? The ones who lose not only suffer the pain of the loss but their whole life is also changed. On top of all that they have to pay out money to therapists because of the trauma they suffered. So there they are bereft first of all and then are out money besides. And all the while others seem to coast through life without a care in the world."

Loss can bring forth still another type of anger. There are some people who handle uncomfortable feelings by denying the feeling (guilt, shame, helplessness) and lashing out in anger at any convenient scapegoat. Because these uncomfortable feelings are part of grief, one should expect some bereaved to snap at others instead of feeling sorrow or pain.

Mr. and Mrs. Zimmer, ages seventy-five and sixty, came for marital counseling because of constant quarreling. The marriage had never been good because of Mr. Zimmer's domineering attitude toward his family. The situation had deteriorated since his retirement. He was around the house all day and had neither hobbies nor interests. Over the past few years he had become increasingly forgetful and this troubled him greatly, because despite the best of medical care, it was impossible to stop the process. Mr. Zimmer took out his frustration and helplessness on his wife. He badgered her with repeated questions, forgot her response, repeated the question sometimes as often as four times in five minutes. She found some relief in volunteer work which took her out of the house a few hours a day, but the evenings and weekends were almost intolerable. She felt she wanted a divorce to escape "his suffocating me" or "I will go under." Psychiatric examination confirmed that there was, in fact, some organic base for his reactions but not enough to account fully for the behavior. It was clear this couple had to be separated, but divorce was hardly the answer at this late stage. Mr. Zimmer was finally placed in a board and care home; Mrs. Zimmer regained her emotional equilibrium and was able to continue living independently.

Research in a study of widows revealed that they felt anger toward close family members after the initial weeks of bereavement. They were angry for overprotection, for control, for lack of support, and for disappointment in expected help from relatives. Widows had most friction with their own mothers, attributed to the conflict over renewed dependency, the mother's expectation of dependency, or the renewal of old conflicts. The study also revealed that death provided an opportunity for the direct expression of antagonisms between widows and their in-laws that had been suppressed during the life of the husband. This was particularly true in the relationship of the widows with female members of the husband's family. There was anger over grievances at the time of the death, in regard to funeral details and lack of interest, at the eagerness of relatives to take over possessions of the deceased, at callousness or withdrawal. As the first year of bereavement progressed, the anger of the widows toward family members and in-laws increased, although that toward friends remained more constant.[8]

Anger Directed Inward

If anger cannot be expressed outwardly, it must go elsewhere. Some people, in an attempt to hide their anger in acute grief, adopt a wooden kind of behavior that gives them a mask-like appearance and robot reactions suggestive of schizophrenia.

A more common way of dealing with unexpressed anger is that it is turned inward and repressed. The result can be depression, nightmares, psychosomatic and organic disorders, ruminations about the dreadful past, and even suicide. Self-torture through nightmares and pains has been considered as a defense against depression through expiation of guilt.[9] Anger repressed and turned against the self rather than being directed outward prevents the completion of the work of mourning.

Mrs. David was suffering from a prolonged grief reaction. It was two years since her divorce from her husband, but she acted as if the loss had occurred in the past few weeks. She talked obsessively about his leaving her, her empty life, her inability to resume working to support her family, and her family's disgust with her continued dependency and grief. She had always helped contribute to the family income as her husband's earnings were insufficient for their large family. Now that she needed more than ever to be the wage-earner, she could not function.

Mrs. David's anger, which rightfully belonged on the lost object, her husband, was concealed in her chronic grief reaction. This enabled her to duplicate the very behavior that she had resented in her husband—his irresponsibility. At the same time it allowed her to punish herself for this self-indulgence, to mobilize people in gratifying long unmet dependency needs, and to avoid the outward expression of anger, part of the underlying pathology predating the loss and contributing to the dysfunctional grief reaction in the first place.

Anger turned inward is common in physical losses. Surgical patients can be angry at themselves for whatever they did that may have necessitated the amputation or surgery. Victims of crime are also prone to anger turned inward. With the increase in robbery, burglary, rape, and other acts of aggression there is a growing concern about the effect of psychological damage on victims. Often the rage victims feel toward their attackers is turned inward on themselves as guilt, impotence, and shame.

Although depression is common in the early reaction in normal grief, it is also probably one of the most common dysfunctional reactions to loss. It can be masked as boredom, underachievement, insomnia, restlessness, a tendency to seek out painful experiences, as well as emotional flatness. Depression has been viewed as the most undertreated of major diseases. Recent government surveys show that, in a given year, 15 percent of adults between the ages of eighteen and seventy-four, or roughly 20 million people, are likely to suffer serious depressive symptoms.[10] Unfortunately, even when the sufferer does receive medical or psychiatric attention, the depression is not always connected with loss, a precipitating factor in all depression.

Another form that anger turned against the self can take is unconscious identification with an aggressor. In this phenomenon the victim gradually assumes the values and even the mannerisms of the captors. It was found among prisoners of war subjected to brainwashing and prisoners in concentration camps. Investigators into victimization have concluded that some unconscious identification with the aggressor is indispensable to survival in people who have been subjected to massive psychic trauma. Repressed anger was also found in the self-reproach of younger concentration camp survivors who felt compelled to repress their rage against murdered parents who failed to protect them from the persecutions they suffered in the concentration camp.[11]

Implications for Intervention

Because anger is such an important component of grief, helpers must be on the alert for it. They should validate it when it emerges spontaneously or gently try to elicit it when it does not. Often a remark such as "People normally feel angry at the person for dying but are afraid to say so because it makes no sense" can bring considerable relief to the bereaved.

The bereaved can surprise themselves with unexpected outbursts of hostility, sometimes to the point that they can even fear loss of control. For example, a young man who had lost his father said: "I walked into my aunt's house and thought I would stay for dinner, as she had invited me to. But my uncle was there, and I remembered how hurt Dad was at his coldness all the years I was growing up. When Dad was dying he suddenly got helpful, and he was very helpful to Mom around the funeral. Then he forgot all about us. He hasn't been around since, and it has been six months. I suddenly knew I would either burst out crying right there in front of everybody or tell him off, and no one would understand. So instead I said I didn't feel well and got out of there. The hypocrite!"

In such an instance the bereaved need a listener who can allow the outburst without retaliating or arguing the merits of the position taken. The bereaved may need the presence of another person before they can let go out of fear that the anger might never stop if they are by themselves. Ultimately, healthy mourning requires that anger must be expressed against the lost object to allow the tie to be broken. Anger displaced to other people such as relatives, friends, medical personnel, and so on, would be better expressed to a neutral helper if the direct attack is unjustified, exaggerated, potentially verbally or physically harmful to another, or if it could bring retaliation.

Although anger needs to be expressed, there are a number of factors that operate to inhibit the expression of anger. These include cultural, social, family, and personal attitudes in regard to the expression of aggression. Many families teach children that it is not acceptable to express anger. When confronted by loss, these people are likely to have difficulty working through their grief because it requires the ability to express a feeling they have been taught should be hidden. The bereaved need to be reeducated and helped to free the anger into verbal expression or constructive activities.

Mrs. Mann was emotionally frozen when she first came for therapy four years after her husband left her. She had also had subsequent losses, including the loss of her job. She had had supportive friends during these crises but had not been able to mourn, nor had it occurred to her friends or relatives that mourning was indicated. At the outset of therapy she was in a state of acute anxiety, unable to cry or to express any other feeling than panic. Her greatest need was to be understood by the therapist, even when some of her thoughts and feelings even to herself sounded "weird, as if I am out of my head." Being understood meant being in contact with another, her assurance that she was not "crazy." With acceptance, assurance that the therapist believed her, and validation that what she had experienced was real to her, she gradually began to be able to admit, with no pressure from the therapist, that in her panic she may have misinterpreted or exaggerated the meaning of experiences she was describing.

Because of her great anxiety and inability to function, Mrs. Mann was seen three times a week. She was told that her anxiety might be relieved if she could express some anger. With encouragement she started to whisper that she was angry, but there was no show of anger. When told she was talking about feelings, not feeling them, she uttered a low moan which was more like the sound of an animal in pain than a human sound. She kept repeating in a whisper "I am so angry and so sad." Slowly she started to pound her clenched fist on the arm of the chair in which she sat. She complained of pains in her neck and arm and was told the pain might be relieved if she could unclench her fist and let the anger flow out freely. Several times the therapist reached out and opened the fingers of her hand to show her how to unclench her fist.

Mrs. Mann spoke repeatedly of her distress at being unable to work at her profession of art teacher. She feared a psychotic break. She was unable to touch her paint brushes or clay. It was suggested she try pounding clay at home as an expression of anger, but under no condition to attempt to do anything creative with it. Creative work belonged to a later period; now was the time for anger and verbal destructiveness in a safe setting. She continued on a level of anxiety and whispered anger.

One day Mrs. Mann appeared for her interview carrying a huge mound of clay. She said she had been unable to touch it at home and brought it to the therapist. She was encouraged to pound the clay and to tell her husband how angry she was at him for leaving her. She began with light glancing blows to the clay, whispering "I am so angry at you." With prompting her blows began to increase in power. There finally was a small indentation in the clay.

Recognizing Mrs. Mann's inability to let go without external support stronger than words, the therapist reached over and held her by the shoulders, much as one would hold a child struggling to vomit. The tears started to flow, but it was not anger that came out; it was deep sorrow and helpless sobbing. As she straightened herself up, Mrs. Mann said, "I had a knot in my stomach and now it is in my throat." "Let's see if we can get rid of it," replied the therapist. This time she turned the woman around and enveloped her in her arms, so that she could cry on the therapist's shoulder. The floodgates finally opened, and she sobbed for some minutes with no word from the therapist. As the tears slowed, she whispered "Thank you" and she was released. Sadly she said, "No one ever holds me like that, for comfort." She spent the rest of the hour in a conventional therapeutic session. She asked whether this now meant that her grief was over and was told no, it was but the beginning of her release of emotions. "When will it end?" she wanted to know. She was told it needs to drain off by itself; no one can tell how long it will take or when new grief can be set off by some reminder, but at least now she had some knowledge of the process.

It should be noted here that what started as anger quickly turned to sorrow. Thus do emotions flow in grief with no predictability as to which emotion will be uppermost. In Mrs. Mann's case she was not ready yet to express anger fully. For too many years she had been taught to repress anger and much more work would be necessary before she could feel comfortable about being angry. The ability to express anger implies a sense of self sufficiently aroused to protest against injustice together with some assurance against the power of one's unconscious destructiveness. In the case described, autonomy had never been fully established, a problem that will need to be resolved before grief work is completed. First there was a need to connect to another in safety, to feel helpless without feeling abandoned. Anger that leads to separation comes later in the psychic process. Only in the safety of a secure relationship can one afford to let go of ties to old attachments. It should be cautioned that the encouragement of such catharsis of anger is not indicated in every situation. In this instance, the ex-husband was well and happy. Were he deceased or in any way damaged, such catharsis could play into fears of one's destructive powers.

Anger does not always get expressed as blatant, loud, or overt hostility. Sometimes it takes the form of irritability, complaints—a combination of anger and helplessness—and even annoyance. Hospital personnel need to understand such behavior in the chronically ill; it is their reaction to the losses sustained by their illness.

Anger in grief may sound quite irrational. Friends, relatives, and professionals who fail to understand this irrational aspect of anger can leave the bereaved feeling confused and guilty over anger, and they may even begin to doubt their own mental health.

Anger with the bereaved may also extend toward the helper as a reminder of the loss and pain. Some people want to withdraw from others when in pain, much as a wounded animal goes off into the woods to recover or die. Helpers should adopt an attitude of compassion and firm insistence in response to this attempt to push them away. This is not the time for self-determination. It is a time when the bereaved remain most in need of sustaining relationships.

Bill Johnson telephoned a therapist friend saying he had a strange request to make. Would she be able to check on the credentials of his therapist to see if he were ethical and competent? Bill had been in treatment for about three years. When asked why he had doubts about his therapist at this late date, Bill could not answer. When asked how he would feel if the therapist was found to be incompetent, Bill said he would be devastated. He wanted to believe he was good. Further inquiry revealed that Bill had always cut off relationships instead of ending them mutually. He was at the point in therapy of attempting to deal with his separations in a healthier manner, spurred on by the interpretations of the therapist. To avoid the pain of loss and grief Bill was trying to find a way to cut off the therapist himself. He was urged to return to the therapist and share with him his doubts and the fact of the telephone call. He did so and later reported that he had "the best therapy session ever" as the result of his dealing openly with his feelings. It should be noted, however, that he obviously had a therapist who was secure enough to deal with his own negative feelings without retaliation.

There is no relationship that is all love. All relationships are ambivalent, depending on the amount of real or fantasied pleasure or pain they bring us. The bereaved must be helped to accept their negative feelings and to forgive themselves for negative feelings held toward the love object during their lives together, as well as for the anger they feel at the pain of being bereft.

Where the rage the bereaved feels toward others he holds responsible for his pain is turned toward the self as guilt, self-castigation, shame, depression, and so on, the helper needs to work toward enabling the externalization of the anger. One clue regarding what the bereaved feels toward others can be found in the names he calls himself. "I'm no good. I'm dumb! I'm hostile! That is why students are dropping out of my class," wailed one young teacher. The decline in student population was due in reality to changing student enrollment, and a nationwide drop in the student population at this level of teaching. This young man had a traumatic history of previous losses. Thus, where other teachers might take the drop in enrollment with equanimity, for him the same loss, reactivating old scars, represented a severe blow to self-esteem. The names he called himself were, in fact, those he would have liked to call his students who chose courses from teachers having a reputation of being easy and nondemanding. The help this young teacher needed was to be shown that his self-denigration was really furious anger at the "dumb" (unambitious) students for leaving his classes.

On the other hand, when people rapidly resort to anger where the underlying emotion is more likely to be anxiety, shame, or yearning, the release of anger alone is not sufficient. What is needed here is a painstaking reconstruction of personality to enable the person to experience a range of feelings previously hidden under angry outbursts. In other words, helpers must be astute at diagnosing the personality and customary defenses of the bereaved and where these are dysfunctional for the bereaved, as in immature explosive personalities, or dangerous to others, as in the case of the paranoid or psychopathic personality, expression of anger needs to be channeled into nondestructive outlets.

"You make this work sound so delicate," remarked one man in an audience where a therapist was speaking on grief work. He went on: "I have been a minister for forty years and have counseled many bereaved people during those years. I never before realized how dangerous working with the bereaved can be. Now I am almost afraid to do damage."

"Your fear is a sign of wisdom," was the therapist's reply.

Notes

1. See Sigmund Freud, "Mourning and Melancholia," in *The Complete Psychological Works of Sigmund Freud, Standard Edition,* ed. James Strachey (New York: Macmillan Co., 1964); and John Bowlby, "Processes of Mourning," in *Grief: Selected Readings,* ed. Arthur C. Carr, et al. (New York: Health Sciences Publishing, 1975), p. 13.

2. Ibid.

3. Erich Lindemann, "The Symptomatology and Management of Acute Grief," *American Journal of Psychiatry* 101 (1944): 141–48.

4. John Bowlby, "Childhood Mourning and Its Implications for Psychiatry: The Adolf Meyer Lecture," *American Journal of Psychiatry* 118 (1961): 485.

5. Melanie Klein quoted in Geoffrey Gorer, *Death, Grief, and Mourning: A Study of Contemporary Society* (Garden City, N.Y.: Doubleday and Co., Anchor Books, 1972), pp. 140–41.

6. Erich Lindemann, "The Symptomatology and Management of Acute Grief"; and Peter Marris, *Widows and Their Families* (London: Routledge and Kegan Paul, 1958).

7. Gorer, *Death, Grief, and Mourning*, p. 149.

8. Ira O. Glick, Robert, S. Weiss, and C. Murray Parkes, *The First Year of Bereavement* (New York: John Wiley and Sons, 1974), p. 194.

9. Emanuel Tanay, "Initiation of Psychotherapy with Survivors of Nazi Persecution," in *Massive Psychic Trauma,* ed. Henry Krystal (New York: International Universities Press, 1968), p. 230.

10. Nathan S. Kline, "Anti-Depressant Medications: A More Effective Use by General Practitioners, Family Physicians, Internists and Others, *Journal of the American Medical Association* 227 (1974): 1158–160.

11. Henry Krystal and William G. Niederland, "Clinical Observations on the Survivor Syndrome," in *Massive Psychic Trauma,* ed. Krystal (New York: International Universities Press, 1968), p. 343.

9/
Guilt and
Shame

Theoretical Considerations of Guilt

It is generally held that guilt, self-reproach, and even fleeting suicidal thoughts can be normal following a major loss, provided they do not continue too long and that the suicidal thoughts do not take on structure and planning. These suicidal thoughts are probably more an expression of the wish to find relief from the pain of grief than a wish for self-destruction.) Freud originally saw guilt as important in melancholia (depression) but not in normal grief; others now disagree. Melanie Klein believes that guilt can account for much of the pain of mourning.[1] However, guilt can be an important element in pathological grief, particularly depression, and should not be ignored. Depressive guilt is dangerous because it can lead to suicide. Competent and early intervention is, therefore, imperative.

Studies of widowhood reveal that marked guilt in regard to loss could be associated with a pathological outcome to the grief process.[2] Guilt can lead to feelings of unworthiness, a desire to atone, self-punishment, and rejection of help from others. Guilt and anger can combine to cause a spiral of increasing isolation.

Ira Glick and his coresearchers found guilt and anger often but not always associated with grief. They concluded that where these feelings were present in early grief reactions, one was likely to find problems of recovery later. These problems included chronic grief, disorganization of life, and general emotional instability. They warned that marked guilt and anger in early bereavement should be seen as a danger signal of abnormal grief reactions.[3]

Guilt can be one of the greatest obstacles to overcoming grief. It can arise from a number of sources and can be conscious or unconscious, recognized or well defended against.

Guilt Associated with the Loss Itself

The crisis of death, divorce, the need to place a family member out of the home, surgery, a geographical move, or other life events causing upheaval and loss in the lives of people can trigger guilt in those responsible for making decisions in these situations.

Guilt following a death can be focused on any part of the terminal process leading to the ultimate loss. Some of the talking and ruminating described earlier may be an attempt to go over this period in one's mind to assure oneself that everything possible was done for the deceased.

The self-reproach need not be logical or realistic. For example, guilt can be focused on questioning the choice of physician or hospital, on neglect or acquiescence to medical treatment, on irritation with or failure to attend to the deceased during the final illness, on being absent at the moment of death or relief that one was absent and the ordeal over, and on one's inability to gratify unreasonable demands of the dying patient. Where guilt stems from the sorrow of being unable to keep a loved one from pain or dying, avoiding discussion of the topic is one way to avoid possible reproach from the dying person.

Guilt is an expected aspect in grief of those bereaved through suicide, for suicide is an aggressive and hostile act toward those left behind, often culminating an earlier stormy relationship. Guilt is increased following a suicide if the body is at first unidentified and lies in the morgue as a John or Jane Doe. That one should die and not even be identified as belonging to anyone represents unconsciously the ultimate in abandonment.

The mother of an adult who had committed suicide kept repeating "If only our last words had not been so angry." Gently, as she was helped to reconstruct the final scene, she came to realize that she had not been the angry one; it was her son who had flounced off in anger, leaving everyone helpless to offer him comfort in his distress. As the mother talked, she realized further that all attempts to help the son over the past few years had been in vain. His self-destructive act was not one of the moment. Still later the mother could take comfort that even the suicide note was an affirmation of her mothering. "Take care of my cat," her son had written. The mother's gratitude was profound as she began to see that she had done all she could, but that some tragedies are outside our power to prevent, even though we may be loving parents. "As sad as I feel," she said, "at least I don't have to carry that burden of guilt."

Parents feel reproach from dying children who beg to be held, to make the hurting stop, when to hold them might interfere with medical procedures. Either way the parent is beset with guilt.

Guilt pervades the lives of almost all people whose loss is brought about by divorce. The divorced person is still labeled by some as being irresponsible, a home-destroyer, or a deserter. The knowledge that one has probably caused unhappiness to children, as well as the oft-repeated message that delinquents and disturbed children come from broken homes, adds to feelings of guilt. The pleas of children for an intact family, for the father's (or sometimes the mother's) continued presence, pleas that must be resisted, stir up pain at the loss and guilt as well.

Parents who are pressured to relinquish their child for adoption without being allowed to work through their ambivalence at the time of adoption are left with unresolved ambivalence and guilt, which is added to the grief and pain of not knowing what has happened to their child.[4] Parents who give birth to a defective child feel guilt over their genes. Parents of a retarded child must deal with feelings of guilt, ambivalence, anger, shame, and sorrow. They tend to blame themselves, each other, and, finally, the child.[5]

In any kind of placement—of children, the mentally ill, or aged relatives—there can be guilt for being unable or unwilling to care for the person at home. Adult children seeking community facilities for sick and ailing elderly parents are often appalled and guilty over the choices open to them. Care in many institutions is notoriously inadequate, facilities are rundown, odors are repugnant, and the children feel they are consigning their parents to a wait for death.

A severe and persevering guilt complex with far-reaching pathological significance is one of the more common psychiatric conditions found in the survivors of persecution experiences and natural disasters.[6]

Guilt stemming from the past relationship to the lost object is quite common:

All the petty irritations, harboured grievances, moods of rejection and disillusion that may have marred their relationship with the dead, present themselves as hostile witnesses to torment the bereaved. Nothing imperfect in the relationship can now be changed or forgiven, and no lingering resentment can be expressed without disloyalty. Hence the bereaved sometimes cling obstinately to their grief and idealise the dead, in expiation of a latent sense of guilt.[7]

There is no relationship that is pure love, and, therefore, no relationship that, when ended, does not leave guilt in its wake. The depth of the negative feelings will be associated with the degree of guilt.

Guilt can also result from a feeling that one should be omnipotent and thus able to have prevented the loss. The feeling of omnipotence finds expression in a variety of ways. "I never should have left the hospital," said one widow. "There we were, having a chat after his dinner. Had I remained he would have kept on talking to me. But I left and he dozed off and he died in his sleep. Had I stayed I might have kept him talking and awake and he wouldn't have died."

Guilt Induced by Lack of Knowledge

Guilt in the bereaved can be induced by others consciously or unconsciously out of an attempt to be supportive or malicious, or through ignorance. Physicians can also induce guilt in family members unwittingly. For example, the rash of articles a few years ago on the theme of "how to keep your husband alive" by avoiding a high-fat diet and by not making demands on him placed the burden of responsibility on the wife rather than on the husband himself. When heart attack or death did come, the result for the woman was more than normal guilt.

Guilt can be induced by others out of a need to defend against their own painful feelings following a loss. Some people handle uncomfortable feelings by repression, denial, and projecting their discomfort on a scapegoat. It is not unheard of that family members blame each other for the death of a loved one in the midst of the pain of early bereavement.

The issues in regard to decision making provide fertile ground for such projections. A woman, still in shock following the death of her husband, became the brunt of her mother-in-law's attacks. "You killed him," she was told, because she had chosen to remain with the original physician rather than to change doctors as her mother-in-law had wanted.

Guilt can be felt in regard to all the aspects of normal grief and those that are particularly foreign to most people—the preoccupation with the loss, repetitive talking, disorganization, a lack of initiative, the expression of negative feelings about the lost object, searching, and so on. Some people have trouble admitting angry feelings toward others who have been good to them. Often the bereaved are reinforced in this behavior by well-meaning relatives and friends with the same conflict. Added to this is the admonition that it is wrong to speak ill of the dead. All this can lead to guilt.

Guilt can also be felt when, for a minute, the bereaved can forget their loss, involve themselves in a moment of pleasure. They then begin to wonder if they have betrayed their loved one by the moment of forgetting, by anticipating new pleasures, new experiences, new relationships.

There may also be guilt over feelings of relief associated with a loss. This can be seen in the death of someone ill for a long time or where the relationship was unpleasant or burdensome. If the death is viewed as a wish-fulfillment, there will be guilt as if the wish caused the event.

Guilt Derived from Personality Factors and from Childhood

Compulsive people suffer from excessive guilt feelings, part of their very neurosis. When faced with loss, they will tend to be particularly hard on themselves. For example, Amy, a sixteen-year-old girl, was shocked to learn that a casual schoolmate, Ida, had suffered a nervous breakdown. Amy had once been invited to Ida's birthday party through a mutual friend. Amy had never invited Ida, and now Amy was overcome by remorse. What could have set off Ida's breakdown? Could Ida have felt rejected that Amy had never extended friendship to her? Without even knowing Ida sufficiently well to be aware of any of the stresses in her life, Amy reproached herself for Ida's misfortune as if she had directly contributed to her loss.

Unresolved guilt feelings stemming from childhood may be set off by a later loss. Mrs. Ashmore could speak of her deceased mother only in the most glowing terms. It was not simply a matter of idealizing the deceased. Mrs. Ashmore had never been able to achieve a sense of autonomy because of the guilt feelings set off by attempts at separating herself from a mother proclaimed by herself and others as being perfect. All her life, whenever Mrs. Ashmore said anything critical about her mother, she was stopped by comments such as "How can you make an issue of such a little thing when your mother is such a wonderful person? Look at the name she has in the community for all the charitable work she does. She is a perfect mother. You ought to be grateful to have a mother like her." Not until her emotional problems flared up in her fifties following the mother's death did she begin to work through a sense of autonomy and the guilt of a lifetime.

Survivor Guilt

Survivor guilt is a term which became part of the psychiatric vocabulary around World War II. It is believed to be based on guilt feelings over being a sole, or nearly sole, survivor of a disaster in which others perished, particularly close ones.

Survivor guilt needs to be seen as part of a total picture known as survivor syndrome, one of the more serious forms of reaction to loss. It is found in almost all survivors of natural disasters, such as floods and earthquakes, and in man-made catastrophes, such as war, the atomic bombings in Japan, and the Holocaust, and is now being recognized in air crashes and hijackings. It is found when people die through violence or in ways not in accord with the ideas of how death should take place in a particular culture. Most of the research comes from studies and clinical work with survivors of concentration camps and atomic bombs.

After an extensive review of the literature on survivors, Klaus D. Hoppe concluded that our traditional psychiatric diagnostic thinking is inadequate to understand the plight and suffering of these people.[8] The subject is one that is highly charged emotionally and by no means understood fully even by the experts. At the same time, the need to deal with the problem increases daily as World War II persecution survivors move into the middle and later years of life, as their children reach maturity and show problems related to their parents' wartime traumas, and as instances of violence increase in society generally. The goal here is to explore some of the issues surrounding survivor guilt; no attempt has been made to reconcile differing points of view.

The possible symptoms found in survivor syndrome are extensive and include all of those found in both normal and pathological grief outlined earlier. In addition, one may often find emotional inability to feel either happy or sad, disruption in development of adolescent victims, permanent damage to healthy narcissism and shame, extensive psychosomatic complaints, physical illnesses related to malnutrition, and "a living-corpse" appearance.[9]

The conditions of suffering are so varied that one needs to be aware of differences as well as commonalities among survivors. For example, the literature distinguishes between a neurosis of the outlawed, with the syndrome of ostracism, and a neurosis of extermination, with syndromes in children of primitive, animal-like motor reactions, in adolescents of autonomous hormonal disorders, in young adults of chronic anxiety, depression, and personality changes, and in chronic depressives of paranoid features.[10]

Other symptoms among concentration camp survivors are day and night anxiety with nightmares about persecution, chronic mourning over murdered family members, and dreams of reviving murdered family members.

One year in a concentration camp has been equated to four years of normal aging, accounting for a general rapid fatigue as a persistent symptom among survivors. Other manifestations of premature aging are irritability, memory disturbances, shortened attention span, and emotional instability.[11]

Children subjected to persecution later showed antisocial behavior. Those forced to hide from persecution displayed symptoms of motoric, play, and movement inhibition and a compulsion to be quiet, combined with a fear of outside noises. There was also a failure to develop proper adult images because adults were as victimized as the children themselves. Other problems were attributed to malnutrition and hunger and separation from the mother, and exposure to an unfriendly environment.[12] Children raised in concentration camps without adults showed a pattern of object relations based on peers rather than authority figures, as well as a propensity for stealing, depression, and withdrawal during puberty.[13] People who were adolescents during the period of persecution show a fixation of identity diffusion, that is, an inability to achieve an integrated sense of identity.

Among victims of enforced labor, a work-torture complex is described, consisting of an ambivalent attitude toward work, a projection onto any authority of the image of the slave driver, and an inability to find meaning in life.[14]

Not all symptoms found in concentration camp survivors are as a result of their experiences in the camps. Some are a result of uprooting, immigration, and other further stresses added to the earlier traumas. For example, many of the emotional dynamics of survivors are expressed in extensive somatic complaints. Hoppe postulates that people "whose survival depended for years on the appearance and functioning of their bodies" suffered a change in total body image cathexis as a result of their experiences. In cases where these complaints are dismissed as hypochondriacal by compensation courts, the humiliations and traumas of the original years of brutalization are further compounded.[15]

Returning now to the guilt aspect of the survivor syndrome, the primary source of survivor guilt has been attributed to the guilt at being alive. Whereas the dying patient asks "Why me?"—"Why have I been chosen for death when everyone else around me continues to live?" these survivors ask "Why me?" in an effort to understand why they were spared death when so many others perished.

Another source of survivor guilt is the feeling of responsibility for the death of others, particularly loved ones. There were many instances when survivors were assured protection of their loved ones if they submitted to certain unacceptable acts. When they refused and later learned of the death of the loved one, depression set in with delusions of having contributed to the death of the other. Even without such a direct connection, there was the feeling that one survived at the expense of another, a feeling enhanced by the selection methods used in concentration camps.

Still another source of survivor guilt in the camps stemmed from the realization that one had committed morally unacceptable acts such as prostitution, informing on others, stealing, and so on, all in the interests of survival. Guilt has also been attributed to the survivor's passivity in submitting to his tormentors, even though active opposition would have been tantamount to suicide.

Severe survivor guilt has further been attributed to unconscious infantile guilt surrounding death wishes toward family members that could not remain repressed because reality intervened and these people were indeed annihilated.

Guilt resulted also from the rejection of the dead, which found expression in the haste with which survivors wanted the dead buried and out of sight. The universal fear of the dead is expressed in our fear of ghosts and spirits who might come back to harm us, the attempt to keep them safely underground by tombstones, and other customs and rituals surrounding burial and remembrance of the dead.

Hiroshima bombing survivors experienced guilt regarding their inability to carry out the last wishes of the dying, particularly the request for a sip of water. Not only were the survivors busy saving themselves, water was withheld because of a rumor that it might be contaminated. In Japanese tradition there is the belief that water can restore life. Thus, in either case the survivors were guilty, whether they gave or withheld water.[16] Guilt was also communally reinforced, in concentric circles moving out from the center of the blast. Each group felt guilty toward those who had been closer to the center.[17]

Another source of guilt in Japan was the result of rumors that swept the city soon after the bomb fell. One rumor was that everyone who had been in Hiroshima at the time of the blast would be dead within three years. Another was that no vegetation would ever grow in Hiroshima again. Still another was that the area would be uninhabitable for seventy or seventy-five years. This fear of epidemic and all-enveloping contamination was unconsciously felt to have a supernatural source, perhaps as a curse or punishment for some form of group wrongdoing that offended the forces that control life and death.[18]

Survivor guilt is not confined to catastrophic world events; it is merely magnified there. It can be found in survivors of accidents where others have been killed, in old people who live on beyond their wishes while watching younger loved ones die, and in parents whose children die. Writer John Gunther describes the pain and agony of parents struggling to prevent the impending death of their son. The mother describes her feelings as follows:

> I think every parent must have a sense of failure, even of sin, merely in remaining alive after the death of a child. One feels that it is not right to live when one's child has died, that one should somehow have found the way to give one's life to save his life. Failing there, one's failures during his too brief life seem all the harder to bear and forgive.[19]

With increasing developments in medical technology, where the power of life and death is no longer left to nature but is placed within the decision-making or technical skill of people, we need to be on the alert for new forms of survivor guilt. These can be found in abortion, in medical heroics, in "pulling the plug," in having family members sign for medical procedures from which the patient does not recover. Stephen M. Sonnenberg has observed that those people who do develop such guilt may be guilt-prone individuals whose lost love objects had served as the recipients of their guilt expiation during their lifetime. In other words, these deceased had been the subject of unconscious aggressive fantasies or wishes. Following their death, when the real event coincided with the aggressive fantasies, guilt surfaced.[20]

Because this subject is so highly charged emotionally, we might well ask how dare we compare the death of a single individual with the catastrophic deaths of the concentration camps or the atomic bombings? It is almost sacrilegious to the survivors of such losses to so devalue the magnitude of their suffering.

Although the literature consistently refers to survivor guilt, another view of the problem has been presented that does make a distinction between victims of persecution and those bereft by ordinary losses. Itamar Yahalom, a psychoanalyst, postulates from his work with survivors that there are two separate dynamics which have been combined in the term survivor guilt. One is guilt as described above; the other is the inability to comprehend the fact of being alive after one has reconciled oneself to being dead. This can occur following repeated threats of death as in the camps, or after a single atomic explosion with its continuing onslaught of deaths during the years that followed. This problem has nothing to do with comparison with others; that is, why should I live when others die? The guilt stems not so much from what one did to stay alive as from the search to answer the question, why did I survive? The real problem is the acceptance of the state of deadness, and the discrepancy between this resignation to death and the reality of being alive.[21] Or, it can be seen in terms of detachment. Just as the wives of some prisoners of war had detached themselves from their husbands during their absence and were unable to reattach when the men returned home, here there is detachment from life with an inability to reattach when death does not occur.

Support for this point of view comes from a recent study of survivors of air crashes and hijackings, in which it was found that some uninjured passengers make no attempt to save themselves after a plane crash because of their feeling of loss of control over the situation and their lack of hope of survival.[22]

Post-traumatic behavior patterns among survivors

People attempt to cope with the aftereffects of traumatization in a wide variety of ways, of which only a few examples will be given here to indicate the complexity of the problem. For instance, following natural disasters such as plagues, earthquakes, fires, and so on, survivors have expiated their guilt through acts of appeasement of God, for example, by erecting churches.[23]

One pattern found among survivors who relocated to a new country after the Holocaust was for people to remarry quickly, reestablish new families as soon as possible, and energetically throw themselves into financial pursuits. Various explanations have been given for this pattern. One is that immediate replacement of loved ones gave an illusion of restitution for the massive losses suffered, providing a way to avoid the reality of the loss and the pain associated with it. Remarriage also relieved loneliness and social isolation, and took care of sexual needs. Economic pursuit provided a channel for aggression, a defense against depression, social alienation, anxiety, and hostility.

The opposite behavior, namely, the inability to remarry or have children or enjoy any aspect of the new life available, was also found in some survivors. Some writers explain this inability to pick up life again as being a result of survivor guilt; the continued suffering served their need to avoid forgiving their persecutors, to remember the dead, and to remind the world of the years of persecution.

In this same vein, Hiroshima survivors who were themselves wounded by the atomic blast showed a pattern of what has been called the "walking dead." This behavior is explained as feelings of guilt being set off by anything that suggests self-assertion, vitality, or even life itself. The guilt cannot find relief through expiation because the pervasive sense of evil has been internalized.[24] The same behavior can also be explained as the inability to partake of life because of detachment from it and the reconciliation to death.

Some of the deep feelings of Holocaust survivors were expressed in their reaction to monetary compensation from the German government. Some survivors were unable to accept this money, equating it with being paid in money for human lives or other irreplaceable losses. Others, by contrast, wanted the money as a sign of recognition of the wrongs that had been done to them, as a token of justice. Among adolescent concentration camp survivors, survivor guilt took the form of indiscriminate aggression against foster parents as an expression of their resisting unfaithfulness to their own dead parents.[25]

Concentration camp survivors tended to do better in Israel than in the United States because aggression could be turned against an external enemy and the persecution of the Holocaust could be seen as an historical necessity culminating in the rebirth of Israel. Also, the survivor group was so numerous there that feelings of exclusion, isolation, and estrangement were minimized.[26]

Damage to children of survivors

It has by now become clear that not only survivors but their children as well carry the scars of their traumatic experiences. Guilt is an important dynamic in these children, aroused when they feel an aggressiveness toward their parents they fear to express. It is as if they wonder how they can attack someone who has already suffered so much. Concentration camp survivor parents also have trouble setting limits for children, partly out of depressive self-preoccupation, and also because of confusion of limit-setting with aggression toward children as a result of what they witnessed in the camps. Survivors' children also carry guilt in regard to normal separation experiences. Survivors tend to be overprotective parents, fearing impending danger to loved ones from outside. Thus, they feel safest when children are physically close. The depressed survivor as a parent was emotionally unavailable to the child out of depression, and also gave the child the image of a weak, frightened, and emotionally dead parent.

Parents varied in how they dealt with wartime traumas. Some felt driven to talk to their children of the "war," which is how they referred to the Holocaust experience, and children in turn experienced guilt over their own good fortune as compared to that of their parents. Other parents maintained a conspiracy of silence about the Holocaust, the atomic bombings in Japan, even about the Japanese relocation experience in the United States. Children grew up without knowledge of their own past, with a break in the continuity of their own roots. Children intuitively know not to break the parental taboo of silence.

In Japan, leukemia claimed thousands of lives among those exposed to the bomb. A reaction to these deaths has been a condition referred to as "Hiroshima A-bomb neurosis," whereby the people affected become weak, hypochondriacal, and obsessed with every physical sign in themselves or their children.[27] There is fear and guilt regarding possible damage to future generations through genetic defects. Despite surface adjustment through marriage and parenthood, there is a lingering fear of death. Children internalize such fears about their own survival.

Differentiating between Shame and Guilt

Another emotion set off by loss is shame. Shame is defined as a painful feeling of having done something wrong, improper, or silly: a loss of reputation, disgrace, dishonor. It is synonymous with humiliation and mortification, the opposite of self-esteem.

To arrive at a more complete understanding of the full emotional content of grief, it is necessary to differentiate between shame and guilt, two concepts often used interchangeably in American society. Helen Merrell Lynd explored this distinction in her exhaustive study of shame as it relates to the search for identity. According to her, Freud postulated that self-reproach (guilt) could become shame if another person heard about the transgression. Thus, guilt might be seen as based on an internalization of parental values, while shame is based on disapproval coming from the outside.[28]

It would follow, then, that shame is developmentally an earlier emotion than guilt, inasmuch as internalization takes place only after repeated external feedback. Franz Alexander connected guilt with a feeling of wrongdoing and shame with a feeling of inferiority.[29] This formulation ties guilt to the conscience and shame to the ego ideal, two aspects of the superego.

The physical manifestation of shame is blushing, an involuntary reaction consistent with the surprise element in shame, another distinction from guilt. Shame alienates and sets one apart, in contrast to guilt, which connects the guilty to another, even if only through punishment. The postulation that shame sets off an unconscious fear of abandonment whereas guilt arouses a threat of mutilation would thus seem well founded.[30]

The bereaved often speak of feeling isolated, cut off, unneeded, lonely. The problem of loneliness, alienation, fear of separation and abandonment is a major theme of modern society and has been dealt with by Freud, Marx, Fromm, Durkheim, Sullivan, and others. The search for ways to escape loneliness pervades modern literature. It also accounts for a proliferation of groups, fads in psychological movements, and the search for quick panaceas.

When the complaint of loneliness is probed one discovers there is often a deeper dread—that without the physical proximity to another, some people begin to question the reality of their own existence. Unconsciously, this fear has dynamic validity. The infant, after all, is dependent on the nurturance of another for survival; alone he would perish. When we are threatened, our basic core—the infantile, vulnerable self—is exposed. A major loss can set off such a threat. The best guarantee against a feeling of isolation and abandonment is a healthy sense of self-esteem and autonomy.

The seeds of later self-esteem are sown in the early months of life through the quality and vicissitudes of the mother-child interaction. The nature of this dyad determines the quality of the child's growing sense of self, his capacity to delay, his sense of basic trust in himself, his mother, future objects, and the world about him. Failure at the early stage of establishing a sense of trust carries the seeds for later distrust, low self-esteem, and feelings of inferiority. Because of this early association between nurturance in infancy and the feeling of goodness about the self, any significant loss throughout life has the potential for setting off feelings of abandonment and low self-esteem.[31]

Shame, or low self-esteem, makes one feel completely exposed, looked at, and sets off the wish to hide, to avoid being seen. Societies use shame or guilt or both in socializing children. "Shame on you! You wet your pants!" is one example of the use of shame as an educational tool. Although guilt appears to be a personal matter, one can feel shame for the shortcomings and failures of others, particularly parents, children, or other close loved ones.

Guilt and shame have another distinction. Guilt can be nullified by acts of confession, atonement, punishment, expiation, or repentance. Shame, on the other hand, cannot be undone. It involves the entire self; it is not a separate act. Once the self is exposed, how can it then be unexposed? Shame is not so much a matter of wrongdoing, as is guilt, but rather a failure to live up to one's self-expectations or ego-ideal. Thus, shame can be expected to occur any time we suffer a loss involving failure.

Failure is sometimes clearly apparent in terms of the socially accepted norms of a society. A student's failure to pass from one grade to another is one example. But shame regarding failure can also be a highly subjective matter not apparent to an observer because it stems from the individual's self-expectations rather than external measurements of achievement.

Shame and guilt are not opposites. They may appear together in reaction to a situation, alternate with each other, reinforce each other, or appear separately.

Shame in loss and grief

Lynd lists the following characteristics central to shame:

1. The sudden exposure of unanticipated incongruity.
2. The seemingly trivial incident that arouses overwhelming and almost unbearably painful emotion.
3. The loss of trust in expectations of oneself, of other persons, or of one's society.
4. A reluctantly recognized questioning of meaning in the world.
5. The threat to the core of identity.[32]

A gift rejected by the receiver is an example of an unanticipated incongruity between the giver's expectations and the response received. The rejection of the widowed and divorced by former married friends is another example. Sudden blindness, a gradual hearing loss, an incapacitating stroke, crippling arthritis, a medical diagnosis of a fatal illness can all leave one feeling strange in a world one thought one knew.

The sudden exposure that Lynd refers to does not have to be to others to bring about shame. The exposure to the self is another important aspect of shame. Where there is in addition the element of surprise in the exposure, shame can be most painful. "Here I had always prided myself on not believing that men are attackers and predators," remarked a rape victim, "and now that part of me that had such faith, a part that I treasured, is gone." This woman had been one kind of person living in one kind of surrounding, and violently, unexpectedly, she had discovered her assumptions to be false.

Concentration camp victims reported feeling shame at their unexpected yielding to physical and mental torture, at their helplessness and defeat, and at their betrayal by their own bodies and minds. They described their moment of surrender as occurring suddenly and against their will after days of courageous opposition to their interrogators.[33]

There are cultural and individual differences as to what one may feel shame about revealing. In Western society it has traditionally been nudity; in other societies being seen while eating is considered shameful. In Western society shame persists regarding the display of certain feelings such as anger, tenderness, and helplessness. Because loss can arouse many of these forbidden feelings, shame regarding their disclosure can complicate the working through of grief.

As to why a seemingly trivial event can set off feelings of intense shame, some theorists hold that such a reaction is neurotic, or, if consistent and excessive, even indicative of psychotic tendencies. Lynd argues, however, that to consider shame over a triviality as a neurotic reaction is to miss the very essense of shame, that is, that normal, healthy people can be profoundly shaken by a seemingly insignificant occurrence.

Children can suffer acute conflicts between the desire to admire their parents and the shame they feel over the exposure of some difference or inadequacy. Poverty, foreign status, mental or emotional illness, criminality, failures, and ineptitude are some examples. And who cannot recall the shame of a clumsy error when wanting to appear chic, of a check returned marked "insufficient funds"?

Loss, which can constitute a crisis, and grief, a period of disequilibrium—both situations that leave the individual without guidelines for conduct—can allow for many errors in judgment and behavior. Because an error can in itself be experienced as a failure, and a failure can be defined as a loss, it follows that these situations are replete with opportunities for embarrassment or shame over trivial situations. In the mixing of peoples from various cultures in our present-day world are opportunities for other trivial errors to abound; the symbols of one culture can mean something entirely different in another. A burp in Western society constitutes a social error; in some countries it is a compliment to one's host.

An experience of shame is very damaging to basic trust, in the sudden exposure of the discrepancy between one's assumptions and reality. Shame can result from misplaced confidence, from the discrepancy between one's self-image and the image others have of one. It is not only the fired employee who feels shame at his failure. The employer who does the firing can feel shame in the loss of trust in his own judgment. "I lost my confidence in my ability to select appropriately when I had to let this employee go," remarked one executive.

Shame goes even beyond the self and loved ones; it may extend to an identification with people generally, society, or the world. It becomes most painful when one sees so much suffering that the meaning of life and the universe itself comes into question. For example, one of the most damaging effects of being raped as reported by victims is the loss of the sense of safety and confidence in the goodness of life. On the same note, other victimized groups suffer deep depression due to the destruction not only of their world but also of basic trust, confidence, and hope in the worth of human life.

Loss of anchorages on which one's identity is based—familiar people, body image, job and social connections—threatens the very core of the sense of identity. As we mature, we lose the belief that our parents are all-wise and all-good. As we grow older, we find often that we must in addition become the protectors of our aged parents, the very ones on whom our original trust was built. Each of these disappointments is a threat to basic identity and a challenge to flexibility in being able to retain the core of identity while at the same time changing and maturing with the thrusts of life.

Shame is also likely to result when one suffers a loss placing one in a category or group formerly looked down upon. Erving Goffman has written a classic text on the way in which each of us feels stigmatized through feeling cast out of a group we consider "normal." Any major loss has the potential for throwing us into a stigmatized group and thus suffering what Goffman has so aptly called a sense of a "spoiled identity."[34]

Shame-related losses

Although we have not yet arrived at the ability to predict behavior with accuracy, some generalities about losses that are likely to bring about shame are possible. Broadly speaking, any loss that touches on an area of narcissistic or emotional investment (and thereby vulnerability) can set off feelings of shame.

Failures provide a constant threat of shame. The greater the emotional investment in success in a particular area, the greater the likelihood of shame. Failures make us feel small in our own eyes and in the eyes of others; feeling less than another is experienced as shameful. Where emotional investment in youth and physical attractiveness is uppermost, the changes brought on by advancing years can also bring deep shame.

Suicide leaves a legacy of shame to those bereaved by the death. In orthodox Judaism the taboo on suicide is so great that a person who takes his own life has traditionally been buried in a separate part of the cemetery, as if his very physical remains might contaminate the others buried near him.

Parents of defective children experience shame at having brought an imperfect being into the world. Adoptive parents feel shame at their infertility. Parents of emotionally disturbed children feel shame that their child-rearing practices or personal emotional problems produced a disturbed child. Shame is felt in connection with physical imperfections, deformities, and certain diseases and types of surgeries. Even victims of natural disasters feel shame, as do victims of man-made catastrophes. Bright students face shame in potential school failures. Below-average students may find the entire experience of enforced school attendance an arena for shame, because they are forced to compete with peers over whom they cannot hope to win.

Despite open recognition that the work world can be exploitative with little regard for the person as such, a job failure can, nevertheless, come as a severe blow to self-esteem. Shame goes with getting a less-than-expected job rating, having a competitor get a desired promotion, and being fired or laid off. Where the major part of one's ego investment has been in the work role, compulsory retirement can evoke deep shame with the loss of major supports to self-esteem. Until the past few decades it was not uncommon for men to die during the first year after retirement. With changing attitudes toward retirement, influenced by a number of factors including modern youth's valuing people for what they are rather than for what they do, it is hoped that such tragedies of discontinuity can be avoided.

Rape is another instance where shame is predominant. The woman who is raped and murdered is a victim. Should she survive, however, she is almost certain to suffer shame as a predominant post-traumatic reaction. We all internalize the social beliefs and stereotypes of our society. A woman must, we are taught, resist sexual attack. To submit passively rather than risk arousing murderous aggression in the rapist by resistance may save her life. Once the crisis is over, however, the fear of death recedes and old stereotypes rise to the surface.

The incongruity in our social values becomes clear when rape is contrasted with robbery. The robbery victim is praised for relinquishing his material possessions without a fight in order to save his life, that is, to choose the lesser of the two losses. But when it comes to rape, the rules change: The woman's honor is at stake! At a time when there are no guidelines to action and common sense would dictate behavior inconsistent with social teachings, the woman is placed in a situation of "unanticipated incongruity." Shame is the inevitable result.

Disapproval or criticism from others, particularly if administered harshly and unremittingly without compensating validation for positive behavior to maintain a healthy balance of self-esteem, can also lead to shame. Young adolescents are particularly vulnerable to shame reactions, especially in regard to body changes. Who does not recall the fear of the teenage girl that her menstrual bleeding will show, or of the boy's uncontrollable erection?

Individual variations in shame reactions

Just as one cannot predict what will constitute a loss to another, so one cannot predict what aspect of a situation will cause another to feel shame. Within a group suffering the same loss, there will be individual reactions.

Some elderly people continue to function despite severe physical drawbacks. Some choose social isolation rather than reveal the tremor of Parkinson's disease. For many it is a badge of courage to carry on despite heart trouble. One elderly man felt so much shame over a coronary that he withdrew all interest in his business responsibilities and refused to leave his home again. Some of the elderly are ashamed at the gnarled fingers of arthritis, preferring to eat alone rather than have others see their deformities. Although some notable women may have mitigated the sense of shame following a mastectomy, there are some women whose own spouses have never seen this disfigurement. The same reaction is true of both some men and women following a colostomy, and even over a minor skin lesion if it is cancerous.

There are also individual differences in shame regarding grief reactions. Some people are ashamed of their anger, particularly when it is directed toward the deceased. Some are ashamed at their relief over a broken relationship. The grief-stricken can feel shame at their need for another, at their disorganization and unproductivity, at crying in the presence of another, or at any of the normal components of acute grief described in this book.

Defenses against shame

Shame can be an extremely painful feeling and people will erect powerful unconscious defenses as well as conscious maneuvers to avoid the pain of this feeling. How many times has an unemployed man left the house in the morning, pretending he was going to work at a job no longer his! Repression is the most primitive and basic defense against feelings of shame, often through denial of the loss itself. Repression can also take the form of screening out the impact of the loss. Overwhelming criticism can push one to the point of despair. If attacks are too massive, the person, to preserve a sense of self, will "turn off" emotionally to any criticism that would arouse shame anxiety. Some people defend against shame by becoming attacking and belligerent, or suddenly finding fault in another to justify pulling away.

Another way to avoid shame is to make a direct attempt to correct whatever is seen as the source of the shame. Such a defense can lead to hasty remarriage as a way to eliminate the stigma of being divorced or widowed.

People shamed by catastrophic experiences may hide their shame through what has been called "a conspiracy of silence," wherein they do not voluntarily speak of the losses, and the listener, if hearing the details would be too disturbing, refrains from asking questions about them.[35]

Blocking out the event is another way to avoid shame. Rape victims attacked without warning in the midst of some routine activity have been known to return to the activity in question immediately following the rape—preparing dinner, washing windows, cleaning house—almost as if the event had never happened.

The rejected child may seek the cause of his rejection in his own flawed self rather than in the possibility that his parent is incapable of loving. To admit the latter would leave him adrift in a meaningless world. How damaging to self-esteem can this same defense be in cases of divorce, desertion, and other types of separation! One may exaggerate his own guilt rather than admit inadequacy in the loved one and in the world one trusted.

The opposite behavior—to blame others for the loss rather than to assume one's own share of the responsibility—is another common defense against shame. This defense is also common in divorce, where it is so often the spouse who is considered at fault, not the self.

The loss of bodily function, whether temporary or permanent, minor or severe, often encourages defenses of denial, egocentricity, hypochondriasis, changed relationships with others, regression, and elaborate fantasies of restitution.

Defenses against aging in American society provide a lucrative business for those promising weight loss, rejuvenation through face lifts, toupees, and other miracle cures for the inevitable toll of passing years. Another defense of the elderly is to ignore infirmity. Some people, to hide the shame of a hearing loss, pretend to hear; this can give them the appearance of senility when their remarks in a conversation are completely off the subject! Shame over dependency can lead some aged to struggle mightily to maintain independence when the capacity to do so is gone. Anyone who has had an elderly parent who refuses to relinquish a driver's license after adequate driving ability is gone, or who refuses household help when no longer able to manage, knows the burden such behavior can place on others.

Hostility and anger are defenses against shame likely to be found in bereavement where shame is a part of the loss. This can be shame at the way in which the death occurred, such as in suicide, a death of cowardice, and so on. Or shame can be associated with the life of the deceased. The anger at such times can often take the form of the need for revenge, as in a vendetta, or it may be displaced to others out of the need to do unto others that which was done to the self. The betrayed husband may go off on a spree, seducing as many women as he can. Sex here becomes a vehicle for anger and aggression. Because aggression often attracts aggression, a person at such a time is in danger of attracting a partner who is by nature destructive. When the anger of the bereaved has been spent, he may find himself in a destructive relationship stemming from his needs at the time of bereavement.

Anger as a defense against shame can also take the form of shocking people. Hospital personnel who deal with amputees or disfigured patients report experiences in which the patient suddenly pulls aside the bed covers in order to see the look of shock or disgust on the face of an unsuspecting person. This behavior can also be looked at as a way in which the patient turns passive behavior into active, an attempt at mastery, by deliberately controlling the shock effect instead of passively enduring it.

Implications for Intervention

Because guilt or shame after loss can be normal or pathological, conscious or unconscious, the therapist must be aware of ways in which to help deal with these feelings, and be sensitive to the need for repairing damaged self-esteem. Ideally, both guilt and shame need to be slowly allowed expression in the presence of an accepting, non-judgmental other so that integration of the feelings can take place and restitution can be facilitated.

The first approach might well be an educational one. It is safe to assume that in our society it is not generally known that guilt and shame are both parts of normal grief. Reassurance must be not only sympathetic but also honest. The bereaved need to be helped to go over their decisions to see that they were made in the light of the best judgment of the moment. One cannot go back and remake earlier decisions with the wisdom of hindsight, gained in part as a result of the very decisions later deplored. Awareness of the normalcy of guilt following bereavement can serve as a guideline for mental health professionals in advising relatives of the elderly or dying.

A middle-aged woman whose mother had suffered a series of strokes, the last of which left her in a coma, was told by her physician to start to make funeral arrangements because her mother would be dead within a few days. The funeral director agreed that this was appropriate, and said that many physicians and clergymen advise relatives of the dying to make final preparations before the death to avoid decisions being made during a state of confusion and distress. To the woman's surprise, however, another physician casually remarked that her mother had a strong heart and could live on for weeks. To have made funeral arrangements under such conditions would have been tantamount to anticipating the death and would have touched too closely on death wishes in her highly ambivalent relationship with her mother.

In anticipating guilt following the death of a significant other, decisions need to be made on the basis of what will cause the least guilt. Thus, more frequent visits to aging parents or to the dying or acts of reparation before death can avoid feelings of guilt. The opportunity to nurse the dying person offers a chance at reparation for prior lacks in the relationship. Relatives should not be kept from the dying patient. The deathbed might be the place to end past hostilities, to make amends, to complete the relationship.[37]

Guilt stemming from relationships to the lost object takes in both lifelong relationships and stresses associated with the final loss. All these feelings of guilt need to be expressed—guilt for sins of omission and commission of a lifetime as well as guilt about negative feelings during the final days and, in many cases, even years. A chronically ill person can impose tremendous hardships on a family. While the ill person is the center of attention the needs of supporters may go unmet. A family can be emotionally as well as financially depleted by the time a person dies, and guilt following resentment toward the one responsible for the depleting is to be expected.

Further, it should be explained that guilt stemming from lifelong ambivalence in the relationship is also normal. We all react toward one another in life in ongoing relationships as if we will go on together forever. It would be too stressful to constantly be on guard lest each encounter might be our last.

Parents guilty over children because of divorce need help not only in expressing their guilt but also in finding ways to maintain contact with their children to the extent of their ability to parent and the realities of the situation. One mother who moved out of town, leaving her child with his father, was encouraged to telephone the child regularly at a prearranged time as a substitute for in-person visits so that she could remain a real and interested figure, albeit distant, in the mind of the child. This plan helped relieve the mother's guilt at being emotionally unable to mother her child. Fathers separated from children by divorce need help to maintain contact with their children for their own sake as well as for the children's. When two adults cannot sustain their marriage it need not mean the children should be deprived of one of the parents. In the final analysis, the parents remain the most important figures in the child's unconscious. They are the pillars on which his personality is built, and, if possible, both should remain real in his life.

Where guilt following loss is induced by others, whether through the glib remark of a caretaking person or the more malicious projection of one's guilt on another, the recipient of this projection needs to be helped to see the source of this attack, through explanation or psychotherapy. The mother of a child with intellectual or emotional problems who explodes with vitriolic hatred toward a teacher she sees as rejecting her child often is herself a rejecting parent, unable to acknowledge or repress adequately her shame and guilt over her own rejection. To many parents having a defective child is experienced as a loss of face and self-esteem. They need to be helped to get in touch with their feelings hidden under their projections. When the attack goes from one parent to another, the stress of a defective child can break a marriage. Early intervention is, therefore, advisable.

Unconscious guilt will not, of course, be spontaneously expressed by the bereaved. It needs to be spotted by the helper in compulsive behavior such as rituals, or sudden religious interest by someone heretofore not religious. It is also revealed in obsessional review of the loss and in the search for meaning beyond the normal duration of such behavior in acute grief. Unconscious guilt is also a component in acts of self-hurt, such as physical aches and pains, neglect of one's health, the onset of real physical illnesses, accident proneness, and self-defeating life choices regarding work and personal relationships.

Where it is safe to do so unconscious guilt should be brought out into the open and discharged as described earlier. When it is safe is a matter of the utmost delicacy and wisdom on the part of the helper. That one should not uncover any material with which one is not prepared to deal is a good rule to follow. Thus, survivor guilt should be dealt with by the routine helper only when it stems from losses within the normal range of ordinary life experiences.

Guilt may be expressed by fixation on a small detail of the loss while deeper survivor guilt may remain unconscious. It may be too much to expect the bereaved by themselves to get in touch with this deeper guilt. Remarks such as "Often people focus on one aspect of the loss as a way of avoiding facing deeper guilt, such as merely the guilt of being a survivor while another is gone," may be helpful. For the bereaved the fact that someone else can speak of a topic means that others have also had the experience; they are not alone, or different.

The bereaved seem to feel relieved to discover the difference between shame and guilt because correctly naming a feeling is an important step in being able to integrate its intellectual and emotional aspects. The bereaved then feel understood, which is one of the deepest gratifications they seek.

Because shame is an isolating experience, it would follow that the opportunity to communicate one's shame to an accepting and understanding person is one way to restore contact and diminish the feeling of isolation. One goal of intervention is to keep the bereaved from feeling abandoned. This may mean that the helper refuses to be pushed away by the bereaved in their thrashing about with the pain of the loss.

It is difficult to expose the pain of shame to one who is viewed as superior or condescending. The opposite, understanding and empathy, would appear to be an important factor in the success of self-help groups such as Alcoholics Anonymous, groups for mastectomy patients, colostomy patients, parents of mental patients, and so on. For this reason the helper must avoid pushing for disclosure of painful material until the person feels a sufficient sense of respect from the helper to risk such disclosure without further loss of self-esteem. For example, in working with the parents of disturbed children, who already may feel shame for their failure as parents, it is sometimes necessary to enlist their help on behalf of their child through their fetching him to the session, and reporting on changes from week to week, before they can begin to look at their part in the creation of the problem.

Self-esteem can also be enhanced by giving recognition to the successful aspects of a person's life. "It is apparent you are a successful person in many areas" is more likely to elicit a reply such as "Yes, but my son's suicide made all that meaningless" than is a direct question regarding the area where the person feels most mortified.

The bereaved can also feel relief when given information regarding the legitimacy of their loss of trust in themselves, others, and the world. People do exclude the bereaved; it is not only that the divorced, the widowed, the maimed, the victimized feel different and exclude themselves. Any misfortune can set off fears of a similar misfortune befalling others, and avoidance of the bereaved can be one way to insure against such a reminder because "out of sight is out of mind."

To counteract shame, the bereaved also need to hear that tears do not indicate weakness, that one can be strong but feel deeply, that confusion and disorganization in the face of loss do not mean incompetence, and that dependency in the crisis of grief need not mean permanent regression.

The bereaved need to be helped to soften the superego by lowering their demands on themselves. "Why not come down and join the human race with the rest of us? Why shouldn't you be disorganized in grief also?" can be a way of suggesting that the internal demand is too high, rather than that the person has failed or done something shameful.

Treatment of survivor guilt

Because survivor guilt is a form of pathological mourning, this condition when severe is one that should be treated by an expert, and not a routine helper. Inasmuch as the main focus of this book is to examine the dynamics of normal grief, which does lend itself to help by people with varying levels of professional skill, no attempt will be made to explore the helping process in pathological grief, of which survivor guilt or the survivor syndrome is one category. To do so might, in fact, tempt unqualified persons to meddle in an area beyond their skill.

The urgency to provide treatment for survivors and their children increases daily. It is a temptation for the well-intentioned to step in to ease the pain with the rationalization that someone has to help these people who now appear at social agency doors in great numbers. Despite the tragedy of cancer, it does not occur to most of us to try to treat it. Caution should also be the watchword against those who would cash in financially on the bandwagon of loss and grief, a long-neglected problem which is now becoming recognized.

In regard to World War II survivors, there are a number of reasons why the problems are now becoming more visible. The survivors themselves are now in their middle or later years and, as has been discussed earlier, later losses evoke unconscious and conscious memories of earlier ones. The middle and later years have their own multiple normal losses, usually now referred to in the literature as mid-life crises and problems of aging. Another reason is that it has taken almost four decades to be able to examine the traumas of World War II victims. The problems presented by their maturing children is one impetus. Many survivors report that during the first decades following the war, they remained symptom-free. It is now believed that denial played an important part in their perception as well as in that of the therapists and experts dealing with financial reparations. The struggle to adjust to a new country took much psychic energy. The fantasy and hope of finding relatives still alive kept many survivors from experiencing the depth of their losses. Even the problems of their children could be held to a minimum while they were young and protected by parents and the structure of public education. All of these problems, however, remained dormant but unresolved.

Henry Krystal, who has worked extensively with Holocaust victims, sagely comments on mankind's tendency to sanctify and adore martyrs but to condemn, suspect, and ignore survivors.[38] At a deep unconscious level, one may tend to suspect survivors of unfair play, collaboration with the enemy, prostitution, and thus they are feared. This fear is converted into blaming the victim for the guilt of the perpetrator. Witness now the surging insistence of some that the Holocaust either did not happen or that reports of victimization were magnified. This problem can no longer continue to be ignored.

The literature is contradictory regarding the value of therapy with survivors and the methods of choice with various survivor syndromes. Some survivors have been reluctant to seek or to use help for a number of reasons, because help symbolized acknowledgment that their perception of self as inferior had been correct. Help also meant admitting that the damage had been successfully inflicted. Help meant the relinquishment of a feeling of omnipotence or superiority demonstrated in survival despite all suffering. Survivors often refused help because of distrust of its sincerity.

For some survivors acceptance of financial restitution from the German government for relatives killed in the Holocaust threatened the continued repression of identification with the aggressor and reactivated survivor guilt. Some handled this by massive denial, others by spending the money on some worthy cause or charity. Some felt by refusing the money they could make the German people feel more guilty. Still another complication in the treatment of survivors is the loss of financial restitution with improvement.

Survivor guilt has been described as the inability to complete mourning because of repressed aggression toward the lost object.[39] It is a temptation, therefore, to think that all that is needed is the externalization of the aggression through catharsis. This simplistic view is an example of the errors that can be made by people with insufficient knowledge of the complexity of the dynamics involved. Experts warn against the danger of inviting catharsis in patients with unresolved grief reactions. Suicide, psychosis, and severe depression can result after what appears to be a momentary relief from emotional discharge. In patients with a clinical picture of disorganization, the external picture may mirror an internal state of disorganization reflecting anxiety from the threat of internalized dead objects coming to life within in an overwhelming, malignant form. The person carries within himself not only the dead objects but also the conviction that his own destructiveness was the cause of his loss, and there is no way to make reparations.[40]

Further problems confronting the therapist working with survivors are: loss of basic trust because of the persecutory experiences; feelings of hopelessness as well as helplessness; masochistic characterological problems due to prolonged enforced regression of the camp experience; resistance at looking beyond the traumatic experience itself to pre-traumatic or infantile experiences that may be connected in the unconscious; disturbances of superego and ego ideal, and of the sense of shame, of work orientation, and other clearly psychiatric problems.[41]

Yahalom found that when therapists attempted to deal with survivors by regarding the problem of survivor guilt as central to their pathology they have often met with failure.[42] If these people have accepted the reality of their own deaths, if they have detached from life, then the problem is how to help them come alive again. Psychoanalytic interpretations are not the answer.

As a final caution to those who would work with survivors of persecution without sufficient preparation, it might be important here to state that some highly skilled therapists have admitted their reluctance to work with these patients because of the severe emotional demands on them, the therapists. It is no disgrace to admit one's limitations and to refer the patient to someone more qualified by training or by life experience. Omnipotence on the part of the helper can be, if not damaging, at least unhelpful to the suffering person.

Therapists working with survivors must be prepared to walk a tightrope between empathy and objectivity, to avoid being emotionally overwhelmed by the onslaught of material dealing with traumas, cruelties, sadism, persecution, and death. They must remain consistently attentive, be humble enough to admit gaps in their own knowledge and experience, and be able to acknowledge errors in their work.

Further, therapists must be constantly aware of their own counter-transferences and the temptation to gratify the needs of the patient, as well as a tendency to withdraw into scientific detachment or anger as a defense against this temptation. They need to have worked through their own guilt feelings about having been spared the suffering endured by the patient. They must be willing and able to accept the projections of the patient without returning them to the patient or internalizing them, particularly those of the aggressor. And last of all, they must be willing to seek consultation from others more knowledgable than themselves and be open to learning from their patients.

In summary, with emotional as well as with physical illness, we must face the tragic reality that not everyone can be saved or helped. We are even beginning to recognize that some young children are emotionally damaged beyond repair. By accepting the limits of our powers, we may be more free to develop our skills in areas where effectiveness is still possible. And again, we must remember that the therapist should stay out of areas where he would be embarrassed or shocked or otherwise not able to hear the truths he would uncover. A young man remarked about his previous therapist, to whom he could not relate: "I felt I had to protect him, that I had experienced things in life he had never dreamed of. Now with Dr. Smith (the current therapist) I feel there is nothing I could tell him that would shock him. He has heard it all before. He doesn't have to show off how bright he is. I tell him something I think is terrible and he just shrugs. His shrug tells me he has heard it all before. It is all part of the human condition. I can show him my strengths and my weaknesses, my idealistic side and my base side, my rational side and my craziness. And he helps me make sense out of it all, and I feel safe." Thus is trust laid down and the core of self-esteem and identity established.

Notes

1. Melanie Klein quoted in Geoffrey Gorer, *Death, Grief, and Mourning: A Study of Contemporary Society* (Garden City, N.Y.: Doubleday and Co., Anchor Books, 1972).

2. Colin Murray Parkes, *Bereavement: Studies of Grief in Adult Life* (New York: International Universities Press, 1972); and Ira O. Glick, Robert S. Weiss, and C. Murray Parkes, *The First Year of Bereavement* (New York: John Wiley and Sons, 1974).

3. Glick, Weiss, and Parkes, *The First Year of Bereavement*.

4. Annette Baran, Reuben Pannor, and Arthur Sorosky, "Opening the Sealed Record for Adult Adoptees—Implications for Practice," Panel Discussion, 3rd Biennial Scientific Conference, The Art and the Science of Clinical Social Work, Institute for Clinical Social Work and Society for Clinical Social Work, Los Angeles, California, 26 October 1975.

5. Sylvia Schild, "The Family of the Retarded Child," in *The Mentally Retarded Child and His Family*, ed. Richard Koch and James C. Dobson (New York: Brunner Mazel, 1971), p. 434.

6. Robert J. Lifton, "Observations on Hiroshima Survivors," in *Massive Psychic Trauma*, ed. Henry Krystal (New York: International Universities Press, 1968).

7. Peter Marris, *Widows and Their Families* (London: Routledge and Kegan Paul, 1958), p. 27.

8. Klaus D. Hoppe, "The Aftermath of Nazi Persecution Reflected in Recent Psychiatric Literature," *International Psychiatric Clinica* 8 (1971): 176.

9. Krystal, *Massive Psychic Trauma*.

10. Hoppe, "The Aftermath of Nazi Persecution," p. 175.

11. Ibid.

12. Ibid., p. 174.

13. Ibid., p. 180.

14. Ibid., p. 178.

15. Klaus D. Hoppe, "The Psychodynamics of Concentration Camp Victims," *The Psychoanalytic Forum* 1 (1966): 81.

16. Lifton, "Observations on Hiroshima Survivors," p. 175.

17. Ibid., p. 184.

18. Ibid., p. 176.

19. John Gunther, *Death Be Not Proud: A Memoir* (New York: Harper and Bros., 1949), p. 258.

20. Stephen M. Sonnenberg, "A Special Form of Survivor Syndrome," *The Psychoanalytic Quarterly* 51 (1972): 58–62.

21. Personal discussion with Itamar Yahalom, psychoanalyst, Beverly Hills, California, 10 July 1978.

22. "Survivors of Air Crashes, Hijacks Often Get Physical, Mental Ills," *Los Angeles Times,* 12 July 1978, p. 6.

23. Stanley Rosenman, "The Paradox of Guilt in Disaster Victim Populations," *Psychiatric Quarterly Supplement* 30 (1956): 181–221.

24. Lifton, "Observations on Hiroshima Survivors," pp. 179, 183.

25. Hoppe, "The Aftermath of Nazi Persecution," p. 180.

26. Ibid., p. 181.

27. Lifton, "Observations on Hiroshima Survivors," pp. 177–78.

28. Helen Merrell Lynd, *On Shame and the Search for Identity* (New York: Science Editions, 1965).

29. Ibid., p. 22.

30. Ibid., p. 67.

31. Gregory Rochlin, *Griefs and Discontents: The Forces of Change* (Boston: Little, Brown and Co., 1965).

32. Lynd, *On Shame,* p. 64.

33. Ibid., pp. 32–3.

34. Erving Goffman, *Stigma: Notes on the Management of Spoiled Identity* (Englewood Cliffs, N.J.: Prentice-Hall, 1964).

35. Henry Krystal and William G. Niederland, "Clinical Observations on the Survivor Syndrome," in *Massive Psychic Trauma,* ed. Krystal, p. 341.

36. Rochlin, *Griefs and Discontents,* p. 322.

37. Glick, Weiss, and Parkes, *The First Year of Bereavement.*

38. Krystal and Niederland, "Clinical Observations on the Survivor Syndrome," in *Massive Psychic Trauma,* p. 343.

39. Ibid.

40. Charles Anderson, "Aspects of Pathological Grief and Mourning," in *Grief: Selected Readings,* ed. Arthur C. Carr et al. (New York: Health Sciences Publishing, 1975), p. 184.

41. Klaus D. Hoppe, "Psychotherapy with Concentration-Camp Survivors," in *Massive Psychic Trauma,* ed. Krystal, p. 217.

42. Personal discussion with Yahalom, 10 July 1978.

10/
Identification
in Grief

Identification in Normal Development

Identification occurs when individuals incorporate within themselves a mental picture of an object and then think, feel, and act as they conceive the object to think, feel, and act. A common misunderstanding of this is that conscious imitation leads to unconscious identification, which is too simplistic a view of the process. Although it is true that children do imitate their parents, this imitation does not automatically lead to identification. Incorporation, the process by which identification takes place, requires certain conditions, which A. Balint describes as follows:

> Its necessary preconditions are an unbroken narcissism, which cannot bear that anything should exist outside itself, and the weakness of the individual, which makes him unable either to annihilate his environment or to take flight from it.[1]

Thus, children take in that which they cannot overcome. Identification is a process for transforming that which is external, strange, and frightening into something internal and familiar. It is lifelong and changes over the years.

Identification goes through several stages. The most primitive form is the merging of self and object in early infancy. As infants begin to differentiate themselves from their mothers, identification takes place along sensorimotor lines. At first it is of the total object by means of magical fantasies of incorporation. Around the second year of life, the desire for a complete union with the mother is relinquished in favor of partial identifications with various characteristics of her and, as the child grows, partial identifications remain the norm. These become integrated as character traits, ego activities, interests, and sublimations. They no longer depend on any ongoing relationship with the object itself.

Throughout all of life identification is an important avenue to security through finding characteristics in others that are similar to our own. Although each of us seeks a sense of uniqueness, feeling different makes for alienation. The healthier the personality, the more the individual can see in himself as well as in others both negative as well as positive traits. The less healthy the person is, the more he is compelled to split off either negative traits, which he can then see and criticize in others, or positive traits, which he can then see and idealize in others. Either leaves him the poorer psychologically because he has failed to "own" all of himself.

Throughout infancy and childhood, identification binds the child to those on whom he is dependent for gratifications and, even more, survival. Fortunate indeed is the child who has kind and loving parents and siblings on whom to depend. The infant searches for similarities to himself in his parents, thus reassuring himself against fears of abandonment, feelings of helplessness, and awareness of his own limitations. As he grows the child expands his arena of relatedness; identifications go beyond parents to siblings, other family members, teachers, friends, characters in literature, films, television, public figures, and so on.

Children do not perceive nor do they identify with the parent as he or she is in reality. Their perception of their parents and the world is always distorted by their own mind, depending on their ego state, level of emotional and cognitive maturity, and personality bent. Thus, the parent with whom the child identifies is the parent perceived through these distortions.

For example, young children believe that adults (parents) have unlimited power, money, and freedom of action. This conviction persists despite evidence to the contrary. They simply do not notice that which does not fit their inner conviction. "I wish I were a grown up so I would never have to do anything I don't want to do," complained one youngster of eight. "Don't you know that Daddy and I have to be at work on time every day," pointed out his mother, who had been working throughout the years of his conscious memory.

"You do?" he asked with surprise, even though every morning the household was organized so that the children could get off to school and the parents to their respective jobs on time. These routine household events that had taken place around him had not been taken in as part of his experience because they did not fit his inner convictions. It would take more than one reminder for him to reconcile himself to the reality of parental limitations.

Children can share in adult power through imitation, which is the outward copying of adult behavior, and also through identification, which is a process of internalization. Children's ego ideals are created through their taking into their own character the qualities of the adults whom they admire and fear, and whom they can neither overcome nor escape. Identification is important to adolescents in elevating their fragile self-esteem during the years that their aspirations outstrip their achievements and before their own competence has been proved.

Identification with parents continues even into the middle and later years. Adults identify with or openly reject the manner in which they observe their parents' approach to aging and death. Whether alive or dead, present or at a distance, loved or hated figures, parents remain the most important figures for identification throughout their offspring's lifetime. Gregory Rochlin summarizes the importance of identification in psychological development as follows: "Identification is the means through which the entire environment, the whole of one's culture, is absorbed into and becomes a part of the individual."[2]

Identification in Mourning: Theoretical Considerations

Identification as a dynamic in mourning has preoccupied psychoanalytic thinkers since Freud. In his early years Freud considered identification with the lost object a process that existed in melancholia but not in normal grief.[3] Later, he began to consider it the main component in normal mourning as well, that is, as a compensation for the loss sustained and perhaps the sole condition under which the object could be relinquished in the external world.[4] The majority of psychoanalysts accept Freud's view, which is expressed by Rochlin as follows:

A substantial reaction to loss seems hardly to have importance unless it carries with it another normal characteristic, an identification with that which is lost. Even if what is lost is but an abstraction like freedom, or some symbol representing what is valued, or a part of one's body or changes in the body as in the loss of function . . . it is the identification which bestows a value. . . . What gives them [losses] their added significance and poignancy is that, by making what we value a part of ourselves, we invariably and unconsciously have invested it with our narcissistic interest. With that increased commitment, losses have profound effects that are dictated in large measure by the extent of the narcissistic involvement associated with them.[5]

Some experts, however, do not agree with Freud in this. For example, John Bowlby and Colin Murray Parkes both claim that evidence does not show identification to be the main nor only process in grief. Bowlby does grant, however, that it is the major component distinguishing the grief of man from that of other species.[6]

Various writers have tried to focus on the nature, purpose, and course of introjection as it relates to both normal and pathological outcomes to loss. Some postulate that pathological or incomplete mourning is related to the primitive, whole object forms of introjection, while normal grief is related to the higher part object forms of identification.[7]

Otto Fenichel turned his attention to the feelings of the bereaved toward the introject. He held that in normal mourning the positive feelings toward the lost object rapidly replaced the negative ones, so that the introjection served to preserve the relationship with the lost object.[8] It is generally agreed that in depression the bereaved are unable to retain good internal objects. One reason may be because of ambivalence toward bad internalized objects; another is that good internalized objects have been destroyed by infantile aggression.[9]

David Peretz also dealt with the nature of the introject. He held that identification with healthy aspects of the lost object can coexist with pathological ones. Identification with positive or idealized aspects will result in increased self-esteem and normal grief; identification with fearful or hostile elements will result in guilt, shame, anxiety, and lowered self-esteem.[10] Identification with a pathological figure or one perceived as pathological, rather than the primitiveness of the identification process, is also believed to account for a pathological outcome in mourning.[11]

Children's resolution of mourning can be complicated when their developmental need to identify with parents makes them vulnerable to taking on the parents' feelings in regard to a loss. In divorce, for example, the parent with whom they live may cast them into the role of the absent parent or vent on them anger meant for the absent spouse. When, in addition, a child, out of a need to identify with the lost object, takes on some aspect of the missing parent's personality, the result can be collusion between the remaining parent and child in a way detrimental to the child's development.

Conversely, children who have lost a parent through death may resist identification with that parent out of fear of their own death. Fear of identification with the dead can result in fear of suicide and denial of the loss. Or, out of the child's need to identify with a parent as part of normal development, identification with a dead parent can lead to the child's committing suicide in order to be, like the parent, dead.

The place of identification in mourning remains a controversial issue. Meanwhile, helpers must proceed with whatever knowledge is available at this time, remaining open to new learning not only from experts but from the bereaved themselves.

Forms of Identification in Loss

Identification in loss can take a variety of forms. One way is with positive aspects of the lost object—in the walk, in facial expression, in interests, values, or tastes of the lost object. Or a mourner may try out various attributes, one after another, before settling on a more lasting identification. This experimental aspect to identification is important in normal grief in that it allows the bereaved the freedom to try on and reject identifications.[12]

Children who lose a parent may identify with some trait of the parent, for example, nurturing through caring for younger siblings, or taking on the interests, mannerisms, tastes, and sometimes the career choice of the dead parent, and so on. The dead or absent parent tends to be idealized by the child, who may then identify with this idealization, risking later problems because of the impossibility of living up to such superhuman qualities in reality. Or the child may identify with a self-punitive or self-destructive aspect of the parent. The child who avoids the pain of unfulfilled yearning for the lost parent by substituting things for people in a need to replace the lost object is vulnerable to serious pathology in the lack of ability to make later attachments to people.

One who has strongly identified with a spouse and then loses that spouse through death may show problems in many areas of functioning. Research has indicated that many marriages are based on processes of mutual identification or projection. In the former instance, when death occurs to one partner, the surviving spouse often succumbs to a paralyzing illness or dies soon after the loss of the mate.[13]

Identification can be with the last illness of the deceased in the form of somatic illness, symptoms, passivity, or lack of interest, as with a young professor who lost a respected and admired older colleague through death from a heart attack. The younger man developed chest pains for which no organic cause could be found. His symptoms were diagnosed as psychosomatic identification with his deceased colleague.

Identification with a dying patient on the part of hospital personnel or caretakers can lead to feelings of helplessness or, as a defense, to anger at the patient followed by guilt and perhaps withdrawal. Out of feelings of helplessness one can feel pressured internally into doing something—anything—to regain a feeling of effectiveness. This flight into activity can result in interventions that are not always timely or needed and may be contraindicated. The same defense of rushing into activity to avoid feelings of helplessness can account for acting out behavior on the part of relatives anticipating a loss or the bereaved after a loss has occurred.

In normal grief some of the feelings of numbness, as well as the lack of emotion, described by the newly bereaved can be forms of identification with the deceased: numbness symbolizes death. As long as these reactions are short-lived, they can be considered part of the normal grieving process.

Several writers have commented on the outcome when a parent identifies with a deceased young child. Some believe it is almost impossible for a parent to do so in any adaptive fashion. It has been observed that a mother who loses a child through death may feel an intense identification with that child, with possible reactions of depression, suicidal ruminations, and even suicide. On a deep level, she has, in fact, lost a part of herself that was meant to continue on after her. On a more hopeful note, however, the case has been cited of a mother who lost a five-year-old son and began to recognize in herself a tendency to be meek and mild, which she was able to connect to the dead child's traits during his final illness. Her identification with the dead child was confined to her mourning period, and she was able to relinquish it once she recognized what was going on and once the acute mourning stage was over.[14]

Identification with a deceased parent can carry the threat of death all through life, not only for children. It is not unusual to find that people expect to die at the age the parent of the same sex died. The suicide of a parent becomes an invitation to the child to follow suit. Mike, a twenty-three-year-old foreign student from an underdeveloped country, was convinced that he would not live beyond the age of thirty-nine because it was at that age that his father and three uncles had died. He made all his family and career plans around that final date. The fact that his relatives had died from diseases that had since come under control seemed to have no impact on his deep-seated conviction of the fate in store for him.

When the image of the elderly parent is grossly negative, adult children may take measures to avoid a similar fate. "I spend every Saturday with my grandchildren," said one middle-aged woman. "This is my insurance for my old age. My mother was a cardplayer. She never had any relationship with her grandchildren. Now she wonders why she is alone, why they don't want to visit her. Why should they? They don't even know her. When she dies, there will be no one to really grieve for her. I see her out of duty, not love. It would have been much better if she had been a caring mother and grandmother who spent time with her family when she was younger. There would be someone to care about her now."

Identification with the lost object is often seen in anniversary reactions, at which time any of the various forms of identification can appear anew even though they did not show up at the time of the original loss.

Finally, one of the more ironic and potentially tragic forms of identification in loss is found in identification with an aggressor. The young child's helplessness at the hands of adult caretakers who can be neither escaped nor overcome is fertile ground for the operation of this defense. Everyone is, therefore, vulnerable when confronted by a situation of loss in which one is at the mercy of another person or group. Physical or verbal abuse, persecution, imprisonment, kidnapping, hijacking, or other similar traumatic situations can bring this defense into operation.

In identification with the aggressor there is no longer an optional or experimental aspect to the dynamic, as in the optional trying-on phenomenon of normal grief described earlier. Now there is an imperative quality to the defense: it is needed for survival. Rochlin describes this behavior as follows:

> In the Nazi prison camps, under terms of desperate deprivation which forced an indifference to others who were sharing a similar plight, life was relieved by bursts of abuse and destructive impulses toward one's fellow prisoners. The prisoners thus unwittingly acquired some identification with their hated jailors. Currying the jailors' favor may have been not only an unmistakable sign of defection but a sign of a return to childhood defenses as well. These defenses in the service of an individual's oldest desires are the familiar ones, such as wishing for special consideration, envy, jealousy, self-interest and a disregard for others, or the consequences, the relinquishing of social aims for egocentric ones, and identifying oneself with the powerful tormentors.[15]

Victims pay a high price through identification with their aggressors, even though it is necessary for their survival. They may be left with serious characterological problems, severe depression, or lasting problems of superego or conscience.

Identification with the aggressor is also found in the self-hatred of people belonging to groups discriminated against by society—racial and ethnic groups, religious groups, the handicapped, the elderly, and the poor are some examples. When born into such a group, people internalize the depreciation of the group of which they are a member. If they later find themselves in a group which they had previously considered stigmatized, such as the elderly, the physically maimed, or the chronically ill, they turn against themselves some of the negative feelings they were socialized into having against such people. The black power and senior power movements are attempts to undo some of this damage to self-esteem.

The Nazis also used identification with the dead as a tool to dehumanize their victims. In the concentration camp situation, as in other instances of victimization, total helplessness was only the beginning of the ordeal for the sufferers. William G. Niederland points out that despite "total degradation to the point of dehumanization" there was not a "full animalization" in the sense of actual loss of humanity.[16] This made for even greater difficulties because the ego ideal, the feelings of rage and shame in seeing themselves dehumanized, remained. Although physically reduced to basic animal level for survival, spiritually, humanely, and psychologically they remained human. He says:

> These changes of the body and of the self-image led to severe identity problems. The identity and ego-ideal were systematically assaulted with an aim to destruction. All taboos were violated; impulses of help or compassion had to be thwarted. The S. S. men made a special effort to impress the prisoners with the fact that they were going to end up in the gas chamber and crematorium anyway. Accepting this identification with the dead was really the ultimate end of giving up one's own identity.[17]

The quality of deadness in survivors, which is distinct from survivor guilt, comes close to identification with the dead that Robert J. Lifton describes in post-traumatic reactions of atomic bomb survivors. These people almost died, inwardly felt they did die, and if not, felt that because only the dead are pure, their being alive was an insult to the dead. Lifton holds that:

> This whole constellation of inwardly experienced death symbolism is . . . the survivor's means of maintaining life, because in the face of the burden of guilt that he carries, particularly guilt over survival priority, his obeisance before the dead is his best means of justifying and maintaining his own existence . . . and a life, which in a very powerful symbolic sense, the survivor does not feel to be his own.[18]

Implications for Intervention

The importance, complexity, and subtlety of identification in mourning cannot be overemphasized. Whereas many of the reactions to loss thus far discussed have been observable in behavior—anger, guilt, shame, searching, anxiety, and so on—identification is an internal process not always revealed in behavior observable by another. Certainly, when the bereaved take on interests, personality traits, values, or other aspects of the person lost to them, it may become readily apparent to significant others that identification with the lost object is taking place. The tendency of the average person is to support positive identifications as an indication of affection toward the lost object and to attempt to interfere with negative identifications. Who would think to question the appropriateness of a positive identification with an admired figure? "He is just like his father" can be taken as a highly prized comment about a fatherless boy.

In the same way, overt negative behavior in children can easily be attributed to identification with a lost parent. "She is as sloppy (dull, wild, disorganized) as her mother" or "He is as irresponsible (exploitative, selfish, self-destructive) as his father" are examples of the above. Whether the behavior is the result of identification with the lost parent, predates the loss, or is part of the normal developmental stage of the child is not at issue here. What is important is that attributing such traits to identification with the lost parent may have a suggestive effect on the child.

The matter of encouraging positive identifications and attempting to break negative identifications with a lost object is not, however, the entire issue here. Identification at any phase of development is one means of insurance against loss in that the bereaved not only is unconsciously like the lost object but also has, in part, become the object. Identification thus serves in the interest of holding on to the lost object internally by making it a part of the self.

As stated earlier, a focus on the lost object is found in the first stage of grief. The inability to move on to the next phase of mourning, that of acute grief, after a reasonable period indicates the refusal at some level to admit the loss, laying the groundwork for much psychopathology.[19]

Fixation on the lost object prevents the bereaved from making attachments to new objects necessary for continued life and growth. Where the loss is of a part of the self rather than of a significant other person, the holding on to the pre-loss self-image can prevent the bereaved from moving on to an integration of a new self-identity.

How, then, does the mental health professional deal with the mechanism of identification? First, he or she must be aware of its significance in loss, and look for it even when overt signs of its operation are lacking.

"My father has blue eyes just like me," said by a man of forty about his father dead for twelve years is an example of how the use of the present instead of the past tense grammatically can reveal that for the bereaved the dead person is still alive and indentified with himself.

In the final analysis, every death makes us aware of our own mortality and of the mortality of loved ones. One widow recalled that at the time of her husband's death, all their male friends feared for their own untimely death; their wives expressed fears that their husbands might die prematurely, and their children had to be reassured that their daddies were not about to die.

The closer the relationship or involvement with the deceased or the bereaved has been, the closer the tragedy hits home, and the greater the likelihood of identification. One instance where identification with the lost object needs to be looked for is when a child's parent dies. The impact of the death of a parent in childhood is a complex and as yet not fully understood matter. "Look at all the people who have lost parents in childhood, and they all made it!" is a common argument against looking more deeply into this most painful subject. Certainly, the child's behavior is not always a reliable clue. In relation to childhood loss it has been stated that:

> In the case of children, especially before adolescence, it is important that identification not become the predominant means. This can interfere with the capacity for recathexis of a new parent figure and progression in the development of relationships and structuralization. . . . Our group found that children are developmentally inclined to deal with loss by identification, so that this frequently presents a danger to the resolution of mourning.[20]

Mary, age four, when told by her mother that her father had died during the night, commented: "Now I will have to be the Daddy." "No," her mother replied. "You are still Mary, my little girl. Daddy is gone. I will take care of you. If I need help, there will be Grandma and Grandpa and other grownups to help me. I will take care of you. But you are still Mary, my little girl."

Erna Furman found that children who identified with a dead parent suffered from severe symptomatology and were arrested in development at the time of the parent's death. Despite the availability of substitute love objects, these children could not make use of them in order to proceed with their emotional development without psychiatric treatment. This was necessary in order to help them undo the identification with the dead parent. She states:

The younger the child, the more he needs the surviving parent's help in differentiating himself and his own fate from that of the dead parent. In many ways this runs contrary to the child's tendency to identify himself with his parent, both developmentally and as a part of the mourning process. The conflict over such an identification is an almost never-ending process, as the child needs to grapple with it on each subsequent developmental level, long after the parent's death and even into adulthood. In working with parents we have frequently noted instances of such a struggle. When the parent had lost a mother or father through death in childhood his parental development and functioning could be interfered with by his conflict over assuming this role.[21]

A study that evolved out of an interest in certain psychoanalytic patients who had suffered parent loss in childhood and who "resisted for much longer than usual the development of a therapeutic alliance and the usual transference phenomena" found a persisting immaturity in adults that correlated with the level of development achieved at the time of the loss of a parent.[22]

Again, the task of the helper is to first enable the bereaved to sever the ties to the lost object. This process includes breaking the internal ties as well. Treatment regarding breaking internalized identifications calls for the highest levels of professional skill as well as an understanding of the dynamics of grief and mourning. One cannot judge from professional titles and degrees alone that a therapist is qualified to work in this area of bereavement.

Treatment should be aimed at the analysis of the identifications as they emerge and are recognized, or as they are recognized symbolically by the therapist and brought to the attention of the patient. What have been called "linking objects" are helpful in facilitating the remembrance of the loss. These might be articles of clothing, photographs, contact with people who knew the lost person, stories, or other tangible reminders of the loss.[23] It is necessary to remember, to grieve, to break the tie, and to go on. The underlying theme of loss and restitution is that although one way of life may be gone, another must be forged. The intermediate step is the painful one of grieving. It is grieving that helps break the tie binding one to the lost object.

Treatment through "re-grief work," that is, the attempt to help the bereaved at a later time bring into consciousness and discharge the emotions around an earlier loss, is not to be undertaken lightly because of the intense pain that can be set off. We are cautioned that attempting such an approach on an outpatient basis is not wise because of the danger of suicide. Rather, a treatment approach with the patient hospitalized up to three months and seen in daily sessions is considered appropriate. A careful assessment of the stability of the personality is recommended in order to evaluate the patient's ability to tolerate the emotional stress of the "re-grief work."[24]

In working with bereavement, it is also necessary that one recognize that in psychological trauma, just as in physical trauma, not all conditions can be corrected. With some victims of massive losses helpers may be unable to undo the full effects of the trauma. For example, therapists working with concentration camp survivors often found that for them the working through of the defense of identification with the aggressor was virtually impossible. To do so would have required their recognition of death wishes toward loved ones who had actually been destroyed. It was impossible for the survivor to be assured that his wishes did not have magical powers when he had witnessed the destruction of the entire world he had known and had been compelled to use identification with the aggressor as a survival defense. Therapists had to be satisfied with their conclusion that the only solution:

> ... workable, but unsatisfactory, ... is afforded by repression, an ego split in which the identification with the aggressor was repressed and walled off. ... Since, in view of the magnitude of the trauma, the repression mechanism seems to have failed in a certain number of cases, ... the conscious awareness of such identification with the aggressor may add to the enormous burden of unconscious guilt and drive the victim into further self-isolation, brooding withdrawal, self-contempt and self-exclusion from human society, or in the case of total denial and projection, into psychotic illness.[25]

Notes

1. A. Balint, "Identification," in *The Yearbook of Psychoanalysis* 1 (1945): 317.

2. Gregory Rochlin, *Griefs and Discontents: The Forces of Change* (Boston: Little, Brown and Co., 1965), pp. 5–6.

3. Sigmund Freud, "Mourning and Melancholia," in *The Complete Psychological Works of Sigmund Freud, Standard Edition*, ed. James Strachey (New York: Macmillan Co., 1964).

4. Freud, "Group Psychology and the Analysis of the Ego" and "The Ego and the Id," in *The Complete Psychological Works*.

5. Rochlin, *Griefs and Discontents*, pp. 38–39.

6. John Bowlby, "Processes of Mourning," *International Journal of Psychoanalysis* 42 (1961): 317–40; "Pathological Mourning and Childhood Mourning," *Journal of American Psychoanalytic Association* 11 (1963): 500–41; and Colin

Murray Parkes, "The Nature of Grief," *International Journal of Psychiatry* 3 (1967): 435–38; and *Bereavement: Studies of Grief in Adult Life* (New York: International Universities Press, 1972).

7. See Melanie Klein, "Mourning and Its Relation to Manic-Depressive States," in *Contributions to Psycho-Analysis 1921–1945* (New York: Hillary, 1940); George H. Pollock, "Mourning and Adaption," *International Journal of Psycho-Analysis* 42 (1961): 341–61; H. Leowald, "Internalization, Separation, Mourning and the Superego," *Psychoanalytic Quarterly* 31 (1962): 483–504; Edith Jacobson, "On Normal and Pathological Moods," *Psychoanalytic Study of the Child, vol. 12* (New York: International Universities Press, 1957), pp. 73–113; Edith Jacobson, "Introjection in Mourning," *International Journal of Psychiatry* 3 (1967): 433–35; Joseph H. Smith, "Identificatory Styles in Depression and Grief," *International Journal of Psycho-Analysis* 52 (1971): 259–66; and Erna Furman, *A Child's Parent Dies: Studies in Childhood Bereavement* (New Haven: Yale University Press, 1974).

8. Otto Fenichel, *The Psychoanalytic Theory of Neurosis* (New York: Norton, 1945), p. 394.

9. Charles Anderson, "Aspects of Pathological Grief and Mourning," in *Grief: Selected Readings*, ed. Arthur C. Carr et al. (New York: Health Sciences Publishing, 1975), p. 183.

10. David Peretz, "Development, Object-Relationships, and Loss," in *Loss and Grief: Psychological Management in Medical Practice*, ed. Bernard Schoenberg et al. (New York: Columbia University Press, 1970), p. 9.

11. Furman, *A Child's Parent Dies*, p. 256.

12. Joseph M. Smith, "On the Work of Mourning," in *Bereavement: Its Psychosocial Aspects*, ed. Bernard Schoenberg et al. (New York: Columbia University Press, 1975), pp. 20–25.

13. See Lily Pincus, *Death and the Family: The Importance of Mourning* (New York: Pantheon Books, 1974).

14. Furman, *A Child's Parent Dies*, pp. 256–63. See also May E. Romm, "Loss of Sexual Function in the Female," in *Loss and Grief*, ed. Schoenberg et al., pp. 178–88.

15. Rochlin, *Griefs and Discontents*, pp. 217–18.

16. William G. Niederland, "An Interpretation of the Psychological Stresses and Defenses in Concentration-Camp Life and the Late Aftereffects," in *Massive Psychic Trauma*, ed. Henry Krystal (New York: International Universities Press, 1968), pp. 65–66.

17. Ibid.

18. Robert J. Lifton, "Survivors of Hiroshima and Nazi Persecution," in *Massive Psychic Trauma*, ed. Krystal, pp. 179–80.

19. Bowlby, "Processes of Mourning," pp. 319–20.

20. Furman, *A Child's Parent Dies*, pp. 256–57.

21. Ibid.

22. Joan Fleming, "The Evolution of a Research Project in Psychoanalysis," in *Counterpoint: Libidinal Object and Subject*, ed. Herbert S. Gaskill (New York: International Universities Press, 1963), p. 76.

23. Vamik Volkan, "A Study of a Patient's 'Re-grief Work,' Through Dreams, Psychological Tests and Psychoanalysis," *Psychiatric Quarterly* 45 (1971): 255–73.

24. Vamik Volkan and C. Robert Showalter, "Known Object Loss, Disturbance in Reality Testing, and 'Re-grief Work' as a Method of Brief Psychotherapy," *Psychiatric Quarterly* 42 (1968): 358–74.

25. Henry Krystal and William G. Niederland, "Clinical Observations on the Survivor Syndrome," in *Massive Psychic Trauma*, pp. 343–44.

11/
Regression and
Helplessness

The memories of past experiences are stored in the unconscious, ever ready to emerge whenever repression cannot be maintained. Stress threatens repression, and a loss represents one type of stress under which a person may resort to the defense of regression, or a return to the past. Although regression has usually been regarded as one of the less adaptive forms of psychological defenses, this view is now beginning to be challenged.

Components of Regression

Regression under stress, if temporary, can be both benign and functional, allowing for a return to familiar ground until equilibrium is restored, energies renewed, and courage mobilized for moving on to new life struggles.

David Peretz summarized the types of regression that can be set off by loss as follows:

> In the event of loss, memories of childhood separations with accompanying bewilderment, confusion, and anxiety as well as associated aggressive impulses are stirred up. Regression can occur at the level of thought, feeling, defense, or activity as well as at the level of social relationships. A

bereaved individual may regress in the form of relationship he seeks in substitution for loss. He may regress in the kinds of more primitive defenses he uses to cope with the feelings stirred by loss. Or regression may occur in the character of the conceptualization he uses to integrate the experience of loss. The degree of stress which provokes regressive behavior varies, of course, from individual to individual.[1]

Psychoanalysts, writing on the trauma of illness, state that the "restorative value of regression has not received attention commensurate with its importance."[2] They cite Virginia Woolf as pointing out that our language does not provide even the words to properly describe regression. She suggested such language would have to be:

> More primitive, more sensual, more obscene, but a new hierarchy of passions; love must be deposed in favor of a temperature of 104; jealousy give place to the pangs of sciatica; sleeplessness play the part of the villain, and the hero become a white liquid with a sweet taste. . . .[3]

Many people have testified to the value of regression during a period of prolonged illness. Such a time allows for the cultivation of inner resources such as imagination, perception, and intellectual development not possible during the course of routine living. For example, Darwin's observations of nature during a period of prolonged illness culminated in his writing the *Origin of Species*. Growth and creative development are not the only outcomes of illness, however; emotional problems can also be expressed in chronic illness. One example is the return to infantile behavior in the gratification of wishes for passivity, and demands for care and for special consideration. In fact, the illness need not even be chronic for regression to take place. "He becomes a baby when he has a cold" has been said by more than one wife about her otherwise mature husband. In the emotionally healthy individual such regression is self-limiting and disappears with the cessation of the illness.

Regression is to be expected as a reaction to a catastrophic loss such as a terminal illness, whether in a child or an adult. Severely ill children may be expected to regress to anger, despair, and detachment or emotional "turning off." The child under age three cannot comprehend death, only separation. Thus, every separation sets off feelings of anxiety regarding the ultimate separation, abandonment. If the anxiety is overwhelming, the separations too frequent or prolonged, as measured by the child's inner feelings of suspenseful waiting, he may "turn off" emotionally.

The ability to tolerate suspenseful waiting develops in the infant with tolerable dosages of waiting that end in pleasure. The baby waits for the breast or bottle and is then rewarded by a good feeding. Mother goes away, then returns to a happy reunion. Later, children learn the stress of waiting for school vacations, birthdays, Christmas, and other holidays. Packages labelled "Do Not Open Until December 25" provide a valuable exercise in suspenseful waiting for an expected, happy outcome. Conversely, other childhood experiences lay down memories in the unconscious of pain rather than pleasure in connection with suspenseful waiting—for example, separations that are too frequent or are prolonged beyond the frustration tolerance level of the child at the time.

Persons with backgrounds of parental rejection are other examples of children subjected to painful, suspenseful waiting. They cannot relax and be sure they are safe. In most instances the rejection is not complete; there is sufficient physical care, at least, to insure their survival. In cases of child abuse, of course, there is no guarantee of even this. Somewhere a blow awaits, whether it is physical or psychological.

In later years, the adults who suffered such painful childhood experiences may resort to various defenses to avoid the pain of suspenseful waiting. Despite all attempts at self-control, they may crumble under the threat of loss. A pending job lay-off, absence from a loved one, threat to their own physical well-being, become unbearable stresses. Any pending loss represents the sword of Damocles hanging by a hair, and in their fantasies there can be but one outcome—the sword falls!

Behavior that on the surface may appear to be heartless or indifferent may sometimes be explained by the person's "turning off" emotionally or isolating feelings to avoid the stress of painful waiting. It is important that the helper perceive this behavior accurately so that the person is not seen as being cold or indifferent. Suicide is an irrevocable form by which vulnerable individuals can escape the pain of suspenseful waiting, a way of cutting down the sword rather than waiting for it to fall. A sensitive exploration of suicidal fantasies that reveal the desire to escape from pain might cut short the need to act out the behavior.

Regression is to be expected in situations of failure, with its accompanying loss of self-esteem. The rejected suitor seeks solace in oral regression to a chocolate sundae. Alcohol consumption can also be another form of regression in disappointment. The social rites of serving food to the bereaved and funeral guests are examples of the deep-seated belief that food can compensate for a loss. Individual alterations in eating patterns of the bereaved—the inability to eat, a sudden desire for food favored by the deceased, a sudden voracious appetite—also reflect regressive reactions in grief. This behavior is normal for the bereaved and is connected to their specific dynamics in the particular grief reaction, that is, restitution for the loss, identification with the deceased, and so on.

Regression in loss can also be found in bowel and bladder changes. People have reported periods of constipation or diarrhea, as well as urinary problems, following a loss. The loss of sexual interest, loss of concern about others, and narcissistic preoccupation with the self are other examples of regression in loss and are to be expected.

Regression may also take place on a thought level. A widower speaks sorrowfully of the loss of his wife. Within a few moments his talk turns to the loss of his mother ten years earlier. On the surface it may appear that the memory of his mother overshadows that of his wife. It may, indeed, be that he seeks relief from current pain in the memory of a more remote loss. On the other hand, it can also be that the loss of one nurturing figure has set off the memory of an earlier similar loss.

Regression in Victimization

People subjected to protracted life-endangering traumas such as concentration camp experiences were reported to have reacted with regression to sadomasochistic, oral, and narcissistic levels. It has been written of these victims that "regression and deforming of the ego were the only reality-oriented adaptations available to the people living in the 'psychotic culture' . . . of Nazi persecution."[4]

Those prisoners who were adolescents in the concentration camps were among the most disturbed survivors. For them the camp experience of personal maltreatment, degradation, and assaults, as well as separation from and loss of family members, came at a time when the normal developmental tasks were those of mastering oedipal conflicts and breaking ties with parental internalized objects. The camp experience forced a regression from the oedipal level to a pre-oedipal, anal-retentive, and sadistic level through the more urgent need to hold on to the real object, from whom there was threatened and real separation through transfer to another camp or death.[5]

Many severe forms of neurosis reportedly went into remission during the trauma of the Nazi prison camps. Later, however, after the victims were released, many of the old neurotic disorders reappeared. Cases like these need treatment by experts in the field of victimization. Helpers should avoid attempting to deal with pathology that demands a degree of skill beyond their ability.

One of the most important forms of regression in loss is the return to earlier ways of relating to people. This brings us to a consideration of helplessness, a complex topic that is the subject of the rest of this chapter. The greater the emotional investment in something or someone, the greater the threat of loss and the greater the reaction when loss occurs. A major loss is unconsciously a basic threat to survival. Because of this deep relationship between loss and survival, a major loss or the threat of one sets off in most people a sense of helplessness.

Psychodynamics of Helplessness and Dependency

Helplessness is being without power to help oneself, being feeble or weak, or feeling incompetent and inefficient. From the point of view of learning theory, "a person or animal is *helpless* with respect to some outcome when the outcome occurs independently of all his *voluntary* responses."[6]

Helplessness in grief can be experienced as extremely painful. There are two aspects to this pain—the helplessness in longing for that which is irretrievable, and the helplessness in facing the future without that which has been lost.

Data from animal studies show that many animal species exist in highly organized social systems of mutual help. The ability to depend on others in the group helps insure survival. If this is true among animals, perhaps it is conceivable that people, too, need others at times of crisis in their lives and loss is such a crisis. Temporary regression to the point of helplessness in the crisis of grief may be considered a normal and healthy reaction in the service of survival and reattachment to others. The ability to depend on others is at the core of human survival.

There are problems with regard to this ideal model, however. The problem may lie within the environment, within the personality of the bereaved, within the situation, or a combination of any or all of these factors. Because of these complexities, one sees in bereavement a muddled picture regarding helplessness. (Some of the typical kinds of problems one encounters will be dealt with later in this chapter under Implications for Intervention.) In the well-integrated personality confronted by one of the normal losses of life (in contrast to victimization), helplessness is usually temporary. Others, however, given the same losses, can feel as abandoned as an infant left to care for himself.

In the final analysis, we are all helpless in the face of cosmic forces. Although we try through much of our lives to control some of the forces impinging on us, it is loss that brings home to us our ultimate helplessness in the face of forces beyond our control. It is foolhardy to claim that man is the ultimate master of his fate. Events beyond our control are a part of the universe in which we have our being. No major loss can be resolved without coming to grips with these universal feelings of helplessness.

The most direct solution to helplessness is through dependence on another person. The *Psychiatric Dictionary* defines dependency as "a form of behavior which suggests inability to make decisions; marked inclination to lean on others for advice, guidance, support, etc. . . . Dependency reflects needs for mothering, love, affection, shelter, protection, security, food, warmth, etc."[7]

Morbid dependency is a form of self-effacement manifested in a compulsive need to surrender to and unite with a stronger person. Alvin I. Goldfarb, one of the leading theorists on dependency and an expert on aging, describes dependency as:

> a complex exploitative maneuver elaborated by one who is or regards himself to be weak, in transaction with another or others whom he considers strong and potentially helpful. The "weak" individual strives to dominate and manipulate the "strong" one, sometimes directly and at other times by emphasizing his own subservience and submission. The tactics employed range from ingratiation and seduction to angry domination and coercion, and provoke emotions ranging from the affectionate to the openly guilty, hostile, and angry. . . . The aim, in essence, is to convert the selected individual into a protector who will . . . help him cope with an environment perceived as hostile and threatening.
>
> In effect, this is a form of magical thinking; it is an attempt, by the use of complex behavior patterns, to gain the powers believed to reside in certain others.[8]

Maturation from dependency to autonomy occurs when major dependency needs have first been optimally met. The optimal conditions seem to be that the needs should have been gratified to a high peak of satisfaction and yet not overgratified to encourage fixation. Babies should nurse to their fill and not be taken from the breast or bottle while still hungry. They should not, however, be kept on the breast or bottle so long or so exclusively that they have no incentive to experiment with new types of food. The same pattern goes on throughout life in movement between dependency gratifications and risk taking. Research indicates that ungratified dependency or punishment dependency, insufficient gratification of dependency, or punishment for dependency, increases the need for dependency as well as the anxiety over it. "In theory, at least, the circle set up not only is vicious, but widens by feeding upon itself."[9]

It has been suggested that total self-sufficiency is probably never achieved. None of us is ever completely independent of the need for a trusted, helpful person who can be called on if necessary. "Originally the person was a parent; later someone else; and eventually, we must depend on our own identifications with internal images from many sources."[10]

Cultural attitudes toward helplessness and dependency

American society is confused about helplessness and dependency. This confusion finds expression in child-rearing practices and in attitudes toward people in need—the poor, the elderly, the sick, and the bereaved. Because all of us, the bereaved and helpers alike, are products of the same patterns of socialization, helpers are likely to have the same cultural bias and to share the same confusions as those they are trying to help. Let us examine some of the discrepancies between psychological theories and cultural attitudes in regard to helplessness and dependency.

Dependency has traditionally had a pejorative connotation in American tradition. It is the independent person who has been considered worthy of social esteem. Not too many years ago taking help from the community was considered shameful. In fact, some extremists refused to enroll in the Social Security program in the early days of its operation because they were unable to distinguish between an insurance program toward which they contributed and "taking charity from the government." It can be argued that our society has come full circle in that all too many people today regard the government as a source for an easy handout. Suffice it to say that many people still feel that seeking professional help for emotional problems indicates a lack of character. For some people even seeking medical care for physical problems carries the same stigma.

Many observers of American life have noted the anxiety and isolation inherent in our definition of freedom as independence. This cultural demand places great stress on the bereaved. Where sorrow propels one toward contact with another for support and comfort, the cultural view of dependency as a neurotic trait indicating weakness of character puts the bereaved in a bind.

Goldfarb exposes the discrepancy between our cultural attitude toward dependency and our societal behavior in regard to it. He postulates that American society socializes children for lifelong dependency while proclaiming self-reliance and independence as virtues.[11] On the one hand, children are encouraged to do things on their own with parents proud about how independent and mature they are for their age. On the other hand, children are given subtle messages to follow parental guidelines. To add to the confusion, peer pressures on the adolescent demand an early emancipation from parents, probably at an age that is earlier than the child's emotional preparedness for it.

In Western society, illness is a crisis during which regression to dependency is permitted, provided it is only temporary. Illness that goes beyond the acute stage into chronicity, however, means that the person has become a threat to others and is considered unproductive and burdensome to family and community by being unable to "give back" to them in exchange for their care. The timetable assigned to a crisis-linked regression has traditionally been about six weeks. Beyond that period the person is considered a psychiatric casualty rather than in a state of crisis. The sanction that accrues to this negative status is that of stigmatization. For decades the bereaved whose grief-related dependency continued beyond this socially prescribed and theoretically pronounced period of regression have been treated as if they had nothing valuable to offer in exchange.

It is understandable that families and friends might become exhausted at the prolonged dependency needs of the bereaved because of stresses in their own lives, often from the same loss. They are, however, the people on whom one feels one has the greatest claim for help and support.

However, many functions which were previously fulfilled by the extended family have now been turned over to professional caretakers in our society. Care of the dead and the ill are among such functions. The funeral industry is becoming increasingly interested in the dynamics of grief and mourning. Unfortunately, such concern is not spreading as rapidly among modern caretakers, including hospital personnel, proprietors of nursing and convalescent homes, and so on. When a person grows old, becomes ill, or is injured, therefore, it means separation from the very people who could be most helpful in offering concern and support. Loneliness and depression can result from separation from loved ones.

People bereaved by other situations—divorce, school or work-related failures, rape, immigration—are also often left to fend for themselves. The conflict surrounding dependency finds its final expression in old age, a time of cumulative losses and increased dependency needs. In working with the middle-aged one discovers that the greatest fear people express about growing old is that of being sick and having nobody there. Because, in reality, there can almost always be somebody there, if only a paid caretaker, the real fear here is that there will be no significant other left on whom one has a right through relationship or affection to make a claim for dependency and care.

In regard to this problem of dependency facing the elderly in American society, it has been said that:

> The elderly person must not only face the imminence of death, but also of the loss of ability to perform tasks for which he had been so thoroughly rewarded, such as walking, writing, reading, and of course that act of such concern to contemporary *and* turn-of-the-century America—control of the elimination processes. With each degree of loss of physical and intellectual

alertness, and equally tragically, with each degree of assumption that this loss will occur, dependency becomes more immediate and very likely more frightening. . . .

The aging individual in our society will perceive his increasing need to be dependent not only as an unfortunate regression, but as a regression to a helpless, disapproved, anxiety-arousing state for which he himself has internalized negative values. His intense feeling of wishing to avoid being a burden to his children reflects his continuing approval of independence, individual happiness, and a limited role for the elderly in our society. If these surmises are true, the self-concept of the elderly is embedded in a web of its own making.[12]

Evaluating helplessness

Helplessness is not a global matter calling for a single approach to intervention. Each case needs to be evaluated as to the type of help-lessness, the form taken, the underlying dynamics, and the kind of intervention needed.

There may be a healthy attempt on the part of the bereaved to regress to temporary helplessness and dependency with adequate supports available to allow for this regression. Mrs. Victor, in planning for surgery, was told by her physician that she must not do any work or bend down for six weeks following the operation. In response to her active questioning, she learned that bending down meant not lowering her head below the shoulders. This meant no cooking, cleaning, pulling on a girdle, tying shoes, putting on stockings, moving so much as a chair, or straining in any way. She arranged for household help every other day for the first week, then for gradually decreasing frequency throughout the period of convalescence. Her husband and adult children took turns staying with her so that she was never left alone. She notified all her friends that she needed company. As a result she enjoyed her period of temporary regression to dependency and made an excellent recovery.

Children need support through tragedies that to the adult may appear insignificant. The loss of pets is one area where parents can be supportive to children in grief. Mrs. Grey, a widow with two young children, was aware of the importance of loss in their lives. Mary, age nine, became hysterical one day when she noticed that the parakeet did not fly. "It's dying and you don't care!" she screamed at her mother. The mother believed that at some deep level Mary was really saying "Daddy died and you didn't stop it so you must not have cared." Gathering up the children and the parakeet in the car, the mother drove to the neighborhood veterinarian. After examining the bird carefully, he delivered his diagnosis: the bird did not fly because it was molting and had lost a tail feather. It was in good health and would fly again. The children returned home reassured and happy, and the mother felt it was time, energy, and money well spent.

Support surrounding the loss of a parent is another matter. Research on parent loss through death revealed that few, if any, parents were able to give young children the full support needed in their grief because the remaining parent was bereaved by the same loss.[13] The loss of a grandparent can also be a trauma to a child, because the parent grieving the death of his own parent is emotionally unavailable to the child. One cannot be helpless and a helper at the same time.

Helplessness about one loss may be displaced and expressed in regard to another. This is one reason why major and minor losses cannot be differentiated; in the unconscious they are all dynamically related. For example, a newly divorced woman had developed a boil on a finger that had to be lanced; the medical procedure carried out under anesthesia involved no physical pain. As the doctor began to lance the boil, however, Mrs. White began weeping helplessly. The physician continued his work. When it was completed, he said gently: "Now, I wasn't hurting you, was I? You weren't crying over the finger. It was something else, wasn't it?" She nodded silently, and although she did not discuss the divorce with him, she was comforted by his tender concern. The helplessness of the situation in which she found herself—the loss involved in the minor surgery which was, nevertheless, an attack upon her body—had set off the helplessness she felt about the marriage moving toward its own inevitable breaking point. The presence of a supportive other, sympathetic but strong, allowed her to regress to helplessness during the procedure.

The feeling of helplessness may be centered on the inability to carry out necessary tasks. This temporary loss of ability to function is a part of normal grief. It can take on extreme forms, however, when the bereaved are confronted by completely new tasks. The woman who is socialized to be dependent on her husband is one such example. In the event of his death or loss through divorce, she may be unprepared to carry on alone, not because she is incapable of doing so, but because she has been socialized to feel that she is. The tasks of picking up her life alone may appear beyond her ability, and she may exhaust relatives and friends or arouse their anger as self-protection against exploitation. Denied the opportunity to learn to handle finances, insurance, car maintenance, home upkeep, and repairs under benign conditions, not to mention her unpreparedness as a wage earner, she is now confronted by all of these tasks and responsibilities at a time of crisis and disorganization in her life. Early bereavement is not the time for learning new tasks or for being expected to perform efficiently in areas where one was formerly rewarded for dependency. Such new widows or divorcees ideally need an opportunity to experience both emotional and practical helplessness, with competent people on whom to lean. Gradually, they need help to take over the tasks formerly handled by their husbands. This new learning can become part of the reintegration of the new personality they will, if fortunate, assume eventually in the process of restitution for the loss.

As an example of how such dependency can be avoided, a professional man who was told he had nine months to live because of an advanced cancer, set about teaching his dependent wife all the business details of their life. She described the pain of trying to struggle with this learning under the conditions of his anticipated death. The man, however, survived and today, fifteen years later, the wife is a competent, participating partner in the marriage and will not have to learn these practical details in the event of her husband preceding her in death as they both move into the later years.

The feeling of helplessness may be situational, due to diminished capacity to cope because of physical illness or other concurrent losses. Each of us has a breaking point. When losses come singly or at least spaced far enough apart to allow for recovery between them, an individual might be able to cope effectively. The same person, in poor health, or faced by too many losses at once, may not have the energy to struggle further. Mrs. Taylor felt burdened with the dependency of her aged father. He had managed to cope effectively following the death of his wife five years before. He continued to live in his apartment, had a cleaning person come in once a week, and was able to prepare his own breakfasts and lunches even though Mrs. Taylor prepared his dinners by cooking several times a week and refrigerating prepared meals.

Following a hernia operation two years later, however, a decided change was noticed in the father. He seemed to lose all initiative in caring for himself. In effect, Mrs. Taylor was now running her father's household as well as her own. If she brought him food, he ate. If she invited him to visit, he came and socialized with her family and guests. If she arranged for it, his apartment was cleaned. If she did his laundry, he had clean clothes. The second loss seemed to be more than he could handle, and he remained in the state of dependency to which he had regressed. He needed an opportunity to share his feelings with a person who could allow him to grieve and eventually to make the decision whether he wanted to live independently or move into an environment where he did not have to take care of himself. One needs to always keep in mind that the rewards need to justify the struggle. "Why should I bother with this artificial leg," asked one old woman, "when the only place I have to go is up and down the corridor in the home for the aged?"

A distinction needs to be made between the emotional feeling of helplessness and inability to function. Despite loss, life does go on for both the bereaved and those intimately associated with them. Where the bereaved are unable to function, someone else may need to take over temporarily, whether it be relatives, friends, a paid homemaker, or in extreme situations even through hospitalization. Decision making is in itself a burden. Judgment needs to be used in ascertaining when the bereaved is capable of taking decision-making responsibility and when this responsibility should be turned over to others. Although it is true that the bereaved must experience helplessness at some point in the grief process before recovery can proceed fully, they should not be pushed into it prematurely. Allowing the bereaved to control situations where judgment is sound may permit a necessary interim period of defense against helplessness.

The feeling of helplessness may be due to the person's being overwhelmed by his own impulses and feelings set off by the loss. Here the bereaved need help in identifying and expressing separately their feelings of anger, yearning, envy, hatred, wish for revenge, dependency, and sexual impulses, as well as their fantasies of retaliation from others for any of these thoughts and feelings.

The feeling of helplessness can be set off by the meaning of the loss to the individual. Aging, a mastectomy, a colostomy, or other bodily trauma can be a severe narcissistic blow to some people, who then see themselves as old, unattractive, and rejected and may regress to an early state of helplessness and the attention-getting behavior of illness and anxiety.

The person with a chronic, progressive illness can be overcome with a feeling of helplessness with each setback. To the patient with bone cancer, every new bone that cracks is a new loss and a reminder of the ultimate potential loss of life itself. One is helpless in the face of the relentless onslaught of the disease process and needs sustaining, tender concern, as well as permission to grieve over the ongoing losses.

The feeling of helplessness may also be manifested as depression. Dr. Howard, aged forty-four, married, and the mother of three children, was aware of being depressed. She attributed it to an early menopause, although she had no menopausal symptoms. Her year-old son had had sleep problems since birth. He woke often during the night, and nothing would comfort him but being held by his mother. Although there was live-in help, Dr. Howard lost sleep every night. This problem with the infant kept her from returning to her profession after the birth of the child. Dr. Howard wondered if the baby might be hyperkinetic and able to benefit from drug therapy, but her husband was against "drugging a baby," as he put it.

The history revealed that the depressive feelings had started six years earlier when Dr. Howard learned that her father had lung cancer. As a physician she suffered deeply, knowing the fate in store for him. Helpless, despite her medical training, she watched him go through years of medical procedures and pain before his final death.

It was in this state of unresolved grief and depression that Dr. Howard gave birth to her son. Her depression made her emotionally unavailable to the infant, thus leaving him unsatisfied and wakeful, further depleting the mother and making it impossible for her to return to her profession, yet another loss. Particularly significant was the fact that in the small community where the family lived there was no one on whom she could be dependent at this time of need in her own life. Her widowed mother, herself a dependent person, turned to the Howard family for fulfillment of her own dependency needs. Unfortunately, there were no psychotherapeutic services available in this small and isolated community that might have been helpful in breaking this cycle of depression and dependency.

The problem of helplessness and dependency in grief is complicated by the fact that there are people who are neurotically dependent personality types; they always look to others to solve problems for them rather than attempt to solve them through their own efforts. For these individuals the helplessness set off by grief would merely exacerbate an already existing pattern rather than represent the benign regression in crisis described earlier. A woman with a postpartum depression may be an example of neurotic dependency. The woman who develops a depression following childbirth (and the same is possible following adoption) can be seen as a dependent, infantile person, one threatened by normal adjustments to life, and now threatened by the dependence of the helpless infant. This has been described well by May E. Romm:

> What a mature woman accepts as a privilege and as a joy [the responsibility of nurturing her newborn child] represents to her a disaster. She mourns the loss of her dependent state. The baby, toward whom she is ambivalent, creates anger and guilt within her. This may account for her fear, which may be turned into action, that she will injure or murder the child. When such rage is repressed by her, it may be internalized with the possibility that she may attempt suicide.[14]

This condition calls for psychiatric intervention.

Defenses and Barriers against Helplessness

We have dealt so far with forms of helplessness one might encounter in bereavement. The inability to regress to dependency and helplessness can also be a problem. All of us function through the development of ego defenses against unconscious feelings and drives. Helplessness is one of the unconscious feelings that, because of the anxiety aroused, often calls for the erection of strong defenses.

Because the resolution of grief demands the experiencing of universal feelings of helplessness in the face of existential loss, those individuals whose major defenses are built around avoidance of feelings of helplessness may be among those likely to have dysfunctional reactions to grief. Thus, the individuals who normally function most competently on the surface may be the very ones thrown more heavily by a major loss as it strikes at the core of their defensive system.

Mrs. Young was a sixty-five year-old widow whose only child lived in a distant part of the country. She planned to take care of herself following surgery for cataracts. The physician who operated on her gave her no instructions for post-operative care except to "take it easy for a few weeks." She did not know exactly what that meant, nor was she secure enough to ask. She planned to return to her home where she lived alone. Her closest friend and former neighbor had recently moved to another community some ten miles away. She still came to help Mrs. Young with the shopping about once a month, and Mrs. Young thought this arrangement would work out fine. However, there was no one to cook, clean, help her dress, bathe, move around the house in her new state of visual disorientation, much less to provide companionship or comfort. She cast aside the suggestion that she spend a few weeks in a convalescent home because "my husband spent seven years in one of those places, and you couldn't get me near one!" When asked who would help take care of her, she replied stoically: "I'll take care of myself! I always have!"

Some people may be unable to regress to a state of helplessness in grief because of responsibility for others. The parent left to care for young children alone is a case in point. The single parent who must work, keep house, shop, cook, clean, drive the children to school, doctor, and dental appointments, has little opportunity to indulge in the regression to helplessness. Other people accustomed to fulfilling the role of the competent person in a family may find that they are not allowed to step out of this assigned role when they themselves are overtaken by a loss.

Mrs. Edwards, aged sixty-four, was referred for psychotherapy following a suicide attempt after the death of her husband. She did not remember any suicide attempt, only that she could not sleep, was worried about it, took a glass of wine, then some sleeping pills, and the next thing she knew she was in the hospital. She felt no need for help. She came only because she had promised the hospital social worker she would do so, and she always kept a promise. Despite her lack of motivation, she came dutifully for several weeks, then stopped coming. The therapist telephoned her and learned she was preoccupied with the care of an aged aunt who had just been released from the hospital following a stroke. After working all day, Mrs. Edwards drove ten miles to take care of the aunt and her apartment, then drove another twenty miles to her own home. She complained that she was exhausted both physically and emotionally but could not see any way out because she was her aunt's only remaining relative.

In response to her request, she was helped to find a nursing home for the aunt in her own part of the city. This cut down her travel time, but she was still not free to deal with her own grief. In fact, she complained of having physical ailments for which she did not even have time to see the doctor. The aunt telephoned her daily, complaining that she was all alone, and asking that Mrs. Edwards visit her. Mrs. Edwards knew she was overdoing the role of caretaker but added "I have been doing this all my life and don't know how to stop now." She was unable to distinguish between the aunt's legitimate needs and neurotic dependency demands, and remained caught in her own neurotic pattern of succoring others as a defense against full awareness of her own needs.

For some people, words and the physical presence of another are not sufficient to enable them to feel safe in regressing to dependency. They may need actual physical support to counteract their fear of "falling apart." Mrs. Paul was widowed following her husband's struggle with lung cancer over a period of eighteen months. She was left with two young sons, ages two and four. Mobilizing her resources and strength, she moved her young family to an urban community where she found work and carried on competently for a number of years. The children grew and were healthy. But there were other tragedies. Just at the point where Mrs. Paul was ready to remarry, her fiance was killed in an automobile accident. The death by drowning of her younger son at the age of twenty-three was the final blow which brought her to therapy.

For weeks she grieved quietly, with tears streaming down her face, but her face was taut, although appropriately sad, angry, sorrowful, guilty. Finally, at one point the therapist said: "I think you need to be held." Going over to where Mrs. Paul sat, the therapist put her arms around her, and suddenly the tears began to flow. Mrs. Paul not only sobbed helplessly, she also shook with what could best be described as an uncontrollable trembling of her entire body. This went on for some minutes as she commented: "I can't stop shaking." Finally, the shaking and crying stopped, and Mrs. Paul was able to allow herself to sit limp and relaxed. She assured the therapist that she would be able to drive home safely.

At the next session Mrs. Paul reported that after driving a few blocks she had to stop because she was crying so hard. It was some time before she could trust herself to drive the rest of the way home. She continued crying at home and found it such a relief because there were no pressing household tasks and she could afford to be helpless. She stayed home the next day from work because she felt "wiped out" and continued to weep. By the following day she was fatigued but somehow deeply relieved and able to resume some routine activities. Later she reflected on the physical support offered her and felt that it had been most meaningful. "I couldn't cry alone," she said. "I resisted crying out of fear that I would just come apart. Do you know I have never been able to let go like this ever in my life. Now I can cry alone at home and get relief from it. But I could not have done it without that first physical support."

Suicidal remarks can arouse anxiety in any helper, but it is important that the underlying meaning be explored. Fleeting suicidal thoughts or expressions such as "It should have happened to me instead of to him" or "It would be easier for everyone if I were dead" may be more expressions of helplessness and guilt than signs of serious suicidal intent. The remark may be an indirect bid for reassurance that one is worthy of attention and concern from others. On the other hand, the guilt, depression, or pain may be severe enough to make the possibility of suicide a real danger.

Normal attempts at regression may be thwarted by family and friends who do not understand the need or cannot tolerate the dependency of the bereaved. This leaves the bereaved wondering what is wrong with them that they cannot mobilize their forces to carry on as effectively as others think they should. This situation constitutes a good example of the blind leading the blind. If the bereaved cannot find someone who can give the help needed both practically and emotionally, one can predict later difficulties. Although the surface appearance may be that of adequate coping following a loss, one can anticipate trouble later, perhaps following a further loss. Buried emotions may be kept underground for years but inevitably will surface into physical, emotional, or behavioral problems.

At times of loss, feelings of resentment among family members can surface as a reaction to the stress under which they are laboring. The healthy person protects himself from revealing vulnerability in the presence of hostile others. Helplessness is such a vulnerability. Feelings in grief are easily shut off by attack, envy, ridicule, or lack of understanding.

Feelings of helplessness can be defended against by "dumping" them on others. Depressed persons are adept at this maneuver. They externalize their helplessness by making others, including would-be helpers, feel helpless. They ask for help but respond with a "yes, but" to every suggestion or offer.

Attacking others is another form of "dumping" uncomfortable feelings, including those of helplessness. Kate Holliday's article, referred to in chapter three, in which she described the changes in her life resulting from a shoulder injury brought a rash of letters to the *Los Angeles Times*. She was attacked in many of the letters for her disgusting self-pity and her ludicrous search for an answer to why the situation had happened. In the course of berating her, the writers referred to their own handicaps and their absence of self-pity. It does not take much imagination to realize that the anger of the letter-writers stemmed from their own barely repressed feelings of helplessness and self-pity, which had been stirred up by her openness.

Some writers on grief claim that those people who choose to enter the medical profession may have greater conflicts regarding loss than the average person, conflicts that may have been an important unconscious motivation in their selection of a profession. Medicine, after all, is devoted to caring for life, and modern technology has made the prolongation of life possible beyond man's wildest dreams. Yet the Hippocratic oath taken by all medical graduates stems from a time in history when medical intervention was crude and fumbling.

The demand this ancient pledge to sustain life makes on physicians who command a variety of life-saving techniques capable of prolonging life beyond the wishes of the patient and the family, and beyond the point where life has any meaning, is awesome and leaves them in an ethical dilemma. Death is inevitable, but the death of a patient represents for physicians a threat to their identity as helpers and is for some a threat to the remnants of childhood feelings of omnipotence which their choice of profession allowed. It is understandable, therefore, that physicians would need to defend themselves against such constant and daily attacks on their self-esteem. One way in which they can do this is by "turning off" emotionally from the dying patient, rather than sustaining him and his family through this crisis in their lives. Ridding themselves of feelings of helplessness by projecting them onto the patient is another way to defend against threats to self-esteem.

Helplessness and dependency in victimization

It would be an error, however, to overlook another type of loss, one that does not end in helplessness but rather begins with it. This is the loss that occurs in such situations as rape, child and wife abuse, concentration camp experiences, kidnappings, and other acts of victimization suffered by one human being at the hands of another.

Studies of concentration camp survivors can serve as a prototype for understanding other experiences of victimization. Chronic starvation, enforced labor, physical attacks, brutality, and degrading forms of abuse resulted in many victims succumbing within a few weeks or months to a state of starvation and death in the concentration camps. For those who did not succumb, "This tactic was an effective means of creating a protracted life-endangering situation, in a state of total helplessness."[15] This psychopathology was engendered by confronting the individuals with a "massive sadistic assault, to which the prisoner could only submit masochistically."[16] Masochistic submission in the interest of survival characterizes other situations of terror as well. Rape victims, for example, report that the most frightful part of their ordeal is the feeling of complete helplessness in the power of another.

The subject of human violence, man's inhumanity to his fellowman, is increasingly receiving attention from students of human behavior. Concern about what appears to be an increasing amount of violence spurs us on to try to understand this behavior in an attempt to control it. The state of knowledge about such violence, however, is still in its infancy. We return to traditional theories of human behavior again and again for answers; the answers may not be in those theories. Just as in physical science and in medicine, the discovery of new forces, planets, disease entities, and illnesses provides a stimulus to new research, so in the study of the human mind, we need to be open to new understanding.

An admission of ignorance is the beginning of wisdom. A professional working with Vietnam War psychiatric casualties admitted that professional helpers are often at a loss to understand the pathology they encounter in these people. Is it due to pretraumatic character problems, cultural factors, drugs, physical or emotional trauma from the war itself, disease of unknown origin, any or all of these, or some other as yet unknown factors?

Survivors of victimization do not need to regress to the point of helplessness as described in the major portion of this chapter. They have already been reduced to this state by their sadistic tormentors. Their difficulty is rather to reestablish trust in human worth and in human relationships. They have been physically, mentally, and morally trampled on by sadists seeking in their acts of violence the illusion of omnipotence to defend against feelings of impotence and emptiness. As Erich Fromm proposed:

> The core of sadism, common to all its manifestations, is the passion to have
> absolute and unrestricted control over a living being, whether an animal, a

child, a man, or a woman. To force someone to endure pain and humiliation without being able to defend himself is one of the manifestations of
absolute control. . . . The person who has complete control over another
living being makes this being into his thing, his property, while he becomes
the other being's god.[17]

It should not be surprising to the helper to find, therefore, that a
common defense among the survivors of victimization is the avoidance of involvement in personal relationships; this includes the relationship with a helping person. Intimacy holds the threat of further
loss. Overt aggression against the therapist, rejection of offers of help,
and other protective maneuvers are among the defenses used. The
helper must also be aware, however, that, "When one is successful in
overcoming the patient's initial fear and aggression, he takes on a
personal responsibility—for thereafter, abandonment of the patient
may destroy him."[18]

Implications for Intervention

Although mental health approaches usually stress the importance
of the person's taking responsibility for his own life, grief remains one
area where it is not only permissible but also essential and healthy that
one turn to another for help. We exist as social beings; without others
we could not survive. None of us can deal with helplessness alone.
Support to the bereaved is a most important element in determining
the ability to recover from a loss.

Sharing grief protects the bereaved from feeling deserted, isolated,
and abandoned to the regression and helplessness which is aroused by
any major loss. Once the grief has been shared with another, the
memory of the support received and of the fact that a supportive
figure exists may help sustain the bereaved through periods of private
grieving. It is helplessness unsupported by the protective presence of
another that can lead to that most dangerous state, a feeling of hopelessness. (This important topic will be dealt with fully in the next
chapter.)

It does not take a professional or an expert to offer support to the
bereaved. Caring, warmth, respect, empathy, hope, and the attempt
to understand are what help connect the bereaved to another human
being and counteract hopelessness stemming from the feeling of
abandonment. Helpers need also to be strong. They do not join the
bereaved in their helplessness. Hurt children do not need their
mother crying with them—this would frighten them even more. They
need a bandage for the scraped knee, reassurance, a hug, and a kiss.
Because of the bereaved's need for strength in the other, it is not
surprising to find that where several people have been affected by the

same loss, they may be of little comfort to each other in grief, although they may be cooperative in carrying out necessary instrumental tasks.

The would-be helper who joins the bereaved in their helplessness can leave them fixated in a state of dependency or, on the contrary, can lead them to dam up their grief so as to protect both the helping person and themselves. It is this need to protect the other and the realization at some level of awareness that one cannot lean on someone as helpless as oneself that keeps the bereaved from being able to mourn either with another who is in mourning over the same tragedy, or with a helper who cannot tolerate dependency.

A mother whose adult son had committed suicide could not "let down" in the presence of her daughter, who had suffered her own traumatic bereavement through the death of her brother. Both women needed outside help to work through the tumultuous feelings set off by the loss. It had to be from someone outside their circle of relationships, where each was free to express her particular range of feelings, both positive and negative, without fear of hurting the other through the pain set off by reminders of the loss or through differences in feelings about the same loss.

It may be the inability of people who have suffered the same loss to comfort each other that contributes to the high rate of marital dissolution that frequently follows in the wake of a family tragedy such as the death of a child, the birth of a defective child, or other traumatic loss. Anger, helplessness, dependency, and other highly charged emotions can break a relationship that is already tenuous or cause one spouse to flee from the pain of the other.

In attempting with one patient to understand why she had failed to receive help from the preeminent psychoanalysts to whom she had gone following the death of her original analyst before her treatment was completed, it became apparent that his death had been such a traumatic blow to the therapeutic community that her grieving could not be endured by her subsequent therapists because her pain threatened to set off their own unresolved feelings about the same loss.

One of the greatest fears of student social workers, and this may be true of other helping professionals as well, is that clients will become dependent on them. "How will I ever get rid of him if that happens?" is the panic-stricken query. To work effectively with grief, therefore, it is necessary that helpers have experienced their own dependency and helplessness in the context of a supportive relationship. Helpers who must defend against their own fear of dependency by seeing themselves only in the helping role will unconsciously feel superior to those who come to them for help. They may even consciously or unconsciously manipulate a patient to remain dependent to meet their own needs.

Gaining one's feeling of self-esteem at the expense of another less fortunate is hardly the essence of therapeutic help. The helper today can become the bereaved tomorrow through a loss in his own life. Ideally, helpers of the bereaved should be those who have experienced their own past losses and come to a healthy resolution of them. Treatment of the bereaved needs to emerge from a compassion based on recognition of the common vulnerability of all human beings in the face of loss.

Regression surrounding normal losses needs to be dealt with by compassion, understanding, and acceptance to enable the growth process to be reactivated, if restitution is a possibility. When decline is inevitable, as in progressive illness, increasing support is called for. Without such understanding the person can be stigmatized as immature and pushed to move forward, a maneuver doomed to disappointment. One of the most sensitive accounts of professional help showing regression, dependency, and helplessness in loss is contained in Janice Norton's account of her treatment of a dying patient.[19] It is her case summary of her treatment during the last three-and-one-half months of life of a thirty-two-year-old married woman, the mother of two children, who died of cancer. Norton's involvement resulted from the fact that everyone else on whom the patient tried to rely—family, friends, the clergy, other physicians—had already abandoned her as well as their roles in her life out of their fear of death and dying. Norton described the essence of her work as follows:

> The treatment of this patient can be simply summarized as a process in which I helped the patient to defend herself against object loss by facilitating the development of a regressive relationship to me which precluded object loss. . . .
>
> In summary, the essential therapeutic tools in the treatment of the dying patient are the therapist's constant availability as an object, his reliability, his empathy, and his ability to respond appropriately to the patient's needs.[20]

Norton stresses that an essential prerequisite to work with the dying patient (and this is but one form of loss) is a conscious acceptance of one's countertransference or feelings set off by the bereaved. These feelings include guilt, injury to healthy narcissism, mobilization of childhood death wishes, reminders of one's own mortality, anxiety, and anger. Without such an open awareness of one's own feelings, defenses against these feelings can intrude in the helping process in the form of denial, false reassurance, repression, overprotectiveness, false optimism, intellectualization, withdrawal, or pushing away. We cannot suffer for another. We can only stand by. Helpers need to become aware of the limits of their effectiveness and avoid the temptation of rushing into activity to counteract feelings of helplessness. Validation of feelings is one key to help. None of us can spare the bereaved pain. We can only let them know that they are not abandoned.

With people who are neurotically dependent personality types expert psychotherapeutic intervention is needed to deal with both the legitimate grief reaction as well as the underlying personality disorder, lest the person drain others or push them away by constant and increasing demands. The clue to this type of personality disorder is contained in the theoretical formulation in regard to dependency outlined earlier in this chapter. Healthy dependency needs when met tend to decrease with the natural push toward growth and autonomy. Neurotic dependency needs when met only increase in magnitude. In short, whether in anticipatory grief of the dying patient or the acute grief following a loss, the bereaved need a helper who can tolerate their regression and helplessness and stay with them both physically, when necessary, and, certainly, emotionally. Abandonment is the greatest fear and danger in bereavement.

Thus far the feeling of helplessness that underlies loss as a part of the existential tragedy for all of us has been dealt with. The therapeutic task here is to assist the bereaved in experiencing their helplessness to the fullest in the presence of a supportive other so that they can then start the road back to some feeling of control over their life, where this is possible.

There is much room for an educational approach as well. Regarding dependence in old age Richard A. Kalish says:

> Any corrective action would necessitate changes in values regarding dependence, helplessness, and privacy. . . . Change to be effective must proceed along two tacks: first, trying to help people at all age levels to accept dependence as natural and appropriate and not place great stress on independent behavior; and, second, to offer people at all age levels, especially children, the opportunity to encounter, learn about, and discuss the problems of aging. Thereby their own later relationships with elderly people and, eventually, with themselves will not involve such a high level of rejection of the often inevitable increase in dependent behavior.[21]

Although Kalish here speaks of aging, the same point may be made about our American values and attitudes toward any loss and the dependency of grief following loss.

Time, space, and the constraints of this book do not permit an adequate exploration of the treatment of various forms of victimization. To gloss over this topic lightly would constitute an insult to the millions who have suffered from man's inhumanity to man. For the purposes of this book, it needs to be stated that the matter of dealing with any aspect of victimization, including regression and helplessness, demands a skilled approach by specialized therapists. Ideally, such helpers should be prepared to face the reality of the horrors visited on the victims without needing to defend themselves against the ugliness of the material, to be cognizant of countertransference pitfalls, to be realistic about the limitations of corrective measures despite the best of intentions, and to appreciate the sensitivity and skill needed for work with victims of experiences foreign not only to our own experiences but even to our ability to imagine. Perhaps the greatest help one can offer these victims is to approach them with a sense of awe and a feeling of humility, and to stand ready to refer them to specialists experienced in dealing with their particular type of victimization.

However, even further caution is needed. All of us, therapists included, are in a position to sit in judgment on both the victims and the aggressors. It is a well-known observation that where answers are lacking, people readily supply their own. Mental health workers must be expected to refrain from fueling the fires of intolerance and to keep an open mind regarding behavior we do not understand.

Our traditional theories on human behavior, be they psychoanalytic, behaviorist, humanist, or from other frames of reference, are not adequate to explain the dynamics of victimization. Neither is our presently constituted legal system adequate to deal with the complexities of crimes committed by people under the threat of death. The matter of the victim's feelings toward his tormentors after the life and death ordeal is over has been one aspect of the victim's behavior that has aroused concern in recent years. How, we ask, can the victims of kidnapping or hijacking have the kind of concern and affection toward their recent abductors that they seem to express after all they have been through? As Hilel Klein states: "no matter what the conceptual or theoretical framework of the psychiatrist, one has to recognize that the experiences of the persecutions have produced damages on a most profound and basic level."[22]

It would appear unlikely, therefore, that the post-traumatic behavior one sees in victims toward their captors can be that of concern and affection. Perhaps we need other theories to explain what we see. Meanwhile, we need to guard against the temptation, discussed earlier, of blaming the victim for the crimes of the aggressor or of rushing, in our anxiety to defend against the helplessness of not understanding, to fit the behavior we see into already prepared theoretical slots.

Notes

1. David Peretz, "Development, Object-Relationships, and Loss," in *Loss and Grief: Psychological Management in Medical Practice,* ed. Bernard Schoenberg, et al. (New York: Columbia University Press, 1970), p. 12.

2. Henry Krystal and Thomas A. Petty, "Rehabilitation in Trauma Following Illness, Physical Injury, and Massive Personality Damage," in *Massive Psychic Trauma,* ed. Henry Krystal (New York: International Universities Press, 1968), p. 281.

3. Virginia Woolf, "On Being Ill," in *The Moment and Other Essays,* quoted in *Massive Psychic Trauma,* p. 281.

4. Emanuel Tanay, "Initiation of Psychotherapy with Survivors of Nazi Persecution," in *Massive Psychic Trauma,* p. 220.

5. Bruce L. Danto, "The Role of 'Missed Adolescence' in the Etiology of the Concentration-Camp Survivor Syndrome," in *Massive Psychic Trauma,* p. 257.

6. Martin E. P. Seligman, *Helplessness: On Depression, Development and Death* (San Francisco: W. H. Freeman and Co., 1975), p. 17.

7. Leland E. Hinsie and Robert Jean Campbell, *Psychiatric Dictionary,* 4th ed. (New York: Oxford University Press, 1975), p. 199.

8. Alvin I. Goldfarb, "The Psychodynamics of Dependency and the Search for Aid," in *The Dependencies of Old People,* ed. Richard A. Kalish, Wayne State University, The University of Michigan Institute of Gerontology, Occasional Paper (Detroit, 1969), p. 2.

9. Richard A. Kalish, "Of Children and Grandfathers: A Speculative Essay on Dependency," in *The Dependencies of Old People,* p. 75.

10. Joan Fleming, "Early Object Deprivation and Transference Phenomena: The Working Alliance," *The Psychoanalytic Quarterly* 41 (1972): 35–36.

11. Alvin I. Goldfarb, "Psychodynamics and the Three-generation Family," in *Social Structure and the Family: Generational Relations,* ed. Ethel Shanas and Gordon F. Streib (Englewood Cliffs, N.J.: Prentice-Hall, 1965), pp. 10-45. See also Margaret Clark, "Cultural Values and Dependency in Later Life," in *The Dependencies of Old People,* p. 59.

12. Kalish, "Of Children and Grandfathers," pp. 81-82.

13. Erna Furman, *A Child's Parent Dies: Studies in Childhood Bereavement* (New Haven: Yale University Press, 1974).

14. May E. Romm, "Loss of Sexual Function in the Female," in *Loss and Grief,* p. 185.

15. William G. Niederland, "An Interpretation of the Psychological Stresses and Defenses in Concentration-Camp Life and the Late Aftereffects," in *Massive Psychic Trauma,* p. 64.

16. Ibid., p. 32.

17. Erich Fromm, *The Anatomy of Human Destructiveness* (Greenwich, Conn.: Fawcett Publications, 1973), p. 322.

18. Hilel Klein, "Problems in the Psychotherapeutic Treatment of Israeli Survivors of the Holocaust," in *Massive Psychic Trauma*, p. 248.

19. Janice Norton, "Treatment of a Dying Patient," in *The Interpretation of Death*, ed. Hendrik M. Ruitenbeek (New York: Jason Aronson, 1973) pp. 19–38.

20. Ibid., pp. 36–37.

21. Kalish, "Of Children and Grandfathers," pp. 81–82.

22. Klein, "Problems in Psychotherapeutic Treatment," p. 248.

12/
Hope, Hopelessness, and Depression

Although hope in humans is considered an ego function, hope and hopelessness may have deep biological roots in prehuman life. Animal studies show that when animals, in experimental situations, in the wild, and in captivity, learn that they are in an inescapable situation where their actions are futile, they frequently die. Autopsies show death from relaxation, a slowed heart rate, and a heart engorged with blood. Researchers have concluded that death was a result of giving up.[1] It has been postulated that this behavior may be an expression of hopelessness, a kind of instinctive suicidal behavior pattern which hastens an inevitable death. Because little children too are known to crawl away and hide when in panic and danger, there may be a thread from animals to little children suggesting a deep biological tendency in humans to end life under hopeless conditions.[2]

The Roots of Hope in Early Development

The human infant begins life more helpless than infants of other species. Compared to animals, human infants have relatively few instinctual responses. By contrast, however, human beings' great capacity for learning leaves them free to make voluntary responses by which they can control aspects of their environment. At some primitive level, infants can calculate the correlation between response and outcome. If the correlation is nil, helplessness develops. If the correlation is positive or negative, it means the response is working. Infants learn, therefore, either to perform that response or to refrain from performing it, depending on whether the outcome is good or bad.

The basic core of personality is established in the first year or so of life during the symbiotic stage of development (three to eighteen months), in which the mother and child, functioning as a unit, are necessary for the existence of each other. During this period it is the mother's sensitivity to the infant's sounds and movements, and her ability to transform these expressions into communication signals for appropriate intervention on his behalf, that sets the stage for the infant's perception of the extent of his ability to influence the source of his comfort. The mother must also take pleasure in this development if the infant is to feel that his life has purpose and meaning, that is, that it is of value to another and that he is thereby worthwhile. From repeated experiences of being helped out of a feeling of helplessness, the infant develops trust and "a basic pervasive feeling . . . that he has the resources within himself to cope with the demands of living."[3] This feeling becomes the foundation for the later stage of mastery, which should include not only the ability to control aspects of one's physical environment (manipulating material objects) but also the experience of being able to influence people on one's behalf—a distinction not always made clear in the literature.

Early development of hopelessness

There are differences of opinion regarding the age at which the infant is believed to be first capable of feeling hopeless. René A. Spitz considers the sleep of the newborn as the prototype of all ego defenses; when tension, whether from within or without, cannot be relieved, the most primitive response is that of withdrawal into sleep.[4] We see the use of this defense under overwhelming conditions throughout life.

John Bowlby delineates three phases of emotional response in young children separated from their mothers for a period of time. The first phase he calls protest, during which separation anxiety is the predominant reaction of the child; this is expressed in angry crying. The second phase is that of despair, characterized by grief and mourning. Hopelessness develops in this second phase. In contrast to the grief of adults, this phase in young children is short-lived. As children realize their helplessness in being able to bring back the mother, their hopelessness increases, and they defend against the pain by emotional detachment. This appears to the onlooker as inactivity and withdrawal.[5]

Spitz found that when children were allowed to withdraw without interruption for a long enough time, they reached an irreversible stage of withdrawal and almost always died eventually of infection or some other cause despite good physical and medical care. This condition he called "marasmus," the "fate of the unmothered infant."[6] It may be concluded, therefore, that "significant object loss in the young child carries with it a highly lethal potential in the absence of adequate intervention."[7]

Physical loss of the mother during early infancy is not the only trauma that can lead to feelings of hopelessness. Other common problems derive from defective early mother-child interactions. These can be due to problems within the child, the mother, or the interaction. The mother who needs to control the child rather than enter into a mutual process of development with him is a source of trauma to the child. External factors such as poverty, lack of physical or emotional supports to the mother, interference from others, illness, or any other factors that prevent the mother from tuning in to her child's cues will leave him feeling psychologically abandoned in his helplessness.

One factor that has received scant attention in child-development literature is the illness or death of a grandparent and its impact on the parent. The grieving or depressed parent is emotionally unavailable to her children. A family crisis centered on an aging grandparent during pregnancy or infancy can thus have serious consequences for children's development.

Later traumas are also important. Erik Erikson postulates that a sudden loss of mother love or care during the weaning stage can lead to acute infantile depression, which can give a lifelong depressive undertone to the personality. Such people, never having known what it is to feel any other way, may not think of themselves as chronically depressed.[8]

The symbiotic stage is followed by the separation-individuation stage (eighteen to thirty-six months),[9] which is not only crucial to normal development but which also holds in it, as does the oral stage, the potential for lifelong problems in regard to separation and loss. The hopelessness underlying some cases of suicide and emotional disorders may stem, not so much from an immediate current crisis, as from failure in development at this phase. Failure can result from traumatic physical separation, from lack of synchronization of the mother's response to the infant's attempts to separate from and return to her, or from the child's interaction with a mother who resists his psychological separation from her entirely.

The mother who needs the infant dependent on her for her own emotional equilibrium will withdraw her emotional support when the child attempts to separate from her as an autonomous individual, and will reward him for regression and clinging. The infantile bind confronting these children gives them the choice of losing the mother if they choose self-actualization, or losing the budding self in order to retain the maternal emotional supplies. Such individuals remain particularly sensitive to life experiences concerning separation and loss. They fail to achieve their full potential in work or in intimate relationships or both. They compromise by living less fully than they might and defend against hopelessness by denial of the possibility of the loss of the mother, by isolation of feelings, and by fixation at this stage of separation-individuation in order to avoid feelings of abandonment so intense they are experienced as "truly a rendezvous with death."[10]

Children given these impossible alternatives defend against the threat of abandonment (made up of depression, rage, panic, guilt, passivity, helplessness, emptiness) by the mother by various mechanisms. Their symptoms may range from neurotic to psychotic, depending on the point in development at which the fixation took place. In adulthood, these people do not relate to others as wholes, but as parts, as determined by their need-fulfilling function. They are unable to imagine the return of someone who has left; out of sight means gone forever. And finally, they are incapable of mourning. Because any loss or separation is experienced as catastrophic, they defend themselves by various maneuvers—leaving before they are left, acting out by finding a substitute thing or person for a threatened loss, pushing away potential relationships, or by emotional withdrawal into apathy.[11]

Apathy, the absence of emotion, corresponds to what Bowlby has termed "detachment," which occurs in the final stage of separation outlined earlier. It is a defense against overwhelming feelings of annihilation and serves in the interests of survival in that the "individual acts as though he were dead in order to avoid death. . . . Living in this restricted, vegetative fashion [serves as] . . . a means of conserving energy in order to maintain life."[12]

Mastery and failure in hope and hopelessness

We have already dealt with the hopelessness that stems from traumas in early development. The educational system exposes the child to further experiences having in them the potential for both failure and mastery. A sense of industry develops out of repeated experiences in mastering tasks that demand effort and struggle. Implicit here are the assumptions that children have the ability to master the task if they apply effort, that the tasks assigned are presented with some sense of progression in difficulty, that there is an expectation of success by significant adults, and that the feeling of success is cumulative and transferable from one learning situation to another.

Where these assumptions do not hold, the school situation can become a lasting nightmare for a child. The learning experience should provide an opportunity for anxiety, frustration, struggle, and stretching to meet expectations that are within attainable limits. Too high expectations can lead to excessive anxiety and feelings of hopelessness and failure. Too low expectations hand children an empty victory and rob them of the self-esteem earned through struggle. Some failure, however, is necessary for healthy growth.

School is not the only avenue of mastery available to the child. Sports, if not geared to the competitive needs of parents, and the study of a musical instrument with a teacher who understands children as well as music provide other opportunities for success through struggle. Depression following success, which is often observed in people after completion of a major accomplishment, can result from feeling that they are being rewarded not for what they are doing, but for what they have done.

Goal Flexibility as a Factor in Hope

How can we say what conditions in life can arbitrarily be called hopeless? Daily we see about us people beset by tragedies whose courage leaves us humble in admiration. How do we account for this capacity to keep going in the face of impossible odds? The situational aspect of hope is the capacity to determine what constitutes a minimally acceptable existence in the pursuit of which one is willing and able to modify goals and aspirations.

The most profound and inspiring examples of the ability to maintain hope through changing goals is found in the testimony of survivors of the death camps of Nazi Germany. In the final analysis, those who survived did so by transcending the temptation to hope for anything but life itself. Having made the decision to opt for life, the survivors then chose to carry on despite every obstacle and horror to which they were subjected. Each particular hope was relinquished until only the hope of life itself was left. As this too ebbed, they were left with the realization that they had lived as long as they could and did the best with what was available to them. This attitude then became in itself the goal of living. Every moment devoid of pain held the promise of pleasure.

Another reason for survival in extremity, as described by Terrence Des Pres, was the compulsion to let the world know what horrors had transpired in the death camps. One survivor of Dachau told Des Pres that the SS guards delighted in telling the prisoners they had no chance of coming out alive and that after the war "the rest of the world would not believe what happened; there would be rumors, speculations, but no clear evidence, and people would conclude that evil on such a scale was just not possible." The survivor struggled between the urge toward silence and the compulsion to bear witness to the horrors endured. Des Pres says: "Silence constitutes the realm of the dead. . . . This is a primary source of the will to bear witness: the survivor allows the dead their voice; he makes the silence heard."[13] The dying charged the living to speak for them. This demand was their tie to a future they would not live to see. For the survivor this became a means of transcending helplessness, a task to carry out in the future so that dead comrades would not be forgotten.

Still another reason for survival in extremity was the wish to resist evil. Capitulating meant selling out to a force that reduced humans to animals. Refusing to compromise was proof that men and women could remain human despite degradation and suffering. Thus the ability to remain future-oriented and to struggle against this evil with life-and-death issues mobilizing the drive toward mastery served to maintain hope in situations of extremity.

The ability to maintain hope through modification of goals is found in more ordinary life situations as well. We know that death is inevitable, yet it intrigues and mystifies us and shocks us each time it occurs. We can deny these fears when young because the future stretches out endlessly ahead. Illness, accidents, and old age shake this denial.

"I hate to think of you getting so old," remarked one woman to her eighty-three-year-old mother. "That's silly," came the reply. "I have one of two choices: I can either keep on getting older or I can die. At my stage of life it is like a woman in her ninth month of pregnancy. There is only one way out. So I enjoy every day to the fullest. When I look at others about me I am grateful for the health I have. I keep busy with activities I can still attend. But I am ready to go at any time. In spite of everything it has been a good life. I only hope that when I die I will go in my sleep, with no suffering."

Here is hope in the face of an ultimate eventuality. But it is hope based on a modification of goals. Who knows what ambitions this woman once had and relinquished? The human being's ability to think forward and backward in time can be used to foster hope. Fantasies of the future and reminiscences of the past can serve to enrich the present moment. This ability was life-saving in the death camps. It is important in the maintenance of morale among the elderly as well. They may even embellish the past to enrich the present.

"Just think," this same old woman remarked. "When your daughter graduates from college, all my grandchildren will be university graduates. In fact, all my children are too. Even your sister went to business college." Here is a woman whose greatest unfulfilled desire was for education. She uses reminiscing about the past, distorted in the service of enrichment, and focus on the future to conclude that her deepest desire is attained, if not by herself, at least through identification with children and grandchildren.

An interesting model has been designed for successful aging based on the ability to relinquish unattainable goals in favor of age-appropriate ones. Four goals for middle age include: (1) valuing wisdom rather than physical powers as youth and strength wane; (2) valuing relationships for their interpersonal rather than sexual opportunities as chances for sexual partners decline; (3) developing the capacity to shift emotional investment from one person and activity to others as children leave home, parents and contemporaries begin to die off, and activities are restricted; and (4) learning to master experiences rather than letting events dictate one's life. Goals for old age include: (1) valuing oneself for what one is instead of what one's work role has been; (2) defining happiness and comfort in terms of satisfying human relationships despite increased bodily aches and pains; and (3) setting aside one's self-centered identity in favor of a vital absorption in doing all one can to improve the world for familial or cultural descendants. This final goal makes even death transcendable.[14]

Modification of goals is seen in those chronically ill and terminal patients who are able to remain hopeful. Hope and denial go hand in hand, but denial is intermittent. Each new treatment restores hope; each setback brings back the reality of the final end. Reports from terminal patients indicate that the ability to relinquish expectations is a factor in maintaining hope. Like the camp survivors, they choose to live for the sake of life itself, relinquishing in turn hope for activities, appearance, career, comfort, and health, in the final analysis, living one moment at a time.

A different kind of goal flexibility is demonstrated by the actor George Burns who, at the age of eighty, began an unprecedented rebirth of his career with an Oscar-winning role in *The Sunshine Boys*. In his autobiography he tells of his early struggles to remain in the theater. His early attempts were all failures; repeatedly he was pulled offstage by a hook. But humiliation meant nothing to him. He changed names, acts, partners, theaters, just to be able to stay in show business. Eventually, as the partner of a great comedienne, Gracie Allen, he attained stardom.[15] Had he set his sights on success, no doubt his repeated failures would have been overwhelming. But with the goal the larger one of simply staying in show business, endurance paid off. Success was the result, not the goal.

Contrast this point of view with that of the young woman who said mournfully, "If I am not married by the time I am thirty, I will commit suicide."

The inability to modify goals is an important factor in hopelessness. It has been postulated that hopelessness comes from the realization that the gratifications one has come to expect are no longer possible and that only regressive behavior will sustain one. Many Nazi concentration camp prisoners who perished did so not from a wish to die but rather because "they could neither accept nor be resigned to the primitive conditions of existence demanded in this type of internment, nor the premise that gratification could only be derived from regression."[16]

A striking example of the life-saving potential of the ability to regress while retaining hope was demonstrated by a nineteen-year-old man who was rescued after surviving eleven days without food or water from the ruins of a ten-story apartment building destroyed in an earthquake in Bucharest, Rumania, in 1977. Doctors were unable to account medically for his surviving without water and food longer than any case in medical history. The youth said he kept hoping all the time that he would walk again, breathe fresh air, go back to work, and see his friends and mother. Although fully aware of what had happened to him, he said that he had slept almost all the time he was buried underground.[17] The feelings of hope were possible for the youth because he could accept the passivity that comes with the feeling of hopelessness; his acceptance could foster hope for a new goal.

The acceptance of passivity is expressed through grieving. Thus, grieving must be a lifelong process accompanying change and growth. What permits some people to endure this passivity and to move on to new goals while others remain tied to old goals, old objects, old self-expectations even to the point of self-destruction? Is it possible to conjecture that it is, once again, the tie to a compassionate and caring other which makes it safe to relinquish old ties without feeling abandoned?

Recognizing Hopelessness and Depression

Hope and hopelessness are feelings inside an individual and as such, if not expressed, can only be inferred by another. The behaviors of hopelessness are varied. An awareness of their forms might alert the helper to danger signals that might otherwise be overlooked.

Probably the most common form of hopelessness is depression, from which millions of people suffer. Although carrying a hopeful prognosis, its danger lies in its potential for suicide or other destructive acts. It is important, however, to outline some differences between the sadness of normal grief and depression. Many people confuse the two and can be heard to say "I am depressed" when, in fact, they are simply sad. At the other extreme, some depressives do not know they are depressed and can be gratefully relieved when their depression is pointed out to them, because then their behavior begins to make sense.

The normally bereaved, despite their sadness, can laugh and show a variety of emotions appropriate to environmental shifts. For example, they can laugh at the antics of an infant even in the midst of grief. Depressives remain downcast regardless of what is going on about them. The bereaved respond to reassurance, support, and comfort; depressives, if they respond at all, require urging, promises, or strong pressure. The bereaved retain the capacity for pleasure; depressives have lost the capacity to have fun. The bereaved dwell on that which was lost; depressives dwell on themselves. The bereaved may be openly angry; depressives may be irritable, critical, complaining, but open anger is missing. The bereaved feel the world is empty but realize their sense of personal emptiness is temporary; depressives feel a prolonged, intense inner emptiness. Both may have physical complaints, insomnia, and changes in sexual interest. The bereaved project a feeling of sadness in others; depressives project a feeling of helplessness, if not hopelessness. Depression may be the dominant or only a partial feature of a grief reaction, and may occur immediately after a loss, gradually, or even after recovery from the grief, or where no grief has been apparent. The bereaved can be helped by a variety of people; depressives need skilled, professional help.

Depression can range from a mild case of the blues to the opposite extreme of psychotic depression, when the feeling of hopelessness is so intense that the person finds ordinary life too great a threat to tolerate. Hopelessness in depression appears as indecisiveness, paralysis about action (why act if everything ends in failure or loss?), increased demands on others, feelings of unworthiness and guilt, and projection of hopelessness onto others. Depressives are convinced that their skills and planning will avail them nothing, that their failures are due to their own incompetence, making reliance on others necessary, and that their previous long-range goals have only resulted in frustration and failure.[18]

Another form that hopelessness can take is the powerlessness that can erupt into violence. This is seen in the poverty-stricken community where apathy in the face of chronic poverty, exploitation, and abuse finds its outlet in suspiciousness, random hostility, defeatism, and self-destructive and aggressive reactions reflecting the constant aggravated stress under which people exist.

An example of powerlessness and hopelessness on the individual level is that of people with poor impulse control who can maintain themselves sufficiently well to get by, so long as they have someone they can tyrannize. Should that balance shift, however, the underlying feeling of powerlessness can erupt into directed or random hostility. The man who holds his wife and children through fear, when finally confronted by divorce action, can become violent in his flailing attempts to restore the control he needs for emotional equilibrium.

Psychopaths live in a state of chronic hopelessness. They are convinced that their powers are impotent not, as with the depressive, because of their own inadequacies, but because others cannot be trusted and are to blame for their failures. To them the future is hopeless; therefore, striving for long-range goals is pointless. They defend against the feeling of hopelessness by seeking immediate gratifications with little regard for the consequences because consequences belong to the future, which is out of their range of interest. They feel alienated, excluded, helpless to change things, and driven by their impulses. Because people have proved untrustworthy and disappointing, they feel free of a feeling of obligation to others, of guilt, and the ability of others to hurt them. They are unable to connect past to present behavior and present behavior to future outcomes.[19]

Suicide, of course, can be the ultimate expression of hopelessness, devastating in its impact because of its dual expression of rage against the self as well as others. The taboos that exist in many societies against suicide point to the universal fear of and attempt to control this behavior. Some suicides, therefore, do not take the form of a direct destructive act against the self. Homicide can serve as a suicidal equivalent where the victim manipulates someone else to carry out the killing. Accidental death is often another suicidal equivalent. Authorities in the United States attribute 80 percent of traffic accidents to the emotional state of the driver. Depression, suicidal intent, alcohol and drug-related impaired brain functioning, impulsive action as a means of recovering self-esteem following a loss, fear of a new responsibility, and rage were some of the emotional determinants found in a study of near-fatal automobile accidents.[20]

A tendency toward an undue amount of sleep may also be a signal of withdrawal into hopelessness. In children, hyperactivity, problems in peer relationships, poor academic performance, hypochondriasis or physical complaints, delinquency, fighting, vandalism, accident-proneness, severe hand-banging and face-beating may also be indicative of hopelessness. The inability of a young person to fantasize about the future may be regarded as a warning sign of hopelessness or even potential suicide.

A suicide attempt differs dynamically from a successful suicide because the attempt has in it a cry for help reflecting an underlying residue of hope. That attempt to reach out to others, whether directly or indirectly, is a "reflection of the balance between hope and despair."[21] The danger in an attempt, however, is that there is always the chance for error. The hoped-for rescuer may not come as expected, or other contingencies may not work as planned, and the cry for help can turn into an accidental suicide.

We have long known of sudden deaths from anthropologists reporting deaths following hex or voodoo curses. We do not have any physiological explanations for these cases, but they have been documented sufficiently to be considered facts. In hex death, the victim hears that he has been cursed. He believes it, feels he is helpless to avoid the curse, becomes passive, submissive, or depressed and dies within a period of hours or days. The Bible also makes reference to sudden death. It says that when the news of Joseph's disappearance reached Jacob, two women of his extended household fell dead from grief.

Death from a "a broken heart" was accepted as part of the normal order of events through the romantic period of the early part of this century; it was even listed as a cause of death on death certificates. We do not hear this expression today. Yet a study of sudden deaths indicates that helplessness was a major contributory factor. Some of the actual precipitating events setting off the helplessness were the death or threat of loss of a loved one, acute grief and mourning, anniversary reactions, and loss of self-esteem.[22] Studies of bereavement point to the first year after loss being a period of high vulnerability to death.[23] In a study of sudden death among one group of workers, the predominating premorbid state appeared to be depression. When these depressed people were provoked to anger or anxiety, death from cardiac arrest followed.[24] It is also becoming increasingly recognized that chronic helplessness constitutes a serious health hazard capable of precipitating physical disease short of death itself.

Implications for Intervention

Although helplessness may be an integral part of acute grief, when helplessness moves to the point of hopelessness the condition may be detrimental to well-being and to life itself. Hopeless people need the help of others to lead them out of their dilemma. They need an outreach approach, not one based solely on their ability to ask for help outright, as the hopelessness in itself may make it impossible for them to do so.

The helper also needs to be sensitive to cues and signals of distress that constitute indirect appeals for help. The response to the cry for help may be the deciding factor in the life of a human being. When the plea goes unheard, or is misunderstood, or its urgency missed, the balance may tip in the direction of hopelessness and despair, and suicide may be the only way out of pain.

"Are you suicidal?" a patient was asked when he sought help following the death of his wife. "No," was his reply, and then he told of a near-fatal automobile accident in which he was involved following the death of his mother ten years previously. He was put on a waiting list for therapy; in three days he was dead of a self-inflicted gunshot wound.

Treatment needs to be geared to the underlying causes of the hopelessness. Where apathy or hopelessness is due to a traumatic situation, the simplest solution, of course, is to remove the source of trauma, where this is possible. Child placement services are set up with such an objective. These children are taken out of an environment that is detrimental to them, either temporarily until the environment can be improved, or permanently if it cannot. In war, removing soldiers from the battlefield to a hospital where they could receive good care (relief from death anxiety and symbolic restoration of the nurturing object) provided sufficient respite for many. Others did not recover until they were actually sent home.

In the concentration camps or prisoner-of-war camps removal from the trauma was not possible, so other means had to be found. J. E. Nardini reported that among Japanese prisoners of war who developed a depressive reaction the most successful treatment:

> Included forced hot soap-and-water bathing, shaving and delousing, special appetizing food, obtaining a few days rest in camp, and if possible temporarily easier work conditions, a mixture of kindly sympathetic interest and anger-inducing attitudes. Victory was assured with the first sign of a smile or evidence of pique.[25]

Viktor E. Frankl[26] described his treatment of fellow concentration-camp prisoners who had given up hope of survival. He spoke to them first of the present, enumerating each comfort, no matter how trivial. He then counted all their losses, insisting that each one was replaceable! He spoke of his own hope in the future and the chance always of a lucky break. He spoke of someone looking down on them in times of trouble—a friend or relative, whether alive or dead, or a God even—with the expectation that they would be found suffering proudly, not miserably, so that their sacrifice might have meaning.

The hopeless person has renounced external object relationships. The procedures described above served to bring back through force, in one case, and through imagination, in the other, the external objects being renounced.

Being helpful to others or caring for pets can serve as a defense against depression. Here people give unto others that which they wish were being given unto them, namely, care. For example, the value of pets or of gardening for the elderly, who are subject to more helplessness-producing situations than any other age group except children, has not been sufficiently developed. The need to care for another living thing can keep an elderly person feeling needed long after significant ties to contemporaries have been lost through death. Helplessness in the elderly can also be held off by allowing them to participate in decisions rather than subjecting them to plans already made for them by others. Voluntary charitable activities or political work for improvement of the lot of the elderly or for some other cause can also hold off depression.

Where hopelessness derives from what has been called "unfulfillable, rather than unfulfilled, desires and wishes focused on impossible aims,"[27] insight-oriented therapy can help identify and modify the wishes. Among these are the wish to be passively cared for without having to communicate to another what one's wishes are, the wish for the perfect, all-giving mother, the wish to possess the oedipal object, the wish that reality fit the mental image.

Treatment of apathy aims at reversing the process by which the person renounced external objects. If the aim of hopelessness is to avoid pain, then it follows that the rekindling of hope leaves one vulnerable to pain again. To avoid this an apathetic person will resist the establishment of an object tie by a variety of maneuvers. Helpers need to be active in stimulating a relationship, yet prepared for distrust, panic, rejection, anger, ingratitude, unwarranted verbal attack, or flight from the relationship and must be on the alert to their own emotional vulnerability to the client's negative behavior.

Once an object tie begins to develop, the person will begin to show a severe hypersensitivity to any threat of loss of the developing relationship. Separations such as weekends, holidays, vacations, or even a change in appointment can represent a catastrophic loss. The person will tend to react as if all had been lost and will readily give way to hopeless despair. There may be quick alterations between a beginning relationship and emotional turning off, depression, or hopelessness, or these feelings may be masked under self-destructive acting out behavior or retaliation through breaking off the contact.

The feeling of emptiness depressed people complain of is similar to the infant's hunger pangs. Just as the infant goes from need to rage to apathy, so does the depression-prone person after a loss go through the same process. The slightest misunderstanding by the therapist can feel like abandonment and bring on a rage reaction or emotional turn-off. Belligerence and anger in the previously hopeless person are, therefore, signs of beginning recovery. Just as hope is abandoned after repeated disappointments, so is hope restored through repeated reality testing to insure that the object is really present. It takes repeated positive experiences before a formerly apathetic person becomes capable of investing in others. The therapist's ability to remain a benign figure despite attack represents one test of reality. In a similar vein, prisoners released from concentration camps had to test over and over again the reality of their freedom before they could accept the fact that they were truly back with loved ones.

Caution should be exercised against the temptation to frustrate the depressive's bid for sympathy, affection, and attention from others. Secondary gain as a motive may actually be a hopeful sign in depressives, because it means they are capable of eliciting at least some response from others. Thus, "patients who use their depression as a way of controlling others may have a better prognosis than those who have given up."[28] At this point helpers must be in touch with their own feelings, conflicts, and defenses against passivity and helplessness in order to tolerate these feelings in others without needing to push toward premature independence or withdraw from the approach-avoidance behavior of the patient. Where hopelessness goes back to disappointment in a significant relationship, it stands to reason that a meaningful change would call for a corrective experience through the establishment of a significant tie with someone who will be nondisappointing. This cannot be achieved by manipulative or short-term approaches. Because overcoming the resistance to forming such a tie may take months, one can anticipate that working with this kind of problem means a commitment over a considerable period of time. Crisis intervention is not the model for this work.

When hopelessness stems from fear of loss because of the struggle for autonomy, the helper needs to walk a tight-rope between encouraging patients' self-determination and protecting them from the self-destructive decisions that might follow if the helper does not hold the person to reality testing.

Mrs. Yale, a woman of fifty, was still emotionally tied to a self-centered, hostile mother. With therapy she gradually succeeded in curtailing her daily telephone calls to her mother and began to seek the friends she had always wanted. In therapy she began to complain about her working conditions—the temperature fluctuations, the lighting, the gossip of other employees. She talked of quitting her job in order to travel for a year. The therapist questioned the wisdom of leaving a job at her age without the assurance of one when she returned. What were her chances of being rehired in the midst of an economic recession with many young people out of work? In fury, Mrs. Yale burst out at the therapist for her negative attitude. What was the use of self-actualizing only to have cold water thrown on her enthusiasm! The therapist held her ground despite the attack and the tirade continued.

After a few such stormy sessions Mrs. Yale revealed that she had the option at her place of employment to take leave without pay for up to a year. She had sufficient savings to cover that period of time and to travel as well. Her attack had been a ruse to test the therapist's concern for her welfare. The therapist had held to reality testing despite the onslaught of verbal attack. In time, Mrs. Yale did leave her job through an early retirement, and in such a way that her financial security was insured.

The individual who has difficulty about the stage of autonomy needs to be worked with carefully in regard to terminating therapy. The therapist must be alert to precipitous endings as a way of warding off painful material, as retaliation for the therapist's abandonment (by taking a vacation or accepting a new patient known to the patient in question, for example), or when symptoms have subsided but the original conflicts have not been resolved. "If you see me trying to run," cautioned one patient, "please don't let me." Thus can the healthy part of the patient's ego join in the alliance with the therapist in the interests of health.

The helper working with loss and grief needs to be aware of the pitfalls of trying to make up to the bereaved for losses they have experienced in the past. In families who have lost a child through death and then applied to adopt a child, for example, the replacement child may be in danger because of the mother's inability to invest emotionally while her grief is unresolved. There may be a tendency to impose the identity of the dead child on the replacement child, and compensation is achieved through guilty overprotection.

Sometimes the helper needs to carry the hope for the sufferer with a firm, kind, confident approach, as in this case of a soldier. Private Will was in a foxhole when he heard the shell coming. He was not aware of being hit but, looking down, he saw blood flowing from his shirt-front. Is this what it feels like to die? he wondered calmly (in his state of shock). He waited for his life to pass before his mind's eye, as all the books said happened at the moment of death, but nothing came to him. Instead, with surprise he watched as the trees slowly turned from green to brown, and then he knew no more.

When Private Will regained consciousness it was in an army hospital some days later. He was a mass of flesh and blood and bones attached to tubes and bottles that took care of his life processes. From time to time he opened his eyes, but for the most part he slept or kept his eyes shut. He had a hazy notion of people moving about but could not tell his dreams from reality.

The chaplain came to see him every day, ignored his closed eyes, greeted him cheerfully by name, wished him well, and promised to return the following day. He always kept his word. For two weeks this pattern continued. One day Private Will overheard the doctors talking about his case. "I guess he's not going to make it after all," they said. "We'll give him one more day and then we'll call it quits."

When the chaplain stopped by that day Private Will finally forced open his eyes. "I guess I'm dying," he said. "Yes, perhaps that's true," replied the chaplain. "But we haven't given up hope yet." And again he went away, promising to return. Private Will closed his eyes again and drifted off into sleep. When he awoke nine hours later his bladder and kidneys had begun to function on their own. From that point on his recovery was steady, and today he is a healthy, active man. "I am sure there was something in the chaplain's interaction with me that saved my life," he said years later in recounting this experience.

Was there something to his speculations? Can hope in itself be a burden? Can the body, free to relinquish even hope to another, reserve its strength for physical recuperation? Using the above example as a prototype, a therapist experimented with holding on to hope for patients too exhausted to carry on alone. Ted, a young man of twenty-seven, came into treatment at the time of the breakup of his marriage following his developing a severe illness. The early months of treatment were spent in his mourning the loss of his wife. As his condition improved, he faced the problem of needing to decrease his medication. To continue on a high dosage of the drug he was taking was dangerous because of serious side effects. Yet, whenever his physician attempted to cut the dosage, his temperature flared, his pain mounted, and the dosage had to be increased even further. He was in a hopeless spiral, with surgery the only alternative.

At this point the therapist commented: "You know, you have grieved for the loss of your wife. But you have not grieved for the loss of your health." "I can't cry," came the reply. "I can't feel helpless without feeling hopeless."

"Let me carry the hope for you," the therapist answered. At this, Ted began gently to weep. The therapist sat silently, comfortably, until the weeping stopped of its own accord. The first words Ted spoke were, "If I were to feel hopeful about anything, the one thing I could feel hopeful about is. . . ." His medical course proceeded uneventfully from that point on and eventually he was able to be off medication entirely. Ted described this experience in his own words as follows: "One session, when I had arrived in unbearable physical pain, I simply released my hold on the prime responsibility: I simply gave up all hope. It was not particularly that I cared to die as a relief from pain, but that for just one moment I simply did not care whether I lived or not. I wanted someone else to take the responsibility for that decision. It was then that my therapist took the hope I had relinquished and, in almost a physical sense, held on to it for me. And in the passage of only a few moments, I was ready to receive it back; given so tenderly that hope no more seemed a burden. From that instant in the midst of physical pain and grief, and then beyond them, I began the discovery of a whole new *joie de vivre*." Sometimes also people need to be given permission to let go when the struggle is too great. It is for them, however, to decide when the pain of life outweighs its rewards.

It is recognized that considerable space has been devoted to the plight and reaction of victims of events that should now be receding into history. It would be fortunate, indeed, if as a world society we could lay these issues to rest. Unfortunately, this is not the case. Mental health workers are being confronted more and more by the physiological and psychological damage done to war victims and their families. The results of infantile and childhood malnutrition of a war-torn world appear today in people in their thirties. As the population ages, the developmental losses of the middle and later years touch off old scars of the physically and emotionally maimed. Furthermore, we are also beginning to see the damage in children born to survivors. The traumas to victims of the Holocaust, the Japanese relocation tragedy, the atomic bomb disasters, and other atrocities of the twentieth century cannot be escaped.

In the early postwar years social workers were cautioned to avoid delving into wartime experiences of refugees because they could not possibly know and empathize with these experiences. Today they cannot afford to ignore these people, or their children, or to segregate them from all others who come for help. The violence rampant in society today makes anyone the next potential victim. Therapists must be prepared to deal with catastrophic loss in the course of their daily work. To work honestly and effectively with victims of loss, they must be open to new theories and new approaches to problems. Cultural variables must also be considered as ethnic and racial groups merge and interact in an open society. The helper from one ethnic group cannot assume that his or her values and truths hold for people from another background. As the world grows in complexity, so must helpers grow in skill and knowledge to keep pace with a rapidly changing world.

Although the focus here has been on implications for treatment of hopelessness after it is recognized, knowledge should also alert helpers to populations at risk for preventive work. The relationship of many childhood losses, particularly the loss of a parent, as factors predisposing children to later psychopathology needs to receive greater attention. Depression and even attempted suicide are particular dangers because of unresolved anger, hopelessness, or identification with the lost object.

Parent loss through divorce is also an increasing problem in American society, and the children of divorce are already receiving attention as a population at risk. The problem of child-snatching, where one parent physically takes a child from the other parent's custody, has become a "noncrime" of staggering proportions, reaching 100,000 cases during 1976.[29] The issue is not only the child's physical safety but his psychological well-being as well. Violence committed by children is increasing alarmingly; statistics indicate that the major juvenile crime rate tripled between 1960 and 1975. A study shows that in 1975, of the twenty-one million arrests of youths between ages seven and eighteen, 4 percent (three times the 1960 number) were for violent crimes of assault, robbery, homicide, or rape. The juvenile justice system has been shown to be inefficient in stemming violent crimes committed by youth, and it is admitted that little is known as to the reasons why certain juveniles commit violent crimes.[30]

Social scientists have deplored the disintegration of the American family for decades. Without arguing this point, it is beyond question that liberalized divorce laws and the sexual revolution have created new potential for multiple relationships, necessitating multiple separations and creating multiple losses. How often can children be expected to separate and reattach? Helpers must become much more attuned to clients at risk who are in need of skilled preventive intervention.

Notes

1. Martin E.P. Seligman, *Helplessness: On Depression, Development, and Death* (San Francisco: W.H. Freeman and Co., 1975), pp. 169–75.
2. Maurice L. Farber, "Suicide and Hope: A Theoretical Analysis," in *Proceed-*

ings: Fourth International Conference for Suicide Prevention, ed. Norman L. Farberow (Los Angeles: Delmar Publishing Co., 1968), p. 297.

3. Ibid, p. 298.

4. Rene A. Spitz, *The First Year of Life* (New York: International Universities Press, 1965).

5. John Bowlby, "Pathological Mourning and Childhood Mourning," *Journal of American Psychoanalytic Association* 11 (1963):500–41.

6. René A. Spitz quoted in Gertrude and Rubin Blanck, *Ego Psychology: Theory and Practice* (New York: Columbia University Press, 1974), p. 41.

7. Larry Dizmang, "Self-Destructive Behavior in Children: A Suicidal Equivalent," in *Proceedings: Fourth International Conference,* p. 317.

8. Erik H. Erikson, *Childhood and Society* (New York: W.W. Norton, 1963), pp. 247–51.

9. Margaret S. Mahler, *On Human Symbiosis and the Vicissitudes of Individuation* (New York: International Universities Press, 1968).

10. James F. Masterson, *Psychotherapy of the Borderline Adult: A Developmental Approach* (New York: Brunner/Mazel, 1976), p. 29.

11. Ibid., pp. 43–44.

12. Ralph R. Greenson, "The Psychology of Apathy," *The Psychoanalytic Quarterly* 18 (1949): 300.

13. See Terrence Des Pres, *The Survivor: An Anatomy of Life in the Death Camps* (New York: Oxford University Press, 1976), p. 36.

14. Robert C. Peck, "Psychological Developments in the Second Half of Life," in *Psychological Aspects of Aging,* ed. J.E. Anderson (Washington, D.C.: American Psychological Association, 1956), pp. 42–53. Reprinted in *Middle Age and Aging,* ed. Bernice L. Neugarten (Chicago: University of Chicago Press, 1968), pp. 88–92.

15. George Burns, *Living It Up* (New York: G.P. Putnam's Sons, 1976).

16. Gregory Rochlin, *Griefs and Discontents: The Forces of Change* (Boston: Little, Brown and Co., 1965), p. 221.

17. Reported in *Los Angeles Times,* 16 March 1977, p. 5.

18. Frederick T. Melges and John Bowlby, "Types of Hopelessness in Psychopathological Process," *Archives of General Psychiatry* 20 (1969): 693–94.

19. Ibid.

20. Norman Tabachnick and Robert E. Litman, "Self-Destructiveness in Accident," in *Proceedings: Fourth International Conference,* pp. 321–27.

21. Dizmang, "Self-Destructive Behavior in Children," p. 319.

22. G.L. Engel, "Sudden and Rapid Death During Psychological Stress, Folklore or Folkwisdom?" *Annals of Internal Medicine* 74 (1971): 771–82.

23. Colin Murray Parkes, B. Benjamin, and R.G. Fitzgerald, "Broken Heart: A Statistical Study of Increased Mortality among Widowers," *British Medical Journal* 1 (1969): 740.

24. Seligman, *Helplessness,* p. 180.

25. J.E. Nardini, "Survival Factors in American Prisoners of War of the Japanese," *The American Journal of Psychiatry* 109 (October 1952): 245.

26. Viktor E. Frankl, *Man's Search for Meaning* (New York: Washington Square Press, 1963), pp. 128–33.

27. Barbara J. Betz, "Passive Expectations and Infantile Aims," *International Journal of Psychiatry* 5 (May 1968): 397.

28. Seligman, *Helplessness*, p. 102.

29. Dave Smith, "Retrieving Stolen Children for a Fee," *Los Angeles Times*, 28 September 1977, p. 1.

30. Study by the Vera Institute conducted on behalf of the Ford Foundation. See *Los Angeles Times*, 9 July 1978, p. 2.

13/
Relief and the
Restoration of Meaning

In the midst of grief, life still must go on. Because our society values so highly the ability to carry on, grief tends to be inhibited rather than allowed expression. The bereaved often blame themselves for the self-indulgence of sadness or feel guilty for moments when they forget their sorrow. In the same vein, they will tend to pride themselves on their coping ability even when it goes to the extent of inhibiting grief.

Loss as Relief

It seems contrary to all that has been said thus far about suffering to now state that normal grief can also have in it the element of relief. Relief is felt when the loss itself is experienced as better than the state that preceded it.

Death can bring relief from suffering and pain, particularly following a lingering, debilitating illness. No matter how loving and devoted a family may be, people do not have unlimited resources, and an exhaustive illness can strain and deplete everyone concerned. The plight of patients kept alive artificially against the wishes and pleas of family members has aroused increasing concern in recent years.

Death can mean not the ending of a relationship but rather the preservation of positive memories before the torments of prolonged medical heroics steal even these from the family. Death can also be felt as a relief if the alternative is a progressively downward course of alcoholism, drug addiction, disfigurement, vegetative existence, or shame.

A widow whose husband had suffered from a chronic heart condition said that following his death it was a relief whenever she heard an ambulance siren to realize that it was not sounding for him. Every telephone ring had been traumatic to her for years. Every minute that he was late coming home from work had heralded possible danger. Death brought relief from suspenseful waiting. For people to whom suspenseful waiting constitutes an unbearable strain, the anticipation of loss may be as painful as the actual loss itself:

> One must remember that even the reality of a fatal prognosis can be a relief from the agonizing ambivalence and struggle with the question of whether to know whether one has to face the great unknown. Sometimes such confirmation can bring even secret gladness and release.[1]

Improved sleep has been observed in family members when death has meant release from the exhaustive responsibilities of the final illness of the deceased, as well as from the accompanying anxiety.[2]

Knowledge of the fate of a loved one, even if the fate is death, can be experienced as a relief in contrast to the suspense of not knowing whether a missing person is dead or alive, suffering, or in torture. Divorce, despite all the heartbreak involved in the breakup of a family, can also bring relief when peace replaces the fighting of an unhappy marriage. The years when children are becoming emancipated from the family home are often volatile ones. Despite the pangs of the empty nest, many a parent has admitted that it is a relief to have the children finally out of the home and peace restored.

There is certainly relief as well as sorrow when family members who present particular problems—the retarded, emotionally disturbed, delinquent, impaired, aged—are removed from the family to community facilities where responsibility can be shared with others. In some families it takes a death to liberate one family member from control or undue influence by another. An autocratic father, a controlling or engulfing mother, a possessive sister or brother, may have a hold on family members that can be broken only by death.

There can even be relief in loss through illness or surgery. Unconscious dependency needs can be met by the socially sanctioned regression into illness. Asked how he felt after a colostomy, one patient remarked, "Wonderful! This is the first time in twenty years I have been free of disease!"

In past years retirement often meant a downhill course to eventual death, sometimes within the first year. More recently, especially for those elderly who are still in good health and in comfortable economic circumstances, retirement has been welcomed as a relief from confinement to a job. Renewed vigor is experienced following their release from stressful responsibilities.

Even the loss of a job can be experienced as a relief if it means getting out of a nonrewarding situation one has been reluctant to leave on one's own. Being fired has for many been a turning point in life that has eventually led to a new and enriching career.

Immigration, whether motivated by the search for a better life or flight from political or economic hardship, can also involve relief. Immigrants from police states, despite grief over the lives they have left behind, often acknowledge that they willingly traded all they treasured of familiar customs, people, values, material possessions, and way of life for freedom and the relief from totalitarianism.

Relief is intermingled with other emotions in grief—anger, sadness, guilt, shame. Each must be experienced and shared separately if loss is to be worked through appropriately. Crying can in itself bring momentary relief. The final relief, of course, is experienced when the acute grief is beginning to subside. This relief brings with it a resurgence of energy, a renewed interest in life, and a transcendance of the grief experience. In the dying patient this relief can come with the ultimate acceptance of death.

Mitigation

Mitigation applies to any event, person, or thing that lessens the degree of pain in grief. Acute grief cannot be tolerated without surcease from the intense pain that it entails. There are healthy and unhealthy types of mitigation. The smile of an infant, the charming antics of a child, the comfort of a pet, the momentary distraction of any ordinary happening of the day—all can help relieve the pain of grief in a healthy manner. Drugs, abuse of alcohol, overeating, indiscriminate sex, and isolation are examples of unhealthy mitigation. Unrelieved pain invites defensive maneuvers; thus, intermittent relief is beneficial to healthy mourning.

Brief moments of forgetting the fact of the loss may occur even during the early weeks of a major bereavement. Widows reported finding dreams of the deceased comforting to them. Often in these comforting dreams the dead person was seen as young. This was interpreted to mean that the relationship had been a rich and happy one and that the grief was proceeding in a healthy way.[3]

Religion and custom have traditionally served as mitigating agents for the bereaved by offering guideposts to behavior and feeling at a time of disorganization through grief. Religion can provide an outlet for guilt feelings, dependence on God, answers to the countless "whys," and avenues for atonement. Through its prescribed rituals religion can also offer a timetable for mourning and allow for expression of grief as well as for the gradual cessation of sorrow. Thus, the bereaved is provided with sanctions for both the articulation and termination of mourning, moving through well-spaced time steps as the days and months go by.

Mitigation through denial of the loss or denial of the feelings around the loss are examples of the early and normal avoidance of pain. Running away from pain can also be done by the taking in of comforting substances such as drugs, alcohol, and excessive food. Another way is the frantic search for replacement of the lost object through the constant search for sex, social activities, superficial, shallow, and numerous contacts—anything to avoid being alone and feeling it. Mitigation can also be sought through the opposite maneuver— the avoidance of social contacts, withdrawal from people, rejection of social overtures, and isolating oneself from people. Some run away from pain through travel (unconscious search for the lost object?) or overwork. Succoring another who is bereaved can also bring avoidance of pain. Although this is a constructive activity, it does not allow the full experiencing of the pain of loss for the bereaved themselves.

Mitigation needs to occur intermittently in the midst of an outpouring of grief. The key to grief is the release of emotions. Any shortcut to the full expression of emotions is a harbinger for future difficulties. The goal orientation of modern society is a hazard to the full expression of grief.

Coping

Integration of loss means the bereaved must come to terms with the significance of the loss in relation to objective reality. In other words, the bereaved must cope with the very real problems of daily living despite the loss and as a result of the loss.

The emotionally healthy individual is able to carry on daily life tasks, regress to dependency and helplessness during a surge of grief, and return again to some level of adequate functioning. This is possible even in acute grief when the daily demands of a job, homemaking, child care, or school can provide a respite to intense grief. One cannot grieve constantly even in acute grief. The regression to helplessness, however, can be experienced as beneficial and as a relief only when the person is assured of support from an understanding other who can allow the full weight of the dependency and helplessness. Without such support, the bereaved feel bereft and abandoned in their sorrow.

"I am grateful that I have to work," remarked one bereaved mother. "My job takes my mind off my grief; I must function there. But when I get home in the evening and on weekends, it all comes over me again. Holidays are worst. But at least I have work in between."

Grief work goes on during those times when task functioning is not required. This is to be contrasted to the commonly held belief that absorption in work can serve as a shortcut to grief. "She is lucky. Having young children to care for shortened her grief" is a misconception that keeping busy with necessary tasks is a way to quickly get over the painful task of grieving. Absorption in necessary or invented activities to ward off grief is one way by which grief is circumvented, only to remain repressed for months or years, ever ready to break forth anew when a later loss occurs or to interfere with subsequent attachments.

In the opposite vein, grief needs to be held in abeyance during times when strength is needed. Ann's mother had courageously attended her adult daughter whenever she was asked to during the three years of Ann's fight against cancer. She respected Ann's attempts to be independent during the stretches of time when she was able to function on her own. As death approached, she and the rest of the family surrounded Ann with warmth, love, and support. It was not the time for breaking down. That came soon enough after death won from them the daughter who had never had the chance for fulfillment of her aspirations. The family physician had seen to it that these aging parents were supplied with appropriate medications for their various ailments so that they would not break down during their ordeal.

The chronic illness or death of an elderly parent is a crisis for every family. Ideally, adult children should share the burden or receive outside support during this time so that grandchildren are not emotionally abandoned during their formative years. Parents of a terminally ill child also need help to avoid neglect of other family members. The same is true where there is a retarded or autistic or otherwise congenitally handicapped child in the family.

The rape victim also must cope with normal problems of living despite the trauma and, in addition, must sometimes return to the scene of the rape, particularly if it took place in her own home. If the rape is reported to the police, there may be police and medical matters with which she needs to deal, and these can mean further traumas to her. Home, one's most intimate space center, and dating, a normal social activity, now become arenas of panic.

In every major bereavement there are a number of immediate decisions that must be made. Following a death, there are practical decisions regarding a funeral, burial, care of children, meal preparation, insurance, obituary notices, housekeeping, visitors, and other loss-related or routine daily tasks. Divorce brings other problems of division of property, financial settlement, child custody, visiting arrangements, expense of dual households, and financial stress when support payments are withheld. Later the widowed or divorced person may need to solve long-range economic problems stemming from the loss. Decisions regarding illness or surgery involve choice of doctor, agreement to medical procedures, use of consultants, care of children and household during the illness, and financial stress.

If possible, the bereaved need to be supported in all of these tasks by relatives and friends able and willing to take over the necessary work, so that the bereaved can be allowed time and energy to grieve.

Some people handle anxiety by rushing to prove their competency in coping. These are the very people who need to be protected from this defense, which will delay their grief work or leave it unresolved. In our society these people, unfortunately, are lauded for their strength, and the maladaptive aspect of their independence is overlooked.

In addition to the somatic and emotional aspects of grief, there is an intellectual reaction to loss. The human being is, after all, a thinking organism. In loss the bereaved are driven by a need to make sense of what happened and how and why the loss came about.

The Importance of Predictability

It has been postulated that any event that destroys one's understanding of the meaning of life can be experienced as a loss and become the forerunner of grief.[4] By this definition, then, loss would occur whenever there is a discrepancy between one's expectations or fantasies and reality, and reality wins out, resulting in an upsetting of confidence in the predictability of our physical and emotional environment.

Many expressions reveal such discrepancies: "How could he die? He didn't even have cancer!" "How could he go so young?" "How could he leave me? He said I was all the world to him." Here are revealed a number of beliefs: because cancer may cause death, death is caused by cancer; death is for the old, not the young; words and actions are consistent, or love is lasting. The discrepancy may be revealed by what is implied as much as by what is actually said. This material has already been dealt with at length in connection with guilt and shame discussed in chapter nine and, therefore, will not be repeated here.

Much that has been said heretofore about basic trust, confidence, dependency, and so on is predicated on the assumption that a certain order of predictability can be expected in both our physical and social surroundings. We are not merely passive objects to whom events happen. From infancy on we learn to impose our own meaning on events and people about us. We take for granted that the earth beneath our feet will be relatively firm; an earthquake, therefore, upsets our predictability about this basic assumption.

Even before the child acquires language and while thought is still registered in the sensorimotor system, the infant draws conclusions about life and events. Some people are soft and cuddly; others are angular and muscular. Some are big; others are little. Some cause discomfort; others relieve it; sometimes the same person can do both.

The sense of meaning laid down in early infancy before the development of speech cannot be recalled through speech because it was registered in nonspeech form. It is rarely possible, therefore, that these primitive meanings will be accessible to the individual for later reexamination as to accuracy. Thus, all of us are left with conclusions about life based on primitive, infantile fantasies, many of which may be erroneous. Some of these fantasies and impressions, confronted by reality, will be corrected. Others will remain unconscious, perhaps erroneous, and will influence responses to later experiences.

Confidence in the predictability of people, things, and events enables us to function with a sense of security, to plan future actions, to graft new knowledge onto old, and through it all to maintain a thread of continuity of perceptions and meaning to life.

As children grow and interact with others, they are influenced by the beliefs and meanings these significant others attach to experiences. Each culture has its own explanations for reality, and it is the parents who are the transmitters of the cultural explanations for nature, people, and events. Children's sense of meaning, therefore, reflect the particular culture into which they were born.

The importance of culture in establishing a base for continuity is seen in the culture shock of immigration, study in a foreign land, or even travel from one country to another. Culture shock is a form of anxiety which results from the loss of perceptual reinforcements from one's own culture to new cues that have no meaning at all, little meaning, or a meaning different from those in the homeland. In culture shock people can feel helpless, irritable, cheated, or disregarded, and may struggle to comprehend, grow, or even to survive in the new environment.[5]

The readiness to take in new experiences depends on the ability to assimilate them into the familiar. Educators have long known this principle of attaching new material to that already known in order to make it understandable and acceptable. Too great a discrepancy between the new and the old makes the new difficult to take in, if not rejected altogether.

It would be wonderful if life did flow in an orderly fashion so that new experiences could painlessly be assimilated into the old. However, life is constantly in a state of flux and change. Some changes are within the realm of the expected. Others are so drastic as to constitute a loss. When a change matches our expectations, there need not be discontinuity of meaning. For example, we expect children to grow and old people to die. The death of an old person, therefore, does not need to create the discontinuity of expectation that the death of a young person would. There can, however, be discontinuity even in the death of an old person. "How could she suffer so when she led such a good life?" reveals the expectation, ingrained in childhood, that good behavior is rewarded and bad behavior punished. In fact, some people go through life in constant surprise to see "bad" people prosper, while the "good" are buffeted about by fate. Their surprise reveals that despite repeated evidence to the contrary, early beliefs still hold. It may be this association between being good and being rewarded that makes us unconsciously feel that the bereaved are in some way responsible for their loss. If misfortune befalls, does it not in some way imply punishment, and doesn't punishment follow a misdeed?

Survival depends in part on our having appropriate knowledge of how to act so as to respond appropriately to events and thereby avoid danger. This knowledge is enhanced by the ability to make predictions based on some continuity of expectations from one experience to another, predicated on a fundamental sense of meaning. Resistance to anything that challenges the meaning we have assigned to certain experiences helps insure our continuing ability to predict events and thus to act appropriately in the interests of survival. A loss that challenges that meaning is, therefore, ultimately and at the deepest level of awareness a threat to survival itself.

Loss as a Challenge to Meaning

Because resistance to change is a survival mechanism, what options are open to us when a change is so radical that it upsets our basic assumptions? One alternative is to ignore experiences that do not fit our expectations. This reaction explains the denial in the early stages of loss and grief. Denial, which was discussed at length in chapter five, then serves to insure the bereaved against psychological disintegration. Persistent denial can also be of value. Peter Marris states: "Those who hold their principles of life to be absolute, universal and unchallengeable may survive in situations of extreme uncertainty, where the more open-minded are destroyed by their inability to derive any intelligible regularity from events around them."[6]

A striking example of the above was found in the concentration camp experience, where the destruction of meaning was one sadistic tool of the Nazi persecutors. Marris says:

> In an account of his experiences in a Nazi concentration camp, for instance, Bruno Bettelheim describes how the prisoners reacted to circumstances which were made deliberately unpredictable. With cruel psychological insight, the camp guards frustrated any reliable accommodation to the prison regime by the capriciousness of their behaviour; a man might be punished if he did what he was told as well as if he did not. Eventually, to Bettelheim's observation, any personality was bound to disintegrate under such treatment, falling into an apathy which extinguished life. But those who survived best seemed to be the two most ideologically dogmatic groups in the camp—the Communists and the Jehovah's Witnesses.[7]

A more benign and healthier reaction to change that involves loss can take place when the loss is gradual or incremental, or where restitution is possible. Examples abound in developmental losses. Babies are introduced to the cup before they are expected to relinquish the bottle. They are put into training pants before they are ready to do without diapers. The pleasures of toddlerhood pale in comparison to the excitement of going to school like "the big kids." In addition, the comforts of home, providing they remain stable and retrievable, offer little competition to the excitement of teenage adventures with peers. Each success lays the groundwork for confidence and security in attempting the next task. Life has a continuity that allows for gradual changes, leaving the sense of meaning intact.

However, other life changes break the continuity and thus represent a loss that is painful rather than easily assimilated into the already known. A school or job failure, a broken love affair or marital break, a geographical move or displacement can represent such a discontinuity. Aging too presents the individual with painful discontinuities. Entrenched values of independence and self-reliance are dysfunctional in the later years, when a good adjustment requires the ability to accept help gracefully as physical, psychological, social, and economic powers decrease. Discontinuity is a major threat to the health of the aging person.

Whenever life is disrupted in any way that takes us by surprise, continuity is threatened, if not altogether broken. Death, murder, rape, burglary, natural or man-made disasters such as floods, earthquakes, tornados, war, fires, hijacking, kidnapping, are examples of events that upset our understanding of the meaning of things. These losses cannot be acknowledged without pain, the pain of grief, the emotional aspects of which have been discussed in earlier chapters. Here our focus is on the mental aspects, the challenge to entrenched meanings. Psychotherapy is in itself an example of an attack on entrenched meanings. Marris well describes this process as follows:

> The experience of psycho-analytic treatment suggests that it is slow, painful and difficult for an adult to reconstruct a radically different way of seeing life, however needlessly miserable his preconceptions make him. In this sense we are all profoundly conservative, and feel immediately threatened if our basic assumptions and emotional attachments are challenged. The threat is real, for these attachments are the principles of regularity on which our ability to predict our own behaviour and the behaviour of others depends.[8]

The loss of basic assumptions, defenses, and emotional attachments through psychotherapy, even though they may be dysfunctional, is accompanied by grief. The way out is, of course, through the discovery of a new and richer sense of meaning.

The Search for Meaning

For life to be tolerable after a loss, there must be a search and restoration of a sense of meaning. Meaning is sought through two questions: How and Why. The how seeks an understanding of the sequence of events that led up to the loss. How exactly did it come about that two airplanes could be in the same place at the same time so as to cause the catastrophic collision in the Canary Islands? What exactly took place in the physical body of this person to cause her life to be extinguished? What went wrong with this marriage to turn what had started out as a hopeful, loving relationship into a destructive and disruptive one? How does it come about that someone so young, handsome, talented, and successful should decide to end his life by committing suicide? How could she die when all the tests were negative?

Widows whose husbands have died suddenly are more inclined to dwell obsessively on the death and to search continually for its cause. This sometimes takes the form of blaming the deceased himself for his negligence in bringing about the death.[9] Although the anger toward the deceased is obvious here, one should not overlook the mental aspect also contained in this example, namely, the attempt to restore meaning following loss.

Still another example of the search for meaning is seen in the following remark: "When my mother died I felt compelled to understand the reason for her senseless death. This search I carried out by reading every book I could find on cancer. Although none of them answered the predominant question in my mind of why, I continued to read them in hopes of making some sense out of her senseless death at the age of fifty-seven."

A young woman sought psychotherapeutic help because of depression over terminal cancer. After reviewing her physical condition and the prognosis (which she chose to deny), she said what she really wanted to do first was to try to understand what went wrong in her last relationship with a male friend. At the conclusion of one session she forgot a book on the table. When she returned the next time she said, "I left a book here last time. I felt good all week. I think I got rid of Bob here. The book was one he had given me to read. I think symbolically it was my way of leaving him here, and last week's session finished the job. I now know what went wrong. Bob was a taker. What I would like to work on now is to understand my part in attracting men who are takers, because Bob was not the first." For some weeks she explored her relationships with men with the joking comment: "I want to solve this problem because I don't want to get around to getting married when I'm 100!" With death in the offing, she still had the need to make sense of an earlier loss, and with the help of denial protecting her from catastrophic awareness of her impending death, she was able to use time from the few months left to her for continued emotional growth.

Some of this questioning of "how" in regard to a loss has already been discussed in earlier chapters, particularly in chapter seven on searching behavior. Searching serves the interests of holding on to the lost object. It allows for a gradual taking in of the loss, thereby lessening the danger of personality disintegration which could result if the full significance of the loss were to confront the bereaved all at one time.

There is another kind of questioning that goes on in grief, however, that pertains to the why of a loss. This why represents the search for meaning. The search constitutes finding answers to an existential problem.

In this search for existential meaning, the widow sounds more like the following: "I keep asking why did it have to be him? He was just starting to make it. We had worked so hard. He was just coming into his own. I look around at all the unhappy marriages—at wives pushing their husbands, husbands being mean to their wives, and I can't understand it. Why us? It's not fair."

It has been postulated by some that life takes on meaning in three different ways: (1) through achievement or accomplishment; (2) through experiencing something of value such as an aspect of nature, a cultural achievement, or another person through love; and (3) through suffering.[10] It is this third aspect of suffering that concerns us here. Some of the repetitious talk and questions of the bereaved are their attempts to find reasons for their suffering.

Mental health is seen to be based on a certain degree of tension between "what one has already achieved and what one still ought to accomplish, or the gap between what one is and what one should become."[11] Chapter twelve on hope, hopelessness, and depression deals with ways in which people have tried to help the apathetic bereaved find new meanings in life after loss in the hope of helping them mobilize energy for living instead of allowing them, whether actively or passively, to end life out of hopelessness.

Death, despite its inevitability, continues to remain a mystery to man and has a profound impact each time it occurs. In death the loss is irretrievable, and the search is for meaning in the death. All religions have attempted to deal with this issue; there is no definitive answer, only one based on faith. Where faith holds, the bereaved can find comfort out of the belief that it is God's will. Others, out of their pain, reject the religious belief on which their former structure of meaning was based, or the belief in God in general.

Because the questions of life and death are in themselves unanswerable, we attempt at least to give meaning to life as it has been lived. The funeral and religious service at the time of death attempt to give meaning to the life of the deceased. The bereaved in turn are comforted by these customs because, through their association with the deceased, if his life had meaning, theirs takes on meaning as well.

Implications for Intervention

Bereavement needs to be looked at in terms of a total family rather than an individual loss. Support, whether by family, relatives, friends, or helpers is the keynote to intervention in loss. Children need support when an aged parent faces placement or death. The widow needs concern after her husband, the hospitalized patient, dies. She needs to know that she counts to the physician or nurse as a person, not just as the wife of the former patient.

The tasks of the helper are to allow the expression of relief and to assist in the restoration of meaning. The helper needs to be able to identify attempts to run away from the pain of grief and slowly, gradually, intermittently bring the bereaved back to the painful task of confronting the memories associated with the loss so as to bit by bit suffer through them and sever the tie to the lost object.

The prescription of drugs needs to be thought through carefully.

During a period of crisis preceding a death, while awaiting the outcome of surgery, or caring for the terminally ill, a relative may well need the support of medication to permit functioning through a long period of sustained anxiety. On the other hand, the too quick administration of drugs after a loss can be detrimental to the working through of grief.

Outside intervention to a family at time of crisis over anticipated loss or acute loss already incurred can provide the support necessary to facilitate coping and allow time and energy for healthy grief work. This support should be a combination of help in the processes of mourning, mitigation, and coping. Where religious belief in the bereaved is strong, it can be used to assist them in their search for meaning. Helpers must be able to set aside their own religious beliefs or lack of them and operate from within the framework of the beliefs of the bereaved persons themselves. For example, the Catholic mother of a severely mentally retarded son was able to find comfort in the thought that her child, because of his affliction, would never have to struggle with the temptation of sin. This comfort should not be denied to her.

Religious explanations, however, should not be relied on with young children. Young children do not understand death in the abstract. They see the death of flies, bugs, pets, and farm animals, and this can become the basis for their understanding of human death. This understanding develops slowly, however, and children under six years of age cannot comprehend the finality of death. If one listens closely to their talk, it will be noted that they deny death through talking as if the deceased will rejoin them at a later time.[12]

Existential philosophy and psychotherapy offer another avenue to the restoration of meaning following loss. From this point of view the basic motivation of all people is to live the life we have been given in the best possible way, to actualize our potentialities to the fullest, to take in the inevitability of our own death or nonbeing, and to use the anxiety aroused by this knowledge to make a free choice as to how we want to use the time allotted to us.

"I'm in a bind," said one young man. "I want a relationship with a woman but, after my wife left me, I was in such pain I wanted to commit suicide. I still cannot understand what kept me from doing it as I even had the pills at my bedside. If I remember correctly, I telephoned my wife and she came over with a friend, and somehow they got me to see somebody, and that helped. But I can't go through that pain again. If I get involved with a woman, I know that sooner or later, even if we both live to be old, one of us has to face loss. If I suffered this much once, how can I go through it again?"

The therapist agreed with his conclusion about loss and added, "Yes, loss is the price we pay for our ties to one another. It is up to each of us to decide whether we want to have only superficial relationships in our lives so that we will not be hurt when they are ended, or to have lives that are experienced to the full and include both sorrow and joy. You seem, however, to be seeking the latter." The man was left to make his own choice, but both sides of the question were addressed.

One of the values with which existentialism deals is the meaning of suffering. By no means is suffering sought as an end in itself. But it is as much a part of life as is joy or happiness, and the way in which we respond to unavoidable suffering determines the meaning we give to life. "I feel a little better this week," remarked one young man in therapy. "I saw some friends, had fun over the weekend, and don't feel quite so depressed."

"You come in here each week as if you are taking your emotional temperature," was the reply. "How you feel at the moment is not the measure of progress in therapy. There may be times when it is quite appropriate and healthy to feel miserable. Grief is one of those, and if you don't feel miserable in grief, then there is something wrong."

The existential choice facing the bereaved is how to deal with the suffering set off by their loss. The question of why the loss occurred may never be answered by any religious or philosophical system of beliefs. Just as a child's behavior can often be understood not by probing for esoteric theories as to causation but by observing the reaction elicited from parents, so is it likely that the why of a catastrophic loss may be understood only in terms of how the bereaved use loss to create a new system of values.

Mental health workers need to help the bereaved find an expression of relief that their ordeal is now ending and creative meaning in their suffering. Only through restoration of meaning can loss become an influence for growth in the lives of the bereaved, and even in the lives of generations that follow them.

Notes

1. Daniel Cappon, "The Psychology of Dying," in *The Interpretation of Death,* ed. Hendrik M. Ruitenbeek (New York: Jason Aronson, 1973), pp. 71–72.

2. Geoffrey Gorer, *Death, Grief, and Mourning: A Study of Contemporary Society* (Garden City, N.Y.: Doubleday and Co., Anchor Books, 1972).

3. Ibid.

4. Peter Marris, *Loss and Change* (New York: Pantheon Books, 1974).

5. Peter S. Adler, "The Transitional Experience: An Alternative View of Culture Shock," *Journal of Humanistic Psychology* 15 (1975): 13–23.

6. Marris, *Loss and Change*, p. 12.

7. Ibid., pp. 12–13.

8. Ibid., p. 10.

9. Ira O. Glick, Robert S. Weiss, and C. Murray Parkes, *The First Year of Bereavement* (New York: John Wiley and Sons, 1974).

10. Viktor E. Frankl, *Man's Search for Meaning* (New York: Washington Square Press, 1963), pp. 175–76.

11. Ibid., pp. 165–66.

12. Glick, Weiss, and Parkes, *The First Year of Bereavement*, p. 164.

14/
Restitution, Substitution, and Depletion

Despite all that has been written thus far about the importance of grief and mourning, recovery from loss cannot take place without the operation of a second dynamic, that of restitution. Restitution means returning to the rightful owner something that has been lost or taken away; restoration; a making up for loss or damage; reimbursement; a reinstatement to a former condition or situation.

How is it possible to contemplate the restoration of that which has been irretrievably lost? The dead do not return; age is not reversible; an amputated limb or breast cannot be restored. How can the damage of rape, flood, war, fire, looting, or other catastrophes be undone?

The Psychic Push toward Restitution

The psychodynamic push for restoration of that which has been lost does not at first differentiate among restoration of the original object, any available substitute, and creative restitution involving the integration of the old with the new. These will be discussed later.

There are several theoretical attempts to explain the impetus for restitution. One position holds that our repeated experiences from early infancy onward of separations, losses, disappointments, and relinquishments, followed by restitution on each occasion, lead us to expect that all losses will be transient, that is, that restitution will follow.[1] For example, mother goes out of sight; mother returns within view. Father leaves for long stretches of time, but returns each night. Older brothers and sisters go off to school, yet come back later in the day. Each night the young child must leave the family circle to go to bed while older family members are allowed to remain together. The young child watches a stool flush down the toilet, yet the next day new stools are produced. Hair and nails are cut, yet grow back. A favorite piece of clothing is outgrown and set aside, to be replaced by new clothes. The bottle is replaced by the cup, and diapers give way to training pants. In these and countless other ways the young child builds up a tolerance to loss and separation, with the expectation that restitution will inevitably follow.

A second impetus for restitution stems not from actual loss itself but from the many experiences of anticipation of loss that we have throughout life in fantasy. The source of these often disturbing fantasies is to be found in the child's unconscious anger, hostility, and destructiveness, which create a gap between the child and significant others. The striving for restitution is, therefore, a continuous process throughout life; because love and hate toward the same love object are part of the human condition. Restitution offers assurance that one's aggressive impulses have not triumphed over those of love, that one has not destroyed the love object. Because aggression is aroused in the child whenever a wish or impulse is frustrated, hostile fantasies toward that which causes frustration, often a parent, lead to a need for restitution to relieve the guilt set off by those hostile fantasies, which go hand in hand as necessary components of the process by which the child is socialized to function in human society and is helped to develop a separate identity.

An important impetus for restitution, then, is children's need to make reparation for unconscious fantasies of their own destructive powers. The hostility mobilized by repeated frustrations from parents remains unconscious but produces guilt, which compels relief through acts of undoing, fantasies of renunciation, sacrifice, and a range of reparative maneuvers.[2]

Children fortunate enough to have parents who allow the verbal expression of rage and anger without reprimand can also build up an awareness that their anger and, therefore, they themselves are not really harmful, because the parent contains the anger without retaliation, obviously survives the aggressive attack, and continues to nurture the child. Thus does the balance between hate and love shift slowly in the direction of love, and eventually children can in turn become loving parents.

On the other hand, the danger of traumatic losses to young children lies not only in the break in continuity, the loss of nurturing figures, and the loss of security in the meaning of life, but also in the fact that reality reinforces unconscious fears of their own destructiveness. Herein lies one danger to children of a break in the family through parental death or divorce, through the death of a sibling, breakdown of a parent, or other catastrophic event.

Restitution alone is not enough to provide the full relief necessary to quell the guilt arising from unconscious destructive impulses and fantasies. Children also seek relief through denial of the loss and through projection of blame on others, defenses that help relieve the burden of responsibility for the losses. Without these additional defenses, restitution for one's losses would be a far more difficult task.[3]

Creative Restitution versus Retrieval or Substitution

Every major loss represents an interruption in continuity of life, a blow to self-esteem, and a break in the sense of meaning in life. Recovery from the impact of such a loss requires, therefore, that continuity be reestablished, damaged self-esteem be repaired, and the sense of meaning be restored. (These tasks can be achieved by retrieval of that which was lost. The myriad forms of searching behavior discussed in chapter seven serve in this attempt.) Thus, restitution is a compelling need by which the individual attempts to restore inner psychological equilibrium, uniting past, present, and future in the cycle from loss and the fear of loss to restitution.[4]

Marlene, a young adult, annoyed her girlfriends with her obsession with buying dishes. Every time she saw a sale of dishes advertised in the newspaper, she begged one of her friends to go shopping with her. She could never decide on what she wanted. Sometimes she even bought dishes and then canceled the order before they were delivered. Her problem was that she liked so many different patterns she could not decide on one. She finally bought a simple white set for her best dishes, and then yearned for all the colorful sets she still did not have. With the help of psychoanalysis, Marlene learned that dishes symbolized food; food stood for mother, the cream pitcher being the ultimate symbol of the source of original food, mother's milk. (She had actually bought one set of dishes because of the shape of the pitcher, and canceled the order when she realized the size and pieces did not meet her needs.) With this understanding her compulsion ended. It was traced to a break in the mother-child unity when her mother had become depressed during her infancy. Her search was for the good mother who had been temporarily lost to her by depression. This was searching and substitution, not true creative restitution.

Substitution of an object to replace the lost object can also serve in an attempt to reestablish continuity, self-esteem, and a sense of meaning. Examples are the replacement of one pet by another and, in very young children, of one need-fulfilling person by another. The latter is possible before the establishment of object relations—the differentiation of one person from all others. With such easy replacement goes denial of differences between people and the importance of any special one. On the surface it may appear as enviable behavior, free of the pain of grief following loss. "Why can't I be like my friends?" moaned one young woman. "When I break up with a boyfriend, I am miserable, but he and my other friends go from one to another with no pain like I have. I envy them. They don't suffer."

She was correct in believing that her suffering was greater than theirs but not in her evaluation of them as healthy. With the investment of the self in another person, the loss of that other person leaves a void and causes a loss of self-esteem. The mere substitution of one object for another does not fill the void left by the loss or restore self-esteem or a sense of meaning. One child cannot replace another. Love on the rebound does not replace lost love. An artificial limb, breast implant, or colostomy bag does not make up for the missing body part.

To understand creative restitution, it is necessary to refer back to John Bowlby's conceptualization of the three stages of mourning described in chapter three. Stage one is concerned with the attempt to retrieve the lost object; stage two with the disorganization and despair following failure of the attempt; and stage three with reorganization of a new life without that which has been lost.[5]

Creative restitution belongs to the third stage of mourning. Reorganization within the life of the bereaved takes place "partly in connection with the image of the lost object, partly in connection with a new object or objects."[6]

The futility of mere replacement is well expressed by this simple tale. A man was walking along a street when he came upon a little boy crying as if his heart would break.

"What's the matter, little boy?" the man asked.

Pointing to the grate in the sidewalk, the youngster answered, "I had a nickel and it dropped down there, and now I lost my nickel."

"Don't cry," said the man. "Here's another nickel."

To the man's surprise, the youngster started to cry even harder.

"What's the matter now?" the man asked with some annoyance. "You lost a nickel and I just gave you another. Why the tears?"

"You don't understand," wailed the child. "If I hadn't lost my nickel, I would now have two nickels."

With the unconscious wisdom of folk tales, the child's tears reveal the importance of the second phase of mourning, the release of grief through which the wound is healed. Grief and mourning are what lie between the searching of the first stage and true restitution of the third phase of the loss cycle.

Without the catharsis of grief, by which the attachment to the lost object is slowly and painfully relinquished, through the repetitious attempts at recovery, and the repetitious disappointments in the failure of those endeavors, some part of the emotional energy of the person remains tied to the lost object. This tie, unless broken, becomes the nucleus for much of the pathology in unresolved grief.

The difference between restitution in the final stage of grief and the retrieval attempts of the first stage is found in the experience or absence of the intervening mourning process. Mourning, it must again be stated, involves first the actual recognition of the loss and second the step-by-step relinquishment of the ties to the lost object. Time alone does not take care of the matter. Grief is a process that must be lived through, at the end of which the bereaved is prepared to extract the essence of the meaning of the lost object and to integrate it through a new sense of self, strengthened by the grief process, into new attachments.

It is not easy for an observer to know from the behavior of the bereaved whether the replacement is true restitution characterizing the recovery period of the loss cycle or an attempt at retrieval of the lost object. The same object can be used for either purpose, and the meaning is to be found in the thoughts and fantasies of the bereaved, not even necessarily on a conscious level.

A widower remarries a few months after the death of his wife. Is this creative restitution or an attempt at substitution? Parents who have lost a child decide to apply for adoption. Is this true restitution or avoidance of the pain of grief through the fantasy of a replacement child?

The fear of loss as well as an actual loss can generate the need for restitution. "Come see our new puppy," invited the Browns. "Ginger is nearing sixteen and we thought we should have another dog around because she can't last many more years. This way we won't feel so bad when she goes."

Characteristics of Restitution

To attempt to list the forms that restitution might take would be to attempt to enumerate everything in life that might be of value to the human being. Because this would, of course, be an impossible and fruitless task, let us rather attempt some conceptualization of restitution to fit the earlier conceptualization of loss discussed at the beginning of the book. Just as loss can be of a person, a part or function of the body, of material things, values, dreams, wishes, hopes, familiar places, a job, one's native land, neurotic patterns, childhood images of self and significant others, so can restitution be in any one or more of these forms, or in others not mentioned.

Restitution for loss can be sought in a number of ways. The search can be direct or indirect; conscious or unconscious; complete or partial; real or fantasied; immediate or gradual; predictable or unexpected; social or secret; healthy or pathological; by deed, thought, or in fantasy, dreams, and other mental processes. No one can decide what constitutes restitution to another, nor what form of search another may take. The search for restitution can precede or follow a loss, and the forms are as varied as life itself.

Direct restitution for the object lost is easy to recognize. The widow or divorcee searches for another mate; the house destroyed by fire or flood is rebuilt; the discharged employee finds another job; the infertile couple adopts a child.

Symbolic restitution is found in the monuments, statues, endowments, buildings, and charities established in the name of a deceased person, or in naming children after the dead. It is found in the value we attach to material articles bequeathed to us by dead loved ones, not so much for their monetary value alone as for their association with the deceased.

A rather grotesque example of symbolic restitution is given by Jordan Scher, who discusses the primitive impulse in society, still rampant, whereby the living are revitalized by death:

> Since Cain slew Abel, and even before, when man slew beast, the mantle, the birthright, the very life stuff of the vanquished or the slaughtered was somehow mystically acquired in a strangely concrete way by the victor or the hunter. It was not uncommon for Greek warriors to eat the heart of a brave and fallen enemy so that they might absorb his strength. It is a not unpopular saying in today's world that if you eat fish, you will have more brain power or if spinach, you will become stronger. Witchcraft was deeply alive with the concept of acquiring, tampering with, controlling, or changing the life stuff of another. Men fear traffic with the dead (and those who conduct such traffic). The evil eye is still feared today since men think it capable of great powers of destruction or control of the life stuff. Even the psychiatrist is feared since it is rumored he can see into and control this life stuff or psyche.
>
> Genocide, or the destruction of one ethnic or culture group by another, is a clear-cut modern reflection of the ancient myth that the death of another means the enhancement of life for oneself, or returning of surplus life stuff to the reservoir from which it can then be reassigned.[7]

Restitution through relationships

Because the human being is a social creature, loss propels us to attempt to restore contact with others. There is thus always the search for an object outside ourselves to accomplish the task of restitution.

The new relationship is not necessarily similar to the old. For example, in his study of widows, Ira O. Glick found various patterns of relationships sought as restitution for the lost husband: (1) remarriage; (2) intimate nonmarital relationship with a man with no desire for remarriage; (3) close relationships with relatives such as sister, mother, or brother; (4) close relationships with children but otherwise isolation from other adults. Younger widows, especially those without children, tended to drift back to their single friends; they tended to feel marginal among former married friends and among widows, who were usually older than they.[8]

Restitution through relationship may be sought through heterosexual or homosexual outlets, of long or short duration. Turning toward a love object of one's own sex is one way of expressing anger at the former heterosexual love object for having left.

Restitution need not be of the complete object. It can be partial, such as in the transference relationships found in psychotherapy, or those that constitute the basis for "falling in love" at first sight. A trait of a love object can be found in someone else. The need to belong to someone can be transferred from the spouse to a child or turned around into caring for a pet; the need for positive feedback can be found in a friend; companionship may come from a variety of others, sharing one interest with one person, another with someone else.

When relationships are disappointing, one can always fall back on love of oneself. One form is the clinical picture of hypochondriasis, an overconcern with the body, wherein morbid attention is paid to details of body functioning, and symptoms, no matter how insignificant, are exaggerated. Investing emotionally in one's body instead of in other people can serve as a protection from competition and social responsibility and gratify deep-seated dependency needs. Although it may be judged neurotic and dysfunctional, hypochondriasis needs to be looked at in the light of alternatives. If there are no significant others available for restitution, as is often the case with the extremely old, it may be a better alternative than suicide.

Restitution through material objects

Food has deep unconscious ties to loss as a form of restitution. Its use at the time of funeral rites as restitution for the lost object has already been mentioned. Food and alcohol are solace for the rejected lover. Money is another form of compensation for loss. This is seen in monetary damages awarded by courts of law, the money left under the pillow of the youngster by the good tooth fairy, and monetary compensation paid by Germany to victims of the Nazi Holocaust.

Material objects become imbued with meaning through association with significant people and memories. Their loss, therefore, cannot be measured in objective or monetary terms, because often they are not only irretrievable but also irreplaceable, as in the case of photographs, family keepsakes and records, or other possessions lost by fire, flood, burglary, and so on.

This same dynamic is found in the fetishist, who substitutes a material object—a shoe, a piece of clothing—for a lost love object. Whereas the latter is labeled pathological, the same dynamic of substitution of a thing for a person is found in the transitional object of the toddler— the blanket, piece of torn clothing, or diaper—an important linking phenomenon in normal development. These transitional objects are children's security blankets during the period of struggling to separate themselves from their mothers.

The elderly learn to replace people by things to which they become attached, things less easily perishable that can be controlled and possessed. The loss of personal items through stealing in nursing and convalescent homes must, therefore, be appreciated as additional losses to the elderly, who are powerless to prevent these cumulative attacks.

A young couple were referred for marital counseling by their family physician to whom the husband had complained of his wife's lack of interest in sex. "She must have another man on the string," was the physician's superficial assessment of the case. During the one and only interview it was soon apparent that the wife was through with the marriage. Her acceptance of the referral was a gesture of her willingness to go along with her husband's attempt to salvage their marriage, but that for her emotionally the marriage was over. It had been a youthful marriage based in part on her rebellion against rigid, religious parents. Once the rebellion wore off, she found she had married a self-centered, coarse, unfeeling man who relentlessly overrode her wishes and emotions.

The crisis came over the issue of a car her parents had given her as a high school graduation gift. She spoke tenderly and almost poetically of her love for the car. Her husband listened coldly as she spoke of her heartbreak when he had insisted on selling the car and buying her one of his own choosing. "But I loved it so," she mourned, as he argued about the danger of her driving such an old car. In exasperation at her inability to understand his professed concern for her safety (masking his excuse for lavish spending), he exclaimed: "But it was four years old already!" Coldly she looked him over and answered quietly, "Our marriage is four years old too," and it was clear that for her his final disregard of the meaning of a possession bestowed by loving parents marked the end of their relationship.

The pain of many divorces is worked out through battle over material possessions. Material objects constitute the essence of the science and art of prosthetics, whereby lives are rehabilitated after the loss of body parts. Material things can be the linkages for ties to the past, providing for continuity from one life experience to another. Items saved from a fire or flood, restored to their original beauty, can become the kernel for emotional restitution and renewed living.

Restitution through mental processes

If reality and hard work fail to bring about restitution, it is still possible to find restoration for loss through the many mental processes available to us as human beings. Gregory Rochlin considers the dream as the most continuous and the greatest source of mental restitution. It allows for the restoration in the unconscious of that which was lost: the unconscious has no restrictions as to time or place. The dream combines the residues of the day with lifetime unfulfilled wishes, thus the wishes fulfilled in the dream can be of the day itself or of past wishes given up or repressed. He says: "It is in the dream that the reality principle gives way to the pleasure principle; the engine of change operates to transform losses into gains."[9]

Fantasy is another important form of restitution. It is a product of the imagination and consists of a group of symbols synthesized by the secondary process or conscious mind into a unified story. In this it differs from the dream, which remains on a primary process (unconscious) level. The fantasy gives the illusion that wishes have been fulfilled and does away with obstacles, transforming pain into pleasure, thus serving the same purpose as the dream. The fantasy may be conscious or unconscious, may precede action or substitute for it. It may take the form of a daydream or a dream at night; in either case it remains an ego function and is more limited than the dream.

A common fantasy is to be present at one's own funeral. Children often fantasize this when angry at parents for punishment. "You'll be sorry when I am dead" is the theme. There are several elements in this fantasy: sadistic pleasure in the grief of the survivors, identification with the mourners over the loss, thus surpassing the limitations of life itself.

Play is children's natural form of expression and communication, their natural language, just as verbal expression later becomes the natural language of the adult. The spontaneous bodily movements involved in children's play are their way of expressing feelings and thoughts and of relating themselves to their world. To articulate their thoughts and feelings is difficult because at times they do not know exactly what they feel or, if they do, they frequently dare not say what they think or feel in the presence of critical adults. Play, moreover, is to the child what free association and dreams are to the adult, the road to the unconscious. Some seriously disturbed children are unable to play. Play has in it some of the same elements of the dream— wish-fulfillment, manifest and latent content, residues of the day's experiences, symbolization, condensation, fantasy, memory, pleasure principal, and working through of conflict. Thus, play is still another important avenue for restitution.

If one pays careful attention to the delusions and hallucinations of the psychotic patient, one will find memories of early object relations, parents. Here then is another form of restitution or retrieval of the lost object. The hallucinations and delusions of schizophrenics can be considered reparations in that through them they try to deal with their unbearable internal state by mentally constructing another world. In this world everything has another meaning, sometimes hidden, sometimes clear, but nearly always a prophetic or symbolic one. They will sometimes perceive them as good, sometimes as frightening, but they always represent an inner perception of the tendencies to restore what was lost through the regression.[10] The schizophrenic attempts to regain the lost object through word representations, because in schizophrenia words and verbal ideas assume the role of objects.

People who survive isolation experiences, such as sailors adrift alone for long periods of time or people buried under snow or earthslides, report that they dealt with the terror of being without others by hallucinations and delusions of having a companion present or by experiencing being at one with the universe.[11]

Mythmaking is the communal form of fantasy and serves in the interests of wish fulfillment. Myths are the cultural form by which the theme of loss and restitution is carried out. The myth of the American frontier hero which has captured worldwide imagination satisfies deep-seated fantasies that good wins over bad, and that what has been lost, relinquished, or stolen will be restored. In the course of the story, however, the formerly weak and helpless hero acquires the attributes of the villain, namely, aggression, now used in the cause of good.[12] Another universal myth is that of a people with a golden past. The prestigious past adds status to the present. The current popularity of genealogical searches testifies to this longing.

Religious beliefs have been a major defense of people in all societies and cultures against the fear of death. Beliefs that offer immortality and resurrection are stimulated by the child's search for causality at an early age, when the belief in magic and the reversibility of death is still strong. Fear of death leads to creative solutions to living.

Freud and others regarded identification with the lost object as a necessary mental condition for the resolution of grief; restitution is achieved through this internalization. Thus, the object can be relinquished in reality because, in fact, it is never given up but kept inside and one can identify with traits, tastes, values, interests, symptoms, illnesses, or other attributes of the deceased.

"I used to be a wallflower, watching my husband be the life of the party," remarked one outgoing, friendly widow. "You would never believe I am the same person. Now I am the center of attention like he was." The extravagant man with a cautious wife may take on her cautiousness with her death.

Anna Freud postulates the thesis that children separated from their mothers tend to take over the mothering role themselves by taking good care of their own bodies. In this way they identify with the lost mother in their caretaking, while their own body represents the infant in the mother's care.

From this point of view, mourning comes to an end when the object that is lost is internalized and becomes part of the ego, enriching it, changing it through incorporating aspects of the object that is lost. Thus, loss through mourning can be a way of enriching the ego. New experiences may set off grief anew; each time, if the bereaved is free to express grief, further bits of grief can be resolved. Anniversary reactions are good examples of this process.

Restoration of self-esteem

To understand restitution, one must appreciate the relationship between loss and self-esteem. Aside from the loss of the valued object itself, any loss has in it the potential for damage to self-esteem. Self-esteem is a vulnerable quality that is affected by a variety of influences. Damage to or loss of self-esteem must be redeemed. Low self-esteem is an unacceptable condition that must be rectified.

A number of avenues are available for the restoration of self-esteem. A severe illness following a catastrophic disappointment may be an unconscious way to restore self-esteem through being cared for; care means being worthwhile and valued. In this attempt at restitution we see regression to an early form of gratification, in that self-esteem begins in infancy in a healthy nurturing experience of the infant.

The loss of some aspect of the self, whether physical or psychological, is most damaging to self-esteem, if not threatening to life itself. In this area we find endless examples of restorative attempts involving both structure and function. These include, for example, the toupee, false teeth, the face-lift, other plastic surgery for physical deformities, eyeglasses and contact lenses, hearing aids, prostheses, and, most recent of all, organ implants.

Self-esteem can be sought by identification with a social movement or cause from which one derives reflected power and glory. For adolescents and young adults, who can submerge their own fragile identity to the context of a larger cause, especially one in which there is a charismatic leader, this is a way by which self-esteem is shored up during a turbulent phase of development. Another means is by religion, whereby the worship of a higher power reflects back on the devotee. Religion also offers inclusion in a social group, release from suffering through salvation, and restitution through the promise of eventual reunion with loved ones in the hereafter.

Self-esteem can be sought through being important in a group, through involvement in meaningful political and social activity, through association with creative, important, or affluent people, or through support of charitable activities. The father of a murdered youth devotes his life to the control of handguns; another parent whose child committed suicide while under the influence of drugs or alcohol makes the elimination of those abuses a cause. As we grow older, self-esteem can be sought through identification with younger idealized objects such as children or students; teaching gratifies the wish to leave something of value to the next generation.

Because self-esteem is not an absolute but rather a relative matter, it can be restored by damaging the self-esteem of another as a way of elevating the self. The sweetness of revenge also lies in the restoration of self-esteem by creating a loss for another.

Therefore, even if the lost object itself cannot be replaced, there can be restoration of self-esteem damaged by the loss. The form need not be the same as that damaged by the loss. Many factors determine the form sought. Some people will regress to dependency and illness; others will find someone to whom they can feel superior; and some will use the experience of loss and grief to develop aspects of strength and character from untapped resources.

Restitution through mastery

Our human limitations are experienced as losses of wish fulfillment and of self-esteem. Such awareness can goad us on to achievement. Mastery restores self-esteem by healing the narcissistic wound that accompanies failure and its accompanying sense of inadequacy. Mastery has to do with the self-esteem that derives from one's own efforts and labor. Examples abound throughout the life cycle. Ideally, children should learn the techniques of goal-directedness by their own efforts in the school situation. They should be given tasks that stretch their capabilities and have the potential for success.

Failure in one area can be compensated for by success in another. Mrs. Jones, an elderly widow, looked back proudly on her life of achievement. As an adoring sister of a brilliant older brother, she had tried to follow in his footsteps, only to fail in medical school. The shame was extremely painful to her, a proud girl. Eventually, she compensated by marrying a physician, but the wound to her own pride remained. While pregnant with their first child, she contracted polio, and after a prolonged illness she was left with a severe physical impairment. With what in retrospect seemed like superhuman effort, she set about regaining as much use of her arms and legs as was possible with the help of the rehabilitative knowledge of those years. She took care of her baby herself and did the housework without any hired help. After her daughter was grown and out of the home, she became active in volunteer work. At the time of her husband's death, when she was in her sixties, she had become a respected community figure in her small town. She had used the physical handicap to regain through mastery the self-esteem lost by the school failure.

The stroke victim struggles to walk again, to speak, and to build up anew functions lost by the illness. The amputee struggles to be proficient in the use of prostheses; the paraplegic or quadriplegic does the same with function. The struggle can bring people to high levels of achievement. Teddy Roosevelt, once declared an invalid, became a model for physical fitness. In 1977, a legless weight lifter broke the world record in the bantamweight class.[13]

Restitution is the ultimate goal of Thomas J. Carroll in his work with the blind. Just as he outlined the multiple and cumulative losses involved in the loss of sight (outlined in chapter two), so does he proceed to outline the means by which the blind person can acquire a new identity in spite of the handicap. His conceptualization of what constitutes restitution is a model transferable to other losses. He outlines the following areas for rehabilitation and restoration:

Training the other senses
Restoration of psychological security
   The sense of physical integrity
   Confidence in the remaining senses
   Reality contact with the environment
   Background and light security
Restoration of basic skills
   Mobility
   Techniques of daily living
Restoration of ease of communication
   Written communication
   Spoken communication
   Informational progress

Restoration of appreciation
  Perception of the pleasurable
  Perception of the beautiful
Restoration of occupation and financial status
  Recreation,
  Career, vocational goal, job opportunity
  Financial security
Restoration of the whole personality
  Personal independence
  Social adequacy
  Obscurity
  Self-esteem
  Total personality organization
Helping the family
Educating the public[14]

The widowed and divorced find restitution in learning to tolerate and even enjoy being physically alone, becoming sole providers for themselves and their children, finding new social relationships, mastering household management problems, developing a deepening awareness of other people and their difficulties, and working toward a new sense of identity. Some return to school, finish education long since neglected or abandoned, start new careers, turn to volunteer or charity work, the arts, or other creative outlets, or support of creative endeavors.

The fear of loss can also act as a spur to mastery. The fear of burglary and rape has resulted in burgeoning businesses having to do with alarm and safety devices to fortify homes against intrusion. Self-defense classes for women are another outgrowth of this fear.

Loss of self-esteem is a most painful experience, and the restoration of that self-esteem becomes important in overcoming the shame reaction in loss. Examples that show this clearly are Alger Hiss's struggle to restore his reputation following his release from prison, the attempt of the Rosenberg sons to clear the names of their parents convicted and executed for treason during the McCarthy era of the early 1950s, and the successful attempts of the parents of the Kent State University victims to establish before the Ohio governor and adjutant general that guardsmen were accountable for their random shooting into the crowd.

Probably one of the greatest tasks of mastery is displayed by political refugees who have had to flee their native country and start anew in a foreign land. For some people this dislocation has occurred more than once. Those who lost loved ones in concentration camps often felt compelled to start new families as soon as possible. Others chose to not reproduce, but found restitution in building careers or businesses and in reestablishing in the new country lifestyles similar to those they had known in the homeland.

Actively working for causes, such as for the prevention of a disease that kills a loved one or from which one is suffering, is another form of mastery. As long as strength, health, energy, and hope last, attempts at mastery continue. They may even go hand-in-hand with hopelessness in that there may be conscious or unconscious relinquishment of hope in one area combined with strenuous attempts at mastery in others. The possibilities are endless and the choices are as wide as life itself. Mastery finds its ultimate expression in creativity.

Restitution through creativity

Rochlin reminds us that the pain set off by loss is so great that it tends to obscure the fact "that losses, real and otherwise, by serving as catalysts of change and forcing substitution and sublimation, play a critical role in psychic development, and especially in that most exalted of human qualities, creativity." Rochlin sees creativity as restitution for the loss of self-esteem suffered when we encounter our human limitations.[15] The nature of the loss seems to matter little in its potential for generating creativity. Rochlin uses the term "creative" to apply to all those productions arising out of an ability to devise new ways to overcome the limitations of reality.

There is a common saying that genius is 10 percent inspiration and 90 percent perspiration. Creative work demands mastery plus talent; without the former, talent can be dissipated. Mastery is the term applied to the effort put into the development of skills, goal-directedness, the ability to struggle, to defer gratification, and to stick to a task to completion. Mastery is an essential ingredient in creative work but does not guarantee it. Despite stereotypes to the contrary, which attribute gross emotional conflicts to the creative artist, Rochlin finds that the creative artist or genius has "emotional disorders and neuroses of the most prosaic variety."[16] He tends to believe that the great works of psychotic geniuses were produced in spite of their illness instead of because of it.

Artists, whether painters, sculptors, writers, or composers, have the fantasy that their production will outlive them and be left for future generations to see. Thus, in striving for immortality they transcend loss.

Contrary to Freud, who felt that eventually reason would conquer the irrational in man, others believe that in both the child and adult wishes will always prevail over learning and knowledge. Young children have great concern about death, which they often see as the cessation of vital functions due to defective interpersonal relationships (such as defiance of authority, hostility, sexual impulses, retaliation), that is, the projection of their own intimate concerns.

Despite intellectual and rational development with age and education, these early fears remain throughout life and stand ready to emerge under crisis. Loss is such a crisis. Loss, therefore, which sets off ultimate fears of death and abandonment and attacks the feeling of narcissism, unleashes forces for change that culminate in creative attempts at living, striving for the extension of one's powers, and the elaboration into vital and sophisticated social institutions underlying the basis of culture itself.[17]

Restitution of a sense of meaning

A severe bereavement makes life meaningless because the object to which the meaning of life was attached, once lost, took with it also the anchorage to which that meaning was attached. In the midst of the initial trauma of loss, the disruption in the continuity of the meaning of life seems irreparable. The thread of meaning has been broken. How can it ever be made whole again?

The bereaved person does not give up the object completely through grieving but draws out from it aspects which are then reattached to new objects. This continuity is necessary for assimilation of the loss, for without it there is a cutting off of one part of life, a break between the old and the new instead of integration. The process of detachment and reattachment begins by the bereaved person reviving the relationship with the lost object mentally. Each memory, so in conflict with the absence of the object in reality, brings home a new disappointment. Repeated nonreward of behavior results in eventual extinction of that behavior. As time goes on, the reality of the loss begins to be assimilated.

The bereaved may begin by talking to the deceased as if he or she were actually present, then wondering what he or she might have said, then dreaming of the person, then making those thoughts his own. If these changes are gradual, the continuity of meaning can be sustained. Gretchen came for help because of a feeling that life held no meaning. Her major symptom was her desire to sleep. She often went to sleep immediately after dinner, yet she knew her job was not so physically or mentally tiring that she should need that much rest.

Exploration of Gretchen's problem revealed that she was not consciously aware of how much she missed her homeland, Germany. Marriage had brought her to the United States, and she had remained despite her divorce because life was economically more secure for her here. She had a well-paying and gratifying profession which could not be duplicated in Germany. Yet in every dream the scene was in her homeland. "But I'm never homesick," she insisted. "It seems your body is here, but your heart is there," she was told. When asked what she missed most, she started to speak of the difference in the observance of Christmas, and then suddenly burst into tears. "I don't even know why I'm crying," she said. "I didn't know I was lonesome. I like to spend Christmas alone here instead of going to parties. Our Christmas was a quiet family affair, going to church . . ." and the tears flowed on. Her lack of zest and complaint of boredom was the key to her emotional life having stopped, so to speak, in the areas touching on family life and homeland, a loss she had endured without going through the process of grief.

Paul Steiner, a sociologist, has conducted lengthy research aimed at discovering the hows and whys of the terror tactics and persecution by the Nazis around the period of World War II. His interviews of some 250 former S.S. men, the group that carried out Hitler's racial policies, showed that the men were eager to talk about the circumstances that led to their becoming actors involved in a process of mass destruction. They told him that they felt their lives had become a burden to them and that telling what they knew of the Nazi persecution was one way to make some restitution. Steiner's work emerged out of his compulsion to understand what had happened in his own life as a Czechoslovakian-born prisoner in five slave labor and death camps and his desire to prevent such horrors from happening again. He considers his research "a study in compliance" and believes that once a nation starts on this path, it is difficult to stop its escalation.[18] Thus grief is mastered, not by forgetting the past, and not by holding on to it, but by abstracting from it the essential meaning of the tie and recreating it to fit the new life which must go on without the missing object.

Opportunities for Restitution

The ultimate ability to overcome grief depends on the availability of resources for restoration of the object, of self-esteem, and of the sense of meaning. Resources are both external and internal. External resources have to do with the availability of acceptable replacement objects, opportunities for experiences elevating self-esteem, and the timing of crucial events facilitating the restoration of a sense of meaning. The age of a person at the time of loss is an important variable. Childhood and old age are the most vulnerable periods in life for restitution.

It is true, for example, that surrogates in the form of adoptive or foster parents or loving relatives can be mobilized on behalf of a child bereft of birth parents and may provide necessary caretaking during the formative years. A gap remains for the child, however, out of the break in continuity with the original parent(s) regardless of the reason for the break.

The ability to find restitution for bodily loss of structure or function may depend on where one lives. If sophisticated medical and rehabilitative services are available, the outcome of the loss may be quite different than if one lived in an isolated location where such knowledge and skill are not accessible.

Timing is of importance in the availability of the ability to find restitution. At the time of a loss, there may be "nothing of value for substitution . . . available or acceptable."[19] For example, when one member of a post-parental couple dies, it is not surprising that the other would turn to adult children for some of the needs formerly met by the spouse. What happens if there are no children, if they live at a great geographical distance, if in-laws object to the shift in relationships, if children are estranged from parents, or if parents fear "reactivating either incestuous relationships or one of the defensive sado-masochistic positions parents and children so frequently assume"?[20]

There are still other problems about restitution in the nature of our society. America has been called a "nation of strangers."[21] To accommodate the demands of our industrialized economy, people move frequently, and with these moves go the sense of rootedness, of community, of continuity with a place and a group. The economic sphere is no substitute for family relationships. The modern business organization or bureaucracy can be dehumanizing in using people as units of production and discarding them when it is expedient or when they reach a certain retirement age, without regard to the impact on self-esteem. "Burn out" is a term that has been applied to the fatigue of teachers, nurses, social workers, and others confronted by the daily impersonality and demands of the bureaucracy. The paycheck alone is no substitute for kindness and consideration from superiors and co-workers. Often to change jobs is no solution. The same problems will exist in the next organization because they are inherent in organizational structure and functions. These modern businesses thrive best in the large cities. The intimacy of the small town is gone.

It is difficult among strangers to maintain a sense of identity because appropriate feedback is missing. No one knows that we are part of the Brown family, or the wife of the town newspaperman or plumber, or a cousin of the minister. These ties to others are part of identity long before our own achievements become the source of self-esteem. The artificial search for intimacy in contrived groups with strangers, over an extended weekend, and even in nude encounters, is not the same as knowing someone over a period of years, sharing joys and sorrows, knowing there is someone to depend on in an emergency, knowing there are people who care about the little things as well as the major events in one's life.

The absence of the extended family and the vulnerability of the nuclear family in the event of loss is another important factor in the availability of resources. The death of a parent is enough of a trauma in any event; when it occurs in a family separated from supportive relatives, the demands on the surviving parent can be overwhelming. The loss of a job, illness of one parent, or chronic illness of a child can also strain the resources of the vulnerable nuclear family.

Liberalized divorce laws and the sexual revolution have created severe problems in regard to loss and restitution. One problem is the marked increase in the number of separations with which both adults and children need to cope. Multiple and blended families present new problems of adjustment. Unfortunately, many people in the helping professions still do not appreciate the severe impact on the personality of the child of the permanent loss of a parent. The outward adjustment or behavior is no criterion for judging the potential for serious underlying problems. These problems may be minimal or even go unnoticed during the school years, because school can provide a structure that hides the underlying turmoil. Graduation from high school, with its demand for decision making, or, for some, leaving school earlier will unmask the problem.

The sexual revolution has also created a situation where the freedom "to do your own thing" has led to the exploitation of many middle-aged and older women. These women think that if only they could discard their less than perfect husbands there would be other men eagerly awaiting them. Often, men who divorce seek younger, attractive women for themselves, and this is socially acceptable. By the middle years they are also at the height of their earning powers. In contrast, the women of forty or fifty, who have spent their adult years as homemakers, when divorced are often without economic skills and feel—and are often regarded by employers as—too old to start competing in the job market. Nor can they readily find a direct replacement for their spouses, because women outnumber men. Remarriage is not always possible not only because eligible men may not be available and emotional attachments may remain with the husband, but also because children may resent a replacement for the lost father. Both widowhood and divorce often mean a woman must become the wage earner, and a decline in family status is suffered because the woman's earnings are less than the man's had been.

The sexual and companion-protector areas are the most unfulfilled aspects of widowhood, and although grief at the loss of the husband fades with time, the loneliness of the widow that is related to the absence of a significant figure does not.

The loss of a grown child through death brings the most distressing and long-lasting grief. Here the opportunity for direct replacement is missing, because childbearing years are over. Restitution must come, then, from symbolic replacement such as involvement in charity work, completion of further education, or devotion to causes related to the life of the child.

One large area for restitution has been seen in the German program of monetary restitution to World War II victims of Nazism. The payment of monetary claims implies responsibility for damage inflicted. Where such responsibility would be denied, facts would be distorted in the interests of rejection of the claims. The reaction of the world when concentration camp victims were first released was to attempt to refuse claims for compensation in the belief that the suffering had ended with the release of the prisoners from the camps. Increasingly, we are becoming aware of the gross psychological as well as physical damage suffered by the victims during the period of their internment. Survivors and their children are becoming more widely known to social agencies and psychiatric services as time goes on. Often the refugees married as quickly as possible in order to reestablish families. Children became the carriers of hope for the parents. Parents were often overprotective of children (how can one punish a child when one has seen children being murdered?) or, conversely, found it difficult to show love.

We have dealt thus far with external resources for restitution. The internal resources have to do with the age of the individual, health, personality, defenses, unconscious processes, flexibility, and, in the last analysis, the state of vitality or exhaustion.

The manner in which we respond to loss in later life follows the pattern laid down in infancy and early childhood of response to similar losses, just as the manner by which "we reorganize our object relations following loss later in life will depend on the kind of success we had in doing so in these earlier experiences."[22] The unconscious is timeless; that is, past, present, and future merge, and earlier unresolved conflicts remain alive in the present. Thus, healthy internalized objects may be the best protection against loss throughout life.

One of the deepest forms of inability to reattach to new objects is found in people who have had problems in regard to attachment and separation during early life. If the mother-child dyad of the early months of life was insufficient, or if it was broken prematurely, or if the mother was threatened by the child's attempts to separate from her in the course of normal growth, that child will have later problems of attachment. There will also be fears of rejection, a vulnerability to loss, a proclivity toward depression rather than grief, and difficulties in meeting commitments. Life will be governed by deep unconscious processes working against attachment to anyone but the mother. Parent loss for the child has the potential for serious problems in regard to later attachments. Even if another love object is available after loss, it does not mean necessarily that reattachment will take place. Emotional ties to the lost object when incompletely severed leave the bereaved with little emotional energy to reinvest in new objects or interests. Reattachment problems are not confined to love objects alone. They may show up as difficulties in meeting commitments to a profession, to friends, to a course of study, to a therapeutic relationship.

Regarding the child who has suffered parent loss, Erna Furman states: "If his mourning was not complete, if its completion did not free sufficient object libido, if he feared a repetition of the loss too much to invest himself fully again, the child was unable to form a new relationship with a parent."[23] A common example of refusal to reattach is found in the rejection of the substitute school teacher by students, often expressed as rebellion or disorder. Substitute teachers know their job is not an easy one.

Flexibility is one important internal resource for restitution. The widow or divorcee who insists that only remarriage or a relationship with a man will do may be in for severe disappointment. Old age results in a larger number of women than men. The woman who cannot find pleasure in relationships with other women, who would "rather die than be seen out having dinner with another woman on Saturday night," is hardly likely to find healthy restitution.

Flexibility in regard to the evaluation of job-related status is another variable in the ability to find restitution. During recent years we have seen a marked change in the relative status of doctors, lawyers, plumbers, academicians, and craftsmen. The person whose self-esteem is anchored to only one kind of work or profession is likely to encounter severe restitution problems in a world as economically unstable as ours is today. One day it is teachers who are superfluous on the job market; the next it is engineers; a third it is college professors. It has been said that we need to be prepared for about four major career changes during a lifetime in the years ahead. The ability to value those who work with their hands as well as those whose work is primarily mental may be an important survival tool in years to come.

For some middle-aged people, internal and external resources are still sufficient to allow for restitution of new relationships and interests to compensate for the loss of self-esteem from the loss of youth, of a changing body image, and the emancipation of children. Important here is the preservation of basic anchorages such as an intact body and body image, a satisfactory home, a solid socioeconomic base, and a meaningful purpose to life.[24] This allows for the continuity of sharing relationships in which one can have the satisfaction of giving as well as receiving. In regard to the middle years:

> For some, the loss of narcissistic gratification through changes in "attractiveness" constitutes the greatest loss [threat] of this period, if not of their entire lives. The failure of long-relied-upon exhibitionism or other narcissistic gratifications and their effects on various kinds of defensive sublimations have not been given the significant place deserved in the onset of middle-aged neurotic decompensation.[25]

Other fears of middle age can result in unhealthy attempts at restitution. Blaming a spouse for one's own decline is not uncommon, particularly in a society where projection of responsibility on others is a major problem encountered by helping professionals. It is true that many empty marriages consummated in early life are no longer tenable after children leave home, and these may now be dissolved. In the search to recapture youth, however, men may turn to younger women, start new families, or become "swingers," with no commitments other than those of their own pleasure and desperate attempt to prove continued potency.

Women may avoid remarriage for fear of a loss of autonomy, objections of children to parental remarriage (which may have been a rationalization for the parent's own reluctance), continuing attachment to a deceased husband because of incomplete mourning, or a refusal to accept the restrictions of marriage again.

Fear can be a deterrent to restitution in the sexual sphere, particularly the fear of impotence in men. If a man fails sexually a couple of times, he loses his confidence and starts doubting his ability to maintain an erection; soon he may consider himself totally impotent and the situation hopeless. During youth a temporary failure can be taken in stride. When it occurs in later life, when a certain decline has already occurred, the man may conclude that sex life has ended. Following surgery, a man may find he is impotent and come to the same conclusion that the condition is permanent. And some elderly widowers or divorced men prefer celibacy to the risking of rejection from a new sexual partner.

Robert C. Peck's model for successful aging discussed in chapter twelve stresses the importance of flexibility in relinquishing unattainable goals in favor of age-appropriate ones as the person ages. Examination of his four goals for the middle-aged and three for the elderly shows that restitution is possible throughout, so that even death is transcendable. It can be concluded that:

The satisfaction of needs is related, then, not only to the ego structure of the individuals concerned, but also to the timing and history of crucial events in the lives of their significant loved ones. . . . In the course of a lifetime, one may need to re-anchor or resecure the self repeatedly in order to restore a sense of self-esteem and worth.[26]

The spacing or convergence of losses is another factor affecting internal resources for restitution. A person may be able to mobilize energy for restorative efforts following a major loss such as the death of a spouse, or of a child, but should major losses come simultaneously or in rapid succession, the effort necessary to start anew to find replacements may be too great. This is particularly applicable to the later years of life, when losses do converge from all sides. The losses of old age, just as the losses of childhood, are often underestimated:

It has often been suggested clinically and supported by popular views that the losses experienced in later life are received with acceptance or resignation and without efforts at restitution. Careful study does not support these speculative ideas. Resignation in the face of serious loss or a threat to life is more illusion than it is fact. No new mental mechanisms develop in old age; none really appear which were not previously present, nor does an unwelcome reality late in life lessen the necessity to use over and over defenses which have been well developed in the past, particularly those which relate to loss.

True resignation and an acceptance of what the Fates offer appear not to be human qualities.[27]

Another example of the operation of flexibility in the aged is a gradual shift in attention and energy from the present to the past, from abstract meaning to concrete thinking, from people to animals and inanimate objects, and from outside to inside. Depression, acting out, alcoholism, drugs are all ways to ward off the panic of the approaching years. The most profound effects of the experience of loss are most often rooted in the fear of abandonment, of object loss. The overriding fear of people in their middle years is not that of death but of abandonment in old age, expressed as "What will happen if I get old and there is nobody there?" If the formation of meaningful relationships is the most important psychic task of childhood, then "the maintenance of meaningful object relationships may truly be said to be the principal psychic task of the later years."[28]

Restitution may be rejected as a way of denying the loss. Many survivors of Nazi persecution refused to file claims for monetary compensation. One reason given was that if they did not get money for their losses, the Germans might feel more guilty. Another was that no money could compensate for the loss of loved ones. How many dollars is the life of a child worth? Or a wife? Or husband? Or eighty-nine

relatives? Still another reason given was that to accept money constituted an admission that the camp experience had been damaging,
and that the Nazis had, therefore, been successful. Refusal to file
served in the interests of denial.

Thus, it can be seen that restitution depends on both the external
and internal factors of available opportunities for replacement objects
and for the restoration of self-esteem, emotional and practical support at the time of bereavement and afterwards, ego strength, unconscious processes, flexibility of character structure, and other factors
enabling the bereaved to avail themselves of outside opportunities.
When restitution is not possible, depletion occurs.

Failure of Restitution—Depletion

It is clear to any alert observer of the human condition that restitution is not always possible. We all know personally or have heard or
read of lives cut short by a bullet to the spine, by an accident or illness,
or of an act of fate or man-made disaster wiping out the dreams of a
lifetime. How do people survive then?

The horror of the Nazi prison camps which so shocked the world is
not only finally becoming recognized for its catastrophic impact on
the victims themselves and their descendants, it also stands as a prototype for understanding current incidents of kidnappings, hijackings,
and terrorist attacks on defenseless people. The resignation, submission, and apparent failure of the victims to resist attack have aroused
the interest and study of experts.

We need to distinguish between apathy, already discussed in chapter twelve in connection with depression and helplessness, and true
depletion. Caution must be exercised in not mistaking the manifest
behavior for the true emotional state:

> Resignation, acceptance, and submission to an unwelcome reality are a
> defense mechanism; a reaction, in other words, to a serious threat. An
> abhorrence of impending deprivation, disappointment, impoverishment,
> in short the threat of a serious loss, is changed at times into resignation or
> acceptance.[29]

Some of the defenses used are isolation, precocious maturity, denial of fright, avoidance of the emotionally threatening event, and
negation (giggling in a crisis, for example).

It was observed that as conditions worsened in the concentration
camps, restitution continued to take place in the form of dreams,
fantasies, and expressed wishes of the victims. These wishes for restitution were not relinquished but rather took on more childlike and
primitive characteristics. Some of these aspects were increased need

for immediate gratification, increased self-absorption, disregard for others, disregard for consequences, the wish for special treatment, envy, and jealousy. The regressive ideation and the regressive behavior that often erupted came into conflict with the internalized value system of the person for, after all, they had been socialized prior to their internment. This conflict, compounded by the humiliations of the reality situation of the prison camps, resulted in a lowered self-esteem, and the result was apathy. Apathy, then, is a defense against full awareness of intolerable feelings of anger set off by conflicts one cannot escape.[30]

Depletion stems from another source, that of exhaustion. Regression, the opposite of creativity, can be lifesaving during short periods of enforced endurance of loss. When chronic, it can lead to depletion. Stanley H. Cath uses "depletion" to refer to more than depression or the ego state of helplessness. Depletion is exhaustion, an emptying out. He also distinguishes between feeling depleted and being depleted. One can feel depleted when libidinal energy "has been so consumed in maintaining repression that the latter must be reinforced by drawing energy from other essential ego functions. But one *is* depleted when, still later, energy is neither available nor evident."[31]

Cath compares depletion to the clinical picture of the "burned out" mental patient, the "low gear" reactions described by Bettelheim in concentration camp victims, the anaclitic depressions in institutionalized children described by Spitz—a combination of "frustration, rage, and then abandonment of object seeking, followed by a regression to a more primitive form of existence at what appears to be a lowered level of metabolism."[32] Depletion can be seen in the advanced elderly and in physically ill people with progressively debilitating terminal conditions.

Depletion is a psychic process more severe than depression. In depression, narcissistically important goals are still maintained; in depletion they are altered, if not altogether abandoned. The depressive reproaches himself. In depletion, self-reproach is partially or completely absent; the superego is emptied out even of guilt. The depressive introjects; introjection is lacking or is again externalized in depletion. In the depressive there is extreme tension between the superego and ego; in fact, depression has even been described as an attack on the ego by the superego. In depletion even this tension is gone. There is partial or complete abandonment of both external and internal reality, increased isolation of thought and feeling, a splitting of the ego, depersonalization, and a withdrawal of energy from the thinking process, from sensorimotor apparatus, and from other ego functions. In fact, improvement in the state of depletion is marked by the beginning of the capacity to be depressed. Again, to turn to the Nazi experience for an example, prisoners released from the death camps started to become depressed after they found themselves safe in the relocation centers.

Notes

1. Gregory Rochlin, *Griefs and Discontents: The Forces of Change* (Boston: Little, Brown and Co., 1965), p. 158.

2. Ibid., p. 163.

3. Ibid., p. 162.

4. Ibid., p. 196.

5. John Bowlby, "Processes of Mourning," *International Journal of Psychoanalysis* 42 (1961): 317–40.

6. Ibid., pp. 319–20.

7. Jordan M. Scher, "Death—The Giver of Life," in *The Interpretation of Death,* ed. Hendrik M. Ruitenbeek (New York: Jason Aronson, 1973), pp. 102–103.

8. Ira O. Glick, Robert S. Weiss, and C. Murray Parkes, *The First Year of Bereavement* (New York: John Wiley and Sons, 1974), pp. 208, 232.

9. Rochlin, *Griefs and Discontents,* p. 166.

10. Otto Fenichel, *The Psychoanalytic Theory of Neurosis* (New York: W.W. Norton, 1945).

11. Bowlby, "Processes of Mourning," pp. 337–38.

12. Rochlin, *Griefs and Discontents,* p. 202.

13. *Los Angeles Times,* 22 March 1977, pp. 1, 5.

14. Thomas J. Carroll, *Blindness: What It Is, What It Does, and How to Live with It* (Boston: Little, Brown and Co., 1961).

15. Rochlin, *Grief and Discontents,* p. 121.

16. Ibid., p. 171.

17. Ibid.

18. Paul Steiner as reported by Harriet Stix, "Coming to Terms with the Nazi Experience," *Los Angeles Times,* 31 December 1975, pp. 4, 7.

19. Stanley H. Cath, "Some Dynamics of Middle and Later Years: A Study in Depletion and Restitution," in *Geriatric Psychiatry: Grief, Loss, and Emotional Disorders in the Aging Process,* ed. Martin A. Berezin and Stanley H. Cath (New York: International Universities Press, 1965), p. 33.

20. Ibid.

21. Seymour L. Halleck, "Family Therapy and Social Change," *Social Casework* 57 (1976): 483–93.

22. Bowlby, "Processes of Mourning."

23. Erna Furman, *A Child's Parent Dies: Studies in Childhood Bereavement* (New Haven: Yale University Press, 1974), p. 68.

24. Cath, "Some Dynamics of Middle and Later Years," p. 25.

25. Ibid., p. 36.

26. Ibid., p. 33.

27. Rochlin, *Griefs and Discontents*, p. 211.

28. Cath, "Some Dynamics of Middle and Later Years," p. 40.

29. Rochlin, *Griefs and Discontents*, p. 212.

30. Ibid., pp. 218–19.

31. Cath, "Some Dynamics of Middle and Later Years," p. 41.

32. Ibid., pp. 41–42.

15/
Loss as an Agent for Change

The push for restitution is so strong a human need that creativity becomes a common daily experience insofar as regression does not replace it.[1] Peter Marris states that loss demands:

> The need to reestablish continuity, to work out an interpretation of oneself and the world which preserves, despite estrangement, the thread of meaning; the ambivalence of this task, as it swings between conflicting impulses; the need to articulate the stages of its resolution; and the risk of lasting disintegration if the process is not worked out. The outcome therefore depends upon the ability to face the conflict and find a way through it: the particular terms in which it is resolved are accidents of personal history.[2]

The end result of the need to reestablish continuity is the creation of a new identity. "Each of us began a new life at that moment," remarked a terrorist victim on his release from a building where he and other hostages had been held.

A New Identity

Erik H. Erikson, one of the concept's leading exponents, defines identity as the "accrued confidence that the inner sameness and continuity prepared in the past are matched by the sameness and continuity on one's meaning for others."[3] The key words here are "inner sameness" and "continuity." In Erikson's formulation, normal developmental identity starts from within and needs validation from without, in contrast to the child's earlier experience of having values and demands arising from without and eventually being internalized. Identity refers to the ability to maintain a sense of sameness and continuity throughout life despite the external changes that come with growth, aging, and a lifetime of experiences. For identity to be maintained comfortably, these changes should come in small doses. A major loss breaks into this continuity catastrophically and thereby constitutes a threat to identity. It is the grieving process that allows for the repair of that sense of continuity by allowing for the taking in and integration of the catastrophic changes in small doses. This new identity does not spring up anew after the process is over. It is the grieving process itself that creates it.

The seeds of a new identity lie dormant and ready to grow into new life even during the disorganization period of the mourning process. These seeds can be seen in the wish that precedes the act, such as the wisp of desire expressed by the bereaved even at the moment of deepest grief. "Maybe I'll return to school some day," says the new widow. The seed can be in the sudden awareness that one has spent a night alone and survived without terror, in fact, with a feeling of peace and quiet. It can be in the feeling of relaxation instead of fatigue after a task is completed. Slowly, the ability to concentrate returns, the foggy cloud of the early weeks of bereavement begins to lift; one by one new tasks are learned, or people are found who can help solve a problem. The keeping busy for the sake of it no longer seems so urgent. There is even meaning and pleasure in a task well done. One day a smile returns, and humor seems to have come back to the world. A new self-esteem is felt in regard to mastering use of a prosthesis, learning to drive a car, handling a checkbook, or making an important decision independently.

The signs of the new identity become even more apparent when the bereaved are able to take active steps toward the future. A change of residence can be one such step, as is the first job since marriage for the divorcee or widow. The resistant amputee who accepts the prosthesis, the burn victim who enters a retraining program, and the refugee who goes to night school to learn the language of his new country are also taking this step.

In some way the person indicates an intent to bend life to a purpose, rather than wait for things to happen. At this point one might say that the waiting, which is unconsciously the wait for the lost object to be returned, is relinquished, and the reality of the loss is becoming the more predominant factor. The balance has shifted from a concentration on the lost object as the major preoccupation to the reality of the present and the hope for the future in a life without the object. Although searching may again recur at times of holidays, anniversaries, and other significant reminders of the loss, searching as the major preoccupation of attention is over.

The restitution which begins with halting steps toward new experiences finds its flowering in the new identity the bereaved forge out of the fire and pain of loss. Identity stems in part from the roles one assumes. The widow loses not only her husband but also the role of wife. What identity does she then take on—that of the widow, career woman, or mother? The choice she makes will determine what direction she will proceed in her growth from the experience. "I feel like a person again," said one widow as she saw herself in the mirror, prepared to go jobhunting after the loss of her husband. For years she kept the dress she had worn as a symbol of the new "me." She had returned to the profession she had followed prior to her marriage and had resumed an old, familiar identity as a bridge to a new life.

It is not unusual to hear widows say that they lost a part of themselves in the loss of their husbands. This is also true when a woman may have achieved a sense of separateness during early adulthood but relinquished it when she married, in response to cultural and social expectations. With widowhood or divorce, she must again seek the separate identity she had known before. Both men and women may have never achieved a sense of autonomy before marriage. For them divorce or widowhood means a challenge not to return to a former state but to find a state of development they bypassed the first time.

Or, to cite another example, some people feel sexually attractive because of an internalized awareness built over childhood years of positive feedback from significant others. Conversely, others depend for their feeling of attractiveness on the validation from the partner with whom they are involved. The loss of the partner, therefore, can impinge on a fragile sense of attractiveness and usher in an identity diffusion similar to that of late adolescence.

Identity is made up of roles, bodily and mental characteristics, family and ethnic affiliations, class, kind of employment, marital and parental status. For example, a widow found comfort in joining a Parents Without Partners group and finding other people with children who were also without mates. After some months, she came to realize that some of them saw their major identity in terms of their roles of divorcee, or widow, or single parent. She decided she wanted something else as her major role identification and left the group in order to forge a different identity based on positive interests, rather than on her loss. The group had served its purpose for her when her loss was fresh; now she was ready to move on.

It is not unusual to hear the bereaved, after the initial pain and trauma have subsided and new identities are slowly becoming integrated, to look back on the loss and grief periods as times of growth. Often they are tempted to say that the experience was meant to happen in order to teach them something they now value. Suddenly they become aware of their capacity to feel envy, a feeling heretofore repressed. Some have a deepened empathy with other people. Others speak of now appreciating the limitations everyone has instead of seeing some people as fortunate and some as unlucky. Success and failure, joy and sorrow, they now say, are the lot of all people. Their loss has opened them to a fuller appreciation of life. Through their grief they have reassessed formerly held values and goals and have come to new conclusions about people and life.

Treatment Implications

The general impression people have is that when a loss occurs, the bereaved go through a period of grief and eventually equilibrium is restored by the acceptance of the reality of the loss. This view of loss misses the appreciation of the complexities of restitution. Loss and the forces it sets into motion, rather than being interruptions in life to be endured and pushed aside as quickly as possible, are part of the life process itself. Freud, in one of his published letters, wrote:

> Although we know that after such a loss the acute state of mourning will subside, we also know we shall remain inconsolable and will never find a substitute. No matter what may fill the gap, even if it be filled completely, it nevertheless remains something else. And, actually, this is how it should be, it is the only way of perpetuating that love which we do not want to relinquish.[4]

Loss, grief, mourning, and restitution thus become a dynamic, universal experience of all life. Human beings, however, in contrast to lower forms of life, have a choice in the forms of restitution they select.

To be helpful to the bereaved, helpers need to be able to differentiate between restoration of the lost object, substitution of an available object, and creative restitution involving the integration of the old with the new. To be aware of the temptation of the bereaved to seek premature replacement objects as a defense against the pain of grief, helpers must be in touch with their own feelings of helplessness in the face of grief and suffering and with the inner urge to do something to relieve the feeling of helplessness.

It is out of such need to do something that even professional mental health workers fall into the temptation of giving advice to the bereaved. The widowed and divorced are urged to remarry. Parents who have lost a child are urged to have another or to adopt. The infertile couple is pushed to adopt a child without due recognition of the need to grieve over the infertility.

Loss, by creating helplessness and passivity, is experienced as a narcissistic injury. To repair this injury, the bereaved need to be given an opportunity to play an active role in moves toward recovery from the loss. This means including them in decision-making processes where possible and appropriate respect for their wishes and opinions. They need to feel that they have some control over their lives to compensate for the catastrophic loss of control which the losses may have meant. Whatever adequacy remains should be respected.

Helpers also need to respect the deep feelings that can be set off by a fantasied loss or the fear off loss, the need to make restitution for fantasied destruction of the love object to relieve the guilt set off by aggressive fantasies, and the importance of acts of undoing, fantasies of sacrifice, renunciation, and other reparative maneuvers.

It is extremely important that professionals understand the impact of early losses on character development. Early losses call forth adaptive responses that eventually become part of the character. Every loss and reaction thereto thus becomes programmed into the personality of the individual. When losses are gradual, anticipated, and benign, and the growing child has sufficient emotional support from loving others, the adaptive techniques developed go to strengthen coping skills, flexibility, problem-solving ability, and creativity. Traumatic losses, however, threaten psychological integrity. It has been postulated that:

> When an object relationship is interrupted by the death of one of the significant participants, a new ego-adaptive process has to be instituted in order to deal with the altered internal-external psychological situation. Where there is a possibility of substitution with little difficulty, the adaptive task may be easily accomplished, as is the case with certain animals and very young infants. But when the lost object has taken on psychic significance in addition to functional fulfillment, the adaptive process involves in part an undoing of the previous adaptational equilibrium established with that object, and the gradual reestablishment of new relationships with reality-present figures. The complex adaptive process instituted in such a situation is called mourning.[5]

Freud, it will be remembered, struggled with the dilemma of why grief should be so painful an emotion, and he failed to find an answer.

Rochlin postulates that the relinquishment of that which has been lost means the relinquishment of the wish for relationships to be unending and things to be enduring.[6] In the fullest sense, this means the relinquishment of all wish fulfillment and the acceptance of the finality of loss and death with no need for the defense of denial. This, it is generally agreed, is beyond human ability.

Loss, if mourned successfully, serves to strengthen and enhance the ego, thus serving as an important aspect of development. No healthy person seeks out a loss for this purpose. But life brings tragedy and adversity to each of us. It is in the ability to endure the pain of grief and the ability to find healthy restitution that growth can be the outcome of suffering.

Professional helpers must appreciate the impact of traumatic loss on young children, with the break in continuity, the loss of nurturing, and the loss of security in the meaning of life. They must appreciate the relief sought through the denial of loss, through the projection of blame on others, the range of restitution maneuvers, and the relationship between early losses and later problems of physical and mental health, separations, losses, attachments, and commitments. Helpers must stand ready to recognize, facilitate, or support opportunities for external resources for restitution, to respect the internal readiness or lack thereof for restitution, the role of temporary regression in grief in the service of mobilizing strength for further struggle, the outcome of failure to find restitution, and the steps in the process of the struggle toward a new identity. They need to help the bereaved to recognize the loss, mourn appropriately, forgive, relinquish, and return to the struggle.

It is important, because none of us can be all things to all people, for helpers to understand the particular population of clients with whom they work and the forms of loss and, therefore, restitution most common to them. These may be through widowhood, divorce, aging, physical disability, being a refugee, displaced person, or victim of violence, and so on. At the same time, because in the unconscious all losses merge, it is necessary to know the significance of loss at each stage of the life cycle. Helpers should be familiar with the pathological reactions to grief and the factors influencing the reaction to loss, so that they can distinguish between normal and pathological reactions, deal with those within their area of expertise, and make appropriate referrals when other skills are needed.

Because help to the grief-stricken is increasing rapidly, the field attracts people who see a need that can be met and turned into quick profit. Research is needed to guide helpers into choosing appropriately among the many modalities available—the individual approach, the group approach, professional or volunteer or self-help nonprofessional leadership, and we need to respect the dangers of uncovering an area with which we cannot deal.

In the loss cycle is revealed the wonder and majesty of the human mind in all its complexities. Past, present, and future merge in the individual's experience with loss, grief, and restitution. Each reaction is unique. As has been said about snowflakes, there are no two alike. But, as with the snowflake, there is a common pattern that all follow.

Loss cannot be understood or dealt with by a here-and-now approach. It demands an openness of mind to what is observed and what is unseen, what is known and what is implied, to the logical and to the irrational, to the concrete and to the symbolic, to the practical and to the mystical aspects of life. It calls forth in the helper the poetic as well as the scientific, the personal as well as the professional, and it bridges the gap between the helper and the one who needs help. In recognizing the universality of loss and grief, we come to appreciate the commonality of all peoples. Loss removes barriers of race, color, creed, class, religion, sex; it is a leveler. But more than that: Through restitution, we can all share in the creative process.

And one final vignette: Mary woke early; the clock said 6:15 a.m. From behind the woven shades she could tell that it was to be another beautiful, sunny day. The electric blanket felt good. She stretched with a feeling of health and vitality. A fleeting thought crossed her mind. There was something special about today. What was it? A birthday? No. A holiday? No. At last she remembered. It would have been her wedding anniversary had her husband lived. Let's see. How many years would they have been married? She subtracted the year of her marriage from the current year and came up with the answer. Thirty. It would have been their thirtieth wedding anniversary. She recalled the wedding, the honeymoon, the parties, the good years of marriage, of babies, of working toward common goals, of friends, and of vacations together. Today she was alone. The children were grown and involved in lives of their own. She stretched again and realized she could not keep her mind on the past. It kept returning to the present. There were few parties, but there were good friends. There was loving and being loved. But most of all her mind kept going to her work. She could hardly wait to get started. Each day was fulfilling in itself. Life was good.

She remembered that at the time of her greatest grief a friend had said, "Life will never be the same. It will be different, but it can be good." She had been angry then, but had held her tongue. She could not argue with her friend, who was the mother of a retarded child and spoke out of the depths of her own sorrow. But she had refused to believe what she heard. How could it be good if it were different, she had wondered then. She now smiled with the wisdom of the years. It had all turned out as her friend had said. She had found restitution for her losses, and life was good, although different from anything she could have imagined then. She stepped out of bed to greet the day.

Notes

1. Gregory Rochlin, *Griefs and Discontents: The Forces of Change* (Boston: Little, Brown and Co., 1965), p. 222.

2. Peter Marris, *Loss and Change* (New York: Pantheon Books, 1974), p. 42.

3. Erik H. Erikson, *Childhood and Society* (New York: W.W. Norton, 1963), p. 261.

4. Sigmund Freud, "Letter to L. Binswanger," in *Letters of Sigmund Freud,* ed. E.L. Freud (London: Hogarth Press, 1961), p. 386.

5. George H. Pollock, "Mourning and Adaptation," *International Journal of Psycho-Analysis* 42 (1961): 341–61.

6. Rochlin, *Griefs and Discontents,* p. 158.

Index